HOUSE SMART

HOUSE SMART

BY:
BRUCE H. WILLIAMS
AND
NATHAN ROSENHOUSE

Printed in the United States of America By:
MARRAKECH EXPRESS

First Published in November,1995
Revised Edition January, 1996
Seventh Printing August, 1997

Printed in the United States of America

Library of Congress Catalog Card Number: 96-92028
ISBN # 0-9651955-0-3

TABLE OF CONTENTS

PREFACE

For more than 20 years, I have been talking to people just like you on the radio about your life and how to avoid getting into trouble in this difficult and problematic world. When I am listening to my callers, it never ceases to amaze me that so many people seem to approach the buying or selling of real estate with a casualness that they would not apply to the purchase of a dress or a suit. Believe me, this approach is courting disaster; yet, time and time again, I talk to people who could easily have avoided the pitfalls and problems that may arise when buying or selling a home. Let me tell you how you can benefit from their mistakes and my experience by learning how to buy or sell your home intelligently and successfully.

The goal of this book is to help you to avoid making mistakes, correct the misinformation that seems to abound regarding the purchase and sale of real estate, and reveal the "insider tips" that I've learned over the years through my own personal experiences. There is one essential ingredient in a real estate transaction. That ingredient is solid and professional advice. In real estate transactions, the most important professional involved must be a real estate attorney. Surely, if you were to have a toothache, you could solve your problem by buying a 69-cent pair of pliers at the local hardware store, screw up your courage and pull your tooth out. I doubt that many of you would do this. Why then, when you are spending tens of thousands of dollars, would you practice do-it-yourself law? It just doesn't make sense.

From my first home, which cost about $10,000 (I was a sophomore in college at the time) to other properties I've purchased costing hundreds of thousands of dollars, one guiding principle has been constant. I have never, at any time, attempted to navigate those waters without the guidance of a competent attorney.

When I purchased my first home, I didn't know a piece of sheetrock from a box of Jujyfruits. When someone talked about a home with a well, I conjured up a vision of my grandmother's house with a pump in the kitchen. That is a fact. I was a city kid and I didn't have a clue as to what a septic tank was, but I learned; oh, did I learn!

It seems like a lifetime ago but in reality it was only 30-odd years ago when I was the proprietor of a nursery school. One of my early patrons was a young attorney in our community, Nate Rosenhouse. Shortly after he became my client, I became his, and over the years, aside from our client-professional relationship, we have become the closest of friends, and "friend" is not a term I use lightly. I will consider myself lucky that in a lifetime I have a half-dozen real friends. I consider Nate to be one of those half-dozen, and I trust that he feels the same toward me. While we do have a close personal relationship, in matters of business it is strictly a business relationship. He is well aware, as any professional should be, that he is responsible for any mistakes made while providing his services and, of course, he takes this responsibility very seriously (and pays his malpractice insurance premiums).

Since he is the guy I rely on in real estate transactions, I have asked him to collaborate with me on this book. We want the reader to understand the real estate sales process, not in legal, technical terms, but from a practical viewpoint. In other words, we want you to participate in your real estate purchase or sales transaction with insider knowledge, gained from our extensive experience.

We have made a deliberate effort in this book to be brief, yet instructive. We hope that this book will help you to understand and be aware of the hazards involved in real estate, and equip you to spot problems, ask searching questions and get the most accurate information regarding one of the most costly transactions you will ever make.

I have examined many books on this subject written during the past 10 years and can state that this work gives the freshest, most up-to-date and savvy information you (not the professionals) can use for your benefit.

Over the years, I have heard countless horror stories from people who have been involved in real estate transactions.

I have concluded that in just about every instance these mistakes could have been avoided with some diligence in getting the right answers and having your attorney at your side.

I wish you success in your real estate ventures.

BRUCE WILLIAMS

Just a word from Bruce's lawyer:

Bruce has been a friend and client for just about 32 years. I'll tell you why I admire this guy. He earnestly cares about people and his listeners sense and understand this. This synergy translates into great radio communication.

My friend is also one of the most versatile and resourceful people I know. He is a problem-solver who knows how to think without being tied down to rigid preconceptions. This man can do more wonders with an ordinary metal hanger than most people can do with a whole set of tools. In business, his inventive ideas keep me hopping.

In this work, we have combined the knowledge, skill and experience of over 40 years each in our careers and business lives. We hope that you will benefit from these insights, which have been hard-won.

NATE ROSENHOUSE

Disclaimer

It is not the intention of the authors of this work to provide legal, financial or advisory services. Our purpose is to inform, stimulate and guide you on the subject of buying and selling a home and to help you to recognize traps and pitfalls. Therefore, we must specifically disclaim any risk, loss or liability, directly or indirectly, resulting from the use or application of any information contained in this book. **The Reader Is Urged To Seek The Services Of An Attorney, Accountant Or Financial Advisor To Review And Analyze The Reader's Specific Situation.**

In order to ensure readability throughout this work, in most cases the masculine pronoun is used.

A NOTE FROM THE AUTHORS

We have made a deliberate effort to be brief, while providing you with the essential information you will need to buy or sell your home. You will observe that this book is printed in larger type for ease in reference. We have also included a glossary and forms.

We urge you to familiarize yourself with the forms, which are representative of instruments you will be asked to sign in a real transaction. Most of the legal terms are defined and explained in the glossary because real estate has its own unique language.

Most of all, we encourage you to ask questions to become an informed consumer. Remember, there is only one stupid question: the one you never asked.

With this in mind, we offer this book. Please send your comments to Post Office Box 503, Elfers, Florida, 34680.

Bruce H. Williams
Nathan Rosenhouse

ACKNOWLEDGMENTS:

We acknowledge with thanks the special contributions of Judith Tallerman, Daniel Puckett, Lisa Fallon, Lynda C. Falkowski, Jean Troide, and Lisa Dempsey, in editing, assembling and compiling this work. We also express our appreciation to All-State Legal Supply Co., Cranford, New Jersey, 07016 and HouseMaster of America, Bound Brook, New Jersey, 08805 for permission to use some of their documents in the form section of this book.

Bruce H. Williams
Nathan Rosenhouse

CHAPTER 1

HOME OWNERSHIP:

THE AMERICAN DREAM

Shelter is one of our basic physical needs. Home ownership satisfies this need, but also satisfies the emotional and psychological needs for financial stability and commitment to a community.

The financial advantages of home ownership are substantial. In fact, the income tax laws are based on an express intention to encourage home ownership by saving you income taxes. This savings is, in effect, a subsidy because Uncle Sam is paying part of your monthly housing expense if you are a homeowner who itemizes deductible expenses on his income tax return.

Let us show you how owning a home is more economical than renting. If you are paying, let's say, $600 per month in rent to a landlord, that would be enough to cover monthly payments on a $63,000, 30-year, 9% mortgage ($507 per month), plus $100 in property taxes. Since you will in the same payment be reducing principal (amortization), at the end of five years you will build up an equity (difference between the value of the property and what you owe on the mortgage) of about $2,600, $6,700 after ten years, $13,000 after fifteen years and $23,000 after twenty years.

Since tenants (those who rent rather than own a home) do not get any income tax breaks for rent payments, the general deductibility by homeowners of mortgage interest, points and real estate property taxes for income tax purposes makes owning your own home advantageous. These income tax savings actually reduce the monthly housing expense of the homeowner. They also represent a forced form of savings. In addition, when the home is sold, there is a good chance that a profit will be made or, at least, the appreciation in value will greatly or entirely offset the housing expense for the years of the owner's occupancy.

After age 55, if you have lived in this residence three out of the last five years, you can make a one-time election to exclude up to $125,000 of gain (difference between the selling price and your adjusted cost basis) from income tax. This exclusion is one of the very best of all tax shelters.

BRUCE'S INSIDER TIP:

I call this the "shelter-shelter." Each time you sell and purchase another house within two years, you postpone paying taxes on the gain and defer the tax until you sell the last house you own after reaching that magic age of 55. Although each gain will reduce your tax cost basis, you can exclude up to $125,000 in profit (the difference between the sales proceeds and your adjusted cost basis).

HOUSEHUNTING: ARE YOU THE HUNTER OR THE HUNTED?

Once you have decided to purchase a home of your own, you have to do some serious planning. The first step is to understand that there are people out there who have also done a lot of planning <u>to take advantage of you as a buyer</u>.

Unless you have engaged a buyer's broker to find a home for you and negotiate its purchase, <u>any other broker you deal with is a seller's broker</u>.

The recent advent of "dual agency," in which the broker represents both parties, does not solve the ethical problem. It simply formalizes the conflict of interest, as an agent cannot loyally serve opposing parties in a legal transaction. It may be legally possible for an agent to represent both parties with a full disclosure and the express consent of both parties, but there is a built-in clash of duties. For instance, if the seller is anxious to sell because he has already purchased a home, can this agent tell the buyer? If the buyer has revealed that he loves the house and is willing to pay more, can this type of agent tell the seller?

In plain language, this means that any broker other than a true buyer's broker is in conflict of interest (a very bad ethical place to be). It is a dirty little secret in the real estate business that a seller's broker owes undivided loyalty to the seller and none to the buyer, except not to misrepresent. Yet, all you have to do is read some of the unabashedly disgraceful flyers and advertisements handed out by brokers to see that they are insidiously inviting buyers to reveal their personal and financial situations on the pretext of forming a professional relationship with them. The truth is that they are by law required to disclose to the seller all the information they have gained from the buyer. So, if you go to a seller's broker to find a home, you can bet you will be asked basic information about your income, debts and amount of cash you have to put down. **Buyer, Be Aware Of This Trap**.

You must exercise discretion in divulging personal financial information to this broker. But in all fairness, while you are seeking information from the broker as to what is on the market, the broker is entitled to know enough about you in order to guide you to appropriate homes for sale. The broker also has a legitimate obligation to the seller to prequalify buyers - in other words, to decide whether they can afford a given home and the financing required. It is a thin ethical line.

You may be startled to learn that in 1983, the Federal Trade Commission, whose statutory duty is to ferret out and prevent deception and fraud, particularly in advertising, made a study of consumer-buyers using seller's brokers. The FTC found that an astounding 75% of these buyers were operating under the false assumption that the brokers showing them homes represented these buyers. Of course, the reality is that both listing and selling brokers actually are the <u>exclusive agents of the sellers</u>.

Only within the past 10 years have state legislatures enacted disclosure laws. Now, 45 states require brokers to reveal their true interests in a real estate transaction. You can thank the real estate lobbies for their disservice in slowing down reform.

BRUCE'S INSIDER TIP:

Now that you know the truth, does this mean you should not use a broker to find a house? Of course not. You should use a broker. However, the operative word is *use*. He can be a valuable asset. Utilize his services as you would a travel agent. You simply cannot *trust* this broker indiscriminately with your intimate financial information. You must not let this broker find out exactly what you are prepared to pay. This broker is not in business for charity or fun. Well, neither are you. You're looking for a house at the best possible price. Ultimately, you are "paying the freight," so don't be a sucker.

By all means, tell the broker about your family, where you will be working, what type of schools your children require, what

kind of community you are looking for, what your hobbies, sports and social activities are. Ask a lot of questions. Shop for your own mortgage. Keep your personal finances private *unless you want the seller to know exactly the highest price you are willing to pay for the home of your dreams.*

HOW MUCH HOME CAN YOU AFFORD?

Undoubtedly, the most critical preparation and planning required of you *before* you apply for a mortgage is a calculation of how much mortgage you can afford based upon your family income, assets, liabilities and credit. Don't be intimidated. The calculation is easy (the payments aren't).

Take the gross (before taxes) average income for the past two years from all sources of everyone who will be an owner of the home and party to the mortgage. Be prepared to document these figures with your income tax returns, pay stubs and other written proof. Next, list all of your long-term (more than six-month installment term) debts. Then, calculate your monthly gross income and your weekly gross income based on 4.3 weeks per month. Most lenders use a 28% ratio, which means that approximately one week's gross income should be the maximum you can afford for monthly housing expense (mortgage principal and interest, real estate taxes and homeowner's insurance).

7

There is another ratio called total monthly debt. This is currently about 36%, which means that your total monthly installment debt should not exceed that percentage of your before-tax monthly income.

Once you have made these calculations, you will determine how much you can afford each month for your mortgage payment by estimating the monthly taxes and insurance and subtracting those sums from the available monthly payment.

When you have arrived at the net available for principal and interest, you must then determine what types of mortgages (fixed; adjustable; 15-, 20-, 25- or 30 year; conventional; FHA; VA; etc.) are available. Next, you must find out what the current interest rate is. This requires shopping around. You will learn how, later on.

Following is a guide to determine how much mortgage you can afford and what the monthly payments will be.

MORTGAGES -- HOW MUCH CAN YOUR FAMILY AFFORD?

This step-by-step worksheet will give you a rough estimate of how much mortgage you can afford.

A calculator will make the arithmetic easier; the worksheet should take about 5 minutes to complete.

Step 1

Enter your gross family <u>Monthly</u> Income (before taxes) on Line A:

Yearly Income

÷ 12

= A_____ **Monthly Income**

Step 2

Multiply line A by 28% and enter the result on Line B:

A_____ x .28

= B_____

The result is about how much you can reasonably afford for a monthly housing expense, including PITI (Principal, Interest, Taxes and Insurance) and MIP (Mortgage Insurance Premium). Remember, this is only a rough estimate. Frequently, a lender will "qualify" you for a monthly payment higher than you can afford.

For instance, large families that have greater expense ratios for items like food and clothing should be extremely careful not to overextend themselves.

Step 3

Multiply line B by 80% and enter the result on Line C:

B_____ **x .80**

= C_____

The result is about how much you can afford for a monthly principal and interest payment.

Step 4

To figure an estimated mortgage amount, choose an interest rate from the following mortgage calculator.

Enter the corresponding factor number on Line D.
Divide Line C by Line D and enter the result on line E.
Multiply Line E by 1,000 and enter the result on Line F.

C_____ **divided by**

D_____ **=**

E_____ **x 1000**

F_____

Line F is approximately how large a mortgage you can afford.

MORTGAGE PAYMENT CALCULATOR

Principal and Interest Only

Interest Rate	Factor for 30 Years (Per Thousand)	Factor for 15 Years (Per Thousand)
7.0	6.65	8.99
7.5	6.69	9.27
8.0	7.3376	9.5565
8.5	7.6891	9.8474
9.0	8.0462	10.1127
9.5	8.4085	10.442
9.75	8.60	10.60
10.0	8.7757	20.7461
10.5	8.97	10.90
10.25	9.1174	11.0510
10.75	9.31	11.21
11.0	9.5232	11.366
11.25	9.72	11.53
11.5	9.9029	11.6819
11.75	10.10	11.85
12.0	10.2861	12.0017

Multiply the number of thousands in the principal by the appropriate factor to arrive at the monthly principal and interest.

For example:

Principal = $100,000.00

No. of Thousands = 100

Factor 30 Years = 8% (7.3376)

7.336 x 100 = $733.76 Monthly Principal and Interest

(level payment per month during entire life of the mortgage loan)

CHAPTER 2

WHAT COULD GO WRONG?

Real estate transactions are fraught with danger, both for buyers and for sellers. Defects in the contract of sale, the property or the title to it can harm both sides of the transaction, as can mistakes during negotiations. Here are some of the more common pitfalls to watch for:

For the Seller

The listing period has certain risks. A seller should carefully discuss with his broker and attorney the vital subject of who will have access to the residence during the listing period. If there is a lock-box, try to make sure that there is a written record of every use of the key, stating the names of the broker, salesperson and prospects, and time and date of the visit. Make those using your home accountable. Don't rely on the loose practice of real estate agents leaving their card if they choose to.

BRUCE'S INSIDER TIP:

There is really no way to make the house secure if it is occupied. If the property is a beach or vacation home or is vacant, there's no problem. But just accept that anyone in the real estate business has access to your home and belongings. There is really no foolproof way to require those who enter to

"log in."   I've sold many a house without a lock-box.   It's simply not worth the worry and potential trouble.

While prospective purchasers are inspecting the home, there are risks such as accidents and falls and the possibility of theft of personal property and even furniture, especially during "open houses." A wise seller will make sure that his real estate agent and any other real estate brokers and salespersons having access to the premises are covered by appropriate liability insurance. This should be clearly specified in the listing agreement.

If the sales agent has control while the seller is not present during these visits, and someone is injured, an investigation will surely be made to determine whether the agent was negligent in providing a safe place for prospective buyers to visit. Of course, the owner-seller of the home and his liability carrier may also have to deal with a claim by the injured party. Take all precautions, in advance of any listing, to make your home safe. Inadequate lighting and cluttered stairs and basements are leading causes of home accidents.

Even before a contract of sale is entered into, certain other critical considerations must be addressed:

A. What if one of the parties becomes incapacitated or dies before the closing of title? Of course, the buyers want the protection of canceling the contract because usually the broker's form contract is silent on this point. The law in most states does not excuse a buyer under these conditions and the buyer's estate would be liable for any contracts or obligations entered into or incurred prior to death or incapacity. The issue should be addressed; perhaps an escape clause should provide for loss of the deposit or part of it.

B. The marital status of the parties selling and buying must be ascertained and stated in the contract. Every party having a legal interest in the property should sign as seller. Every party intended to acquire title and sign the mortgage should also sign the contract as buyer. Do not allow one spouse to sign for the other unless there is a written power of attorney, a copy of which you retain. A common excuse is that the other spouse is "out of town on business." A party not binding himself in the contract could balk at the time of closing.

Contingencies To Protect The Buyer

The contract of sale _must_ clearly discuss and specify everything that has to happen or be done before it becomes binding.

1. The most common contingency involves the mortgage the buyer is applying for. This is called the **Mortgage Financing**

Contingency. To avoid misunderstanding, the amount, type, terms and duration of the mortgage, a limit on the number of points and other specifics about the mortgage should be clearly spelled out. The buyer should protect himself from a change in financial condition, such as job loss or casualty, because the mortgage commitment issued by the lender will be conditional upon no substantial negative change in the buyer's financial standing. The contract should also state which party should pay for the mortgage application and any costs in connection with the application. Commonly, this is a buyer's expense, but in a weak market the seller may agree to pay to "sweeten the deal."

2. Are there **Inspection Contingencies** in the contract? The contract should provide for a termite inspection, structural inspection, potability report, percolation test, smoke detector compliance certificate, certificate of occupancy on resale, if required, and a radon test, and state who will pay for repairs. It is possible for a seller to set a monetary limit on his obligation to repair (often expressed as a percentage of the sales price) or to provide for the cancellation of the agreement instead of making any repairs if the monetary limit is exceeded. Does the contract allow the buyer to waive the contingency and accept the premises in an "as is" condition if the seller refuses to make any repairs?

3. Other **Environmental Contingencies** to be addressed in the contract of sale:

a. Toxic Waste - Soil and water contamination from corrosive materials spilled on the ground presents an immediate danger to health and safety and has resulted in strict federal and state regulations imposing severe penalties and clean-up obligations. A thorough history of the use of the property (before and after development) is indicated. Former farm properties pose particular hazards, such as underground oil tanks and fertilizer storage sites. In past years, it was a customary practice on some farms to bury waste on the "back forty."

b. Flood Zone/Wetlands/Riparian Rights - The U.S. Army Corps of Engineers has drawn up maps for every region of the country showing where the flood zones are. Even if a small portion of the property is in a flood zone, a lender may require flood insurance. It is, however, possible to obtain an exemption with the assistance of the municipal engineering official.

"Wetlands" are areas where the water table is so high that construction of a dwelling is prohibited. When purchasing a home bordering on the ocean, a river, lake or stream, you must obtain representations from the seller as to the property owner's rights and obligations with respect to free flow and navigability and possible violations by seller.

BRUCE'S INSIDER TIP:

Very often the flood zone designation can be eliminated if you can prove that the classification was erroneous. When I was a town mayor and councilman, I helped many a resident to do this. In one case, the official Corps of Engineers map showed a stream on a particular property but did not show elevations. Further investigation determined that the stream was 25 feet down in a gully. The property was removed from the flood zone classification, and this eliminated an annual expense for flood insurance.

c.   Lead Paint - Flaking and ingestion of lead by children as detected by a blood test are serious environmental concerns in older homes. Therefore, provision for an inspection in the contract of sale is indispensable.

d.   Asbestos - Usually, encapsulated (sealed) asbestos is not a hazard, but asbestos insulation of pipes and in attics, common in some older homes, can become free-floating and cause injury and

19

even death; "clam shells" around pipes and 30 to 40 year-old heating systems insulated with asbestos are the leading culprits. Also, asbestos floor tiles are covered under asbestos removal laws and can be expensive to remove.

e. Underground Fuel Tanks/Sink Holes - Provision for the removal or filling with sand of underground fuel tanks to prevent seepage into the water supply should be included in the contract. A modern method of neutralization is to fill the tank with plastic material that expands, hardens and becomes solid. Sink holes present unique problems relating to the stability of the site; this possibility must also be covered in the contract.

f. Urea Formaldehyde Insulation/Fire Retardant Plywood - It has been proven that toxic fumes emanate from these materials when they burn; be aware of these hazards. Decide whether you wish to proceed with the purchase or negotiate with the seller to remedy the condition.

g. Proximity to Toxic Waste Sites - Courts in some states have held that brokers and sellers of new homes who knew or should have known of the past existence of toxic waste sites near the dwelling had a distinct duty to disclose this important fact to a prospective buyer. The contract should have an express representation by the seller, at the very least, that he has no knowledge of any such condition.

BRUCE'S INSIDER TIP:

You are now aware of the importance of asking the real estate agent as many questions as you can think of. It is up to you to advise your attorney of the information you have uncovered about the house and neighborhood. One of the most valuable services performed by the buyer's attorney is to obtain effective representations in the contract as to adverse environmental conditions. Contingencies allowing cancellation of the agreement must be considered. Fraudulent concealment is very difficult to prove, and you are much better off canceling the contract than having to sue after inheriting the seller's problems.

4. **Title Contingencies** must also be addressed. If the title is defective and seller cannot cure the defect (solve the problem), is the buyer entitled to the return of his expenses for search and survey? The seller can and should place a monetary limit on these expenses to protect himself. Most attorneys for buyers will discourage a client from purchasing a residence built on a lot whose title is based on adverse possession or foreclosure of a tax

lien because of the undue expense in certifying that there is a valid title. It is advisable to have a cancellation clause in the contract to protect the buyer. "Marketability of title" is the standard. This is usually defined as "such title as will be insured by a reputable title insurance company doing business in the state where the property is located at regular rates."

5. **Zoning Ordinances, restrictions of record, variances and subdivisions**. If there are any contingencies of this kind they must be expressed and specifically stated in the contract. Most contracts have a representation by seller to the effect that there are no violations of the zoning ordinance of the municipality where the property is located and no restrictive covenants of record that will interfere with the use of the dwelling as a residence.

If the contract is subject to the seller's obtaining a subdivision or variance, this must be in writing and a time limit specified. Variances are exceptions to the zoning ordinance of the municipality that are considered usually by a zoning board of adjustment. Subdivisions are the separation of a larger tract into two or more smaller lots usually considered by a planning board of the municipality.

6. Is the contract subject to the **sale by buyer of his own home**? A seller may be ill-advised to allow such a contingency in the

contract of sale because it inhibits the seller from making his own plans for relocation. However, in a buyer's market, a seller may have to concede this point in order to keep a deal alive. The parties should also be aware of the common requirement of banks and of mortgage companies that an applicant must sell his existing home as a condition of a mortgage commitment. This creates a situation in which the seller must not only sweat out his buyer's mortgage application but also his buyer's buyer's application for financing. Such an untenable situation dictates that the seller have his attorney provide remedies in the contract for failure of either mortgage application, such as liquidated damages to compensate the seller for the lost time in taking the house off the market during the mortgage contingency period. Alternatively, the house could stay on the market with a right of first refusal in the buyer if a new buyer is found. Of course, if the market is weak, sellers must be flexible and make concessions.

All of these contingencies must have definite time limits and standards of compliance. To avoid dispute, the contract of sale must precisely spell out who is responsible for paying for and carrying out the search or inspection, and the time limits.

There are significant matters that title companies do not search for in connection with the purchase of a home. Some of these matters can create serious practical difficulties and should be taken up in the contract of sale. For instance, if the purchase involves a condominium or a cooperative, the bylaws may require written permission of the board of directors of the condo association or cooperative corporation as a condition of sale. It is up to the buyer's attorney to require the seller to produce the consent.

Condominiums and cooperatives are different. In a condominium, the buyer owns a specified lot or compartment in space (such as an apartment in a high-rise building) plus a fractional undivided interest (a percentage interest) in the common areas (such as walkways, recreational areas, lobby, elevators, etc.). In a cooperative, you are buying a share of stock in a corporation that owns all of the facilities, including the living space.

There are hidden perils in purchasing condos and co-ops.

1. Is the reserve fund for replacement of major items, such as elevators, recreational areas, sprinkler system, adequate?

2. Is the next door neighbor a nuisance or disreputable? Remember, he is an owner, not a tenant, and since he has as much standing as you, he cannot be removed very easily.

3. Has the board of directors maintained the common areas?

4. Has the board paid its bills on time?

5. Is the board considering a refinancing of its debt? If it does, the occupancy fees or common charges may rise.

6. Has the buyer requested comparable sales figures on similar units from the broker?

A good real estate attorney will pose these questions to his client. He may also recommend a property risk service, which will issue a report based on past minutes and financial statements of the board of directors and a report summarizing services and nuisances in the neighborhood. This service can also offer advice as to requirements of the board for approval of the prospective buyer, if required.

Before entering into a contract, find out if there are any restrictions such as no tenancies or limitation of the number of guests or how often you can allow others to use the unit. Often, extra fees may be imposed on the owner for the privilege of renting. Of course, any representations made by the seller or the agent in this regard should be written into the contract of sale.

In addition, it is necessary to have a representation in the contract that the seller of such unit has not violated any of the bylaws and is fully paid in his dues and there are no assessments against the unit. If permission is withheld, the sale can be blocked until there is compliance.

If the property to be purchased is an investment where there are tenants, there may be rent control or rent leveling in the municipality, and this should be covered by a representation from the seller. The title search will also not uncover building code violations. The buyer takes over the seller's problems if this area is not addressed in the contract of sale. The buyer or his attorney must make inquiries of the municipal building department and any noted violations must be cleared up at seller's expense prior to closing of title. Otherwise, the buyer inherits the seller's problems.

7. Surveys. A buyer should always have a survey. Usually, if there is a recent survey that the seller made when he purchased the premises and if that is acceptable to the title company and lender, the survey can be used with an affidavit from the seller that there have been no changes. If there have been changes in the size and location of the building or buildings on the premises, fences, pools, or the like, there must be a new survey with a new metes and bounds description (legal description giving courses and distances) prepared by a licensed surveyor. Almost all lenders and title companies require this. The new survey will show setbacks and may show irregularities that could become violations

of the filed restrictions of record or the zoning ordinance of the municipality. The survey may also reveal encroachments of such things as buildings and fences on an adjoining property or an encroachment on the property to be purchased. Ordinarily, the title company will examine the new survey very carefully to make such a determination, as it will be insuring the survey and title for both the lender and the buyer. The buyers will then have an "option to cancel" instead of accepting seller's problems blindly.

There also have been cases where the survey of a lot showed that a house had been built on the wrong lot or that the lot was smaller in area than bargained for. The survey will also come in handy later on if the buyer wishes to install a fence, hedges, shed, garage or a swimming pool or has a boundary line dispute with an adjoining property owner. It is easier to sell a property by showing it on a survey, as the buyer may be spared the expense of making a new one. More about surveys later.

Many of the risks outlined above (even when lawyers are involved) result in expensive lawsuits and enormous delays, which can have a serious impact on the parties' finances and lives. This raises the compelling question: Can real estate brokers and title companies protect the parties to a real estate transaction? Remember, they are not permitted to give legal advice or practice law. Yet, there are many areas in this country where attorneys are not customarily used. Is it advisable for someone entering into a large financial transaction to leave himself so vulnerable to so many risks just to save a relatively small amount of money? A word to the wise should be sufficient.

BRUCE'S INSIDER TIP:

I would never buy or sell a house without an attorney representing me right from the start of serious negotiations. Brokers, salespeople and title companies have their own motivations and cannot disclose to you what they don't know. There is an increasing trend in the law to require greater disclosure in real estate transactions, but there are too many things that can go wrong. The attorney is the only professional who will advise and protect you with undivided loyalty. Attorneys are most needed to head off trouble by anticipating potential problems based on their experience and use of their skill to provide for remedies. You and your lawyer must work together to create a laundry list of what could go wrong with your unique sale or purchase.

CHAPTER 3

BEING REALISTIC ABOUT

REAL ESTATE PEOPLE

OPEN·HOUSE

Who Are The Players?

It is quite important to know the different categories of people who work in the real estate industry. Real estate salespersons and brokers are licensed in all states which require that they pass a written exam. The distinction between salespersons and brokers is that the salesperson must be supervised by a licensed broker, who must maintain an office open to the public. The broker's exam is much more difficult, and someone must have a certain amount of experience before he can take it. The term "Realtor" is a designated trademark of The National Association of Realtors, to which approximately 40% of the licensed brokers and salespersons belong.

Who Are Appraisers?

A real estate appraiser is usually a licensed broker who has taken advanced courses in valuating real estate. Only twenty states have licensing requirements based on the 1989 federal standards enacted by Congress after hearings disclosed that as much as 50% of all losses during the savings and loan scandals were attributed to faulty or fraudulent appraisals. Many appraisers are affiliated with professional associations such as American Institute of Real Estate Appraisers or the National Association of Realtors and are thus authorized to use the designations of those organizations next to their names (MAI and RM). Banks and mortgage companies invariably engage appraisers to evaluate properties for mortgages. Individuals or companies use them for various purposes, such as setting a price for sale or condemnation by a governmental authority.

BRUCE'S INSIDER TIP:

You simply cannot rely on the lender's appraisal, which tends to be conservative, particularly in a buyer's market. It is made for financing reasons and could well be below fair market value. Even though you pay for the appraisal, it is made for the benefit of the lender, and you probably will not get a copy from the lender, because it is afraid of liability if you rely on the appraisal. This appraisal is simply not a guaranty to you of value or condition. Banks and mortgage companies demand conservative appraisals to increase their "cushion" on mortgage loans. The savings and loan crisis resulted, in large part, from overly optimistic and inflated appraisals.

Seller Beware!

It is essential for sellers, when dealing with salespeople, to determine the extent and limitations of their authority. For instance, if the salesperson promises to have an agreed number of "open house" parties to attract prospective buyers, this may be just a lure to get the listing. When in doubt, confirm the authority of the salesperson by speaking directly to the broker and insist that whatever is agreed upon be put in writing. After all, the real estate agency will require you to put the listing of your property in writing. If you have a special arrangement as to a commission, you will not be happy if the arrangement is not accepted or renounced when it comes to the attention of the broker, who usually must approve the listing.

If you have previously shown the house or discussed selling the house with some prospective buyers, then consider specifically excluding them from the listing (so that if you sell directly to one of them, you don't have to pay a commission).

 **BRUCE'S INSIDER TIP:**

Don't tell your broker, at the outset, that you are under pressure to sell because you have already bought a new house. Your agent may take advantage of this fact by prematurely lowering the price. Just calculate what the reduction in the commission will be for every thousand of dollars in reduction of price. Very little. It is to the agent's

advantage to have a quick sale. The lower the price, the more likely it is that the house will move in a hurry.

The "Standard Commission"?

Don't ever be bulldozed into accepting the "standard commission." There is no such thing. Even if it is printed in the listing agreement, you can always negotiate the rate of commission. In fact, any real estate salesperson or broker who tells you that your house cannot be placed on a multiple listing system unless you agree to a certain rate of commission is acting in restraint of trade and violating the federal antitrust laws, as well as the Real Estate Settlement Procedures Act, which applies to virtually every residential real estate transaction in the United States where there is a mortgage.

In some jurisdictions, the listing agreement <u>must</u> have a provision that states: "As seller you have the right to individually reach an agreement on any fee, commission, or other valuable consideration with any broker. No fee, commission or other consideration has been fixed by any governmental authority or by any trade association or multiple listing service."

TYPES OF LISTINGS

Sellers must also be aware that there are different types of arrangements for listings. These are:

Exclusive right to sell, where a particular broker is entitled to the commission agreed upon if anyone sells the property during the listing period, including the owner (the most common type of listing).

Exclusive agency, where the owner agrees not to employ another broker during the listing period.

A nonexclusive agency, where the property is listed with a number of brokers and the commission goes to the broker or salesperson who first produces a buyer ready, willing and able to sign a contract accepted by the owner.

In some states, there are circumstances in which the commission agreement need not be in writing (where the owner negotiates with a prospective buyer introduced by a broker and the broker protects his commission by sending a written notice to the owner). However, that is beyond the scope of this book. Generally speaking, there are laws requiring that all real estate listings and agreements of sale be in writing.

It is also possible for a seller to be liable for a commission for some period of time after the expiration of the listing period if the buyer was introduced to the property by the broker during the listing period. This is a very common clause in listing agreements, the "carry-over provision." Also, if a conspiracy between the buyer and seller to wrongfully deprive a broker of his commission can be proven, the buyer may be liable for damages.

It is very inadvisable to attempt to circumvent the broker's commission. Some buyers attempt to induce sellers to wait for the listing period to end and then sell them the house at a lower price. If the broker has an exclusive right to sell and has introduced the buyer to the house or can prove that the broker's ad or sign brought the house to the buyer's attention, then you can expect that the commission will be pursued relentlessly. If the agent has found a buyer at an acceptable purchase price, then he has performed a valuable service and has earned the commission. If you attempt to beat him out of the commission, in plain language you are a thief.

Attorney Review

We highly recommend that both sellers and buyers involve their attorneys very early in the game to review any contracts,

including the listing agreement, and the legal situations and risks involving brokers and agents before agreeing to purchase or sell real estate.

What Hat Is the Agent Wearing?

Although brokers and salespersons usually have more contacts with prospective buyers than with the owners, a buyer must be acutely aware that the broker and salesperson are ultimately working for the owner-seller, who pays the commission. (Of course, there are special situations where buyers engage a broker to find a house, in which case the buyer sometimes pays the commission, but this is the exception, not the rule.) In the usual situation, no matter how sincere the broker sounds, or how many coffees or lunches he treats you to as a buyer, be assured that brokers are vigilant to protect their own commissions and are expected to be finally and exclusively loyal to the seller. It is doubtful that the broker or agent will ever see you again after the closing of title.

BRUCE'S INSIDER TIP:

Of course, there is always the "listing broker" and the "selling broker," but you can be certain they both work for the seller,

who pays them both a commission. Sometimes the selling broker refers to himself as the "buyer's broker." Don't take this too seriously.

BUYERS MUST BE PARTICULARLY CAUTIOUS IN DEALING WITH BROKERS

The vast majority of real estate agents are honest professionals. However, as in any profession, there are sharks out there. The following are factors to be aware of. Without a buyer, there is no transaction. Without a closed transaction, there is no commission. Brokers represent sellers unless a special arrangement is made. This places a heavy burden on a buyer to learn how to spot a disingenuous broker or salesperson. Here are some guidelines:

a. If the broker discourages you from being represented by an attorney or from speaking directly with the seller, <u>watch out</u>.

b. If the broker pressures you to sign a written offer (which becomes a contract when signed by the seller) without all of the details and specific contingencies being discussed, explained and expressed clearly, it's not just a warning flag; it's a clear signal to end the relationship immediately.

c. If you are told by the broker that another broker or salesperson intends to show the house "tomorrow" and you must act now, that's a sales technique. If you're not ready to make an offer, resist the pressure.

d. If you find things out about the house after speaking to such people as neighbors, building inspectors, or the town clerk, that the broker did not disclose to you (bad schools, zoning problems, drainage difficulties, nuisances such as an incinerator in the area, the proximity of high voltage electrical lines, a suicide or murder at the premises) you have a right to question how honest or competent this agent is.

e. Watch out if the broker seems to be pushing one or two particular houses and not showing you others you know are for sale in the same price range. Some sellers offer the selling agents incentives (anything from television sets to all-expense-paid vacations) to promote their homes over others. This may be legitimate from the seller's perspective but can be a serious detriment to a buyer.

f. Make sure the broker and agent aren't showing you houses in your price range listed exclusively by them or their agency (so that they get both ends of the commission) to the exclusion of other houses on the market. This technique is not legitimate and you should terminate your dealings with that broker immediately.

Don't get stuck in a "price range," because you can make a bid on any house in any definite price range. All the seller can do is say "no" or extend a counteroffer. You might be very surprised when your offer is accepted. Some people have an exaggerated idea of what their house is worth and after a rude awakening, they become more realistic about price. Ask the broker to show you the price history of any house you may be interested in. If a house has been on the market a long time, you can bet it has been overpriced and the seller will entertain an offer much lower than the asking price. Don't be put off if the broker tells you that the seller will be insulted by your offer. It is the agent's duty to convey all offers to his seller.

Don't give a broker too much information about your finances. You can be sure it will in some way be used against you.

A Buyer Must Be Aware That It Is Not In The _Broker's Best Interests_ To Have Contingencies In The Contract Of Sale. Yet, This Is The Buyer's Greatest Protection. The reason is simple: Contingencies kill deals (but can save your bacon). To the broker no deal means no commission.

Form Contracts of Sale

Invariably, if there is a broker or salesperson in the picture, he or she will initially draw up the contract of sale. These form contracts, although designed by attorneys to allow real estate people to fill in blanks, are very often inadequate to protect the parties, particularly the buyer. Most attorneys for buyers add their own riders to such form contracts to customize them to the specific transaction. This will be covered in more depth in Chapter 5.

In many states there are consumer-protection regulations requiring that these real estate sale contracts be written in simple language, and some states also require a notice such as the following:

"THIS IS A LEGALLY BINDING CONTRACT THAT WILL BECOME FINAL WITHIN THREE BUSINESS DAYS. DURING THIS PERIOD YOU MAY CHOOSE TO CONSULT AN ATTORNEY WHO CAN REVIEW AND CANCEL THE CONTRACT."

Many brokers advise buyers that they will not convey a bid on their behalf unless they sign an "offer." **This offer is invariably in the form of a contract that can become binding <u>when signed by</u>**

the seller. If absolutely necessary, a buyer can sign such a contract _only if it_ _**specifically must be approved by buyer's attorney within a designated period of time**_.

Shockingly, there are many areas of the country and even sections of certain states where it is rare for an attorney to represent either of the parties. In those areas, the brokers or salespersons prepare the contract; order the abstract of title and title insurance, the survey and inspections; and arrange for a mortgage for the Buyer. All of the adjustments at closing and disbursement of funds are made by a representative of the title company, and the closing is also held at the office of the title company.

Some states have a prescribed form of contract, which brokers _must_ initially use, but this is of limited protection because a uniform contract cannot specifically cover unique circumstances.

Some, but not all, jurisdictions require that the broker furnish the seller with a _disclosure form_ to fill out concerning various physical and environmental conditions of the property in question and the history of the dwelling, and that this be turned over to a buyer at the time that a contract is signed. The problem is that often at the bottom of the disclosure form there is a disclaimer by the broker that although he has made all efforts to ensure the accuracy of the information, he takes no responsibility for the information contained in the form.

One state is considering exempting real estate brokers and agents from the duty to reveal that a particular house has a history of ghosts. If the agent knows of this reputation, why shouldn't he or she disclose this to the buyer? This raises the specter of the real estate lobby. (We couldn't resist it.) Because of the vulnerability of buyers, in particular, one state (New Jersey) now requires that brokers give the following notice in writing to all buyers and sellers:

"1. I am a real estate broker. I represent the seller, I do not represent the buyer. Furthermore, both the seller and the buyer should know that it is in my financial interest that the house be sold and that the closing be completed. My fee is paid only if that happens. The title company has the same interest, for its insurance premium is paid only if that happens.

"2. I am not allowed, and I am not qualified, to give either the seller or the buyer any legal advice. Neither the title company nor any of its officers are allowed to give either the seller or buyer any legal advice. Neither of you will get any legal advice at any point in this transaction unless you have your own lawyer. If you do not hire a lawyer, no one will represent you in legal matters either now, or at the closing. I will not represent you and the title company and its officers will not represent you in those matters.

"3. The contract attached to this notice is the most important part of the sale. It determines your rights, your liabilities, and your risks. It becomes final when you sign it - unless it is canceled by your lawyer within three (3) business days - and when it does become final you cannot change it, nor can any attorney you may hire thereafter change it in any way whatsoever.

"4. The buyer especially should know that if he or she has no lawyer, no one will be able to advise him or her what to do if problems arise in connection with your purchasing this property. These problems may be about various matters, including the seller's title to the property. They may affect the value of the property. If either the broker or title company sees that there are problems and that because of them you need your own lawyer, they should tell you. However, it is possible that they may not recognize the problems or that it may be too late for a lawyer to help. Also, they are not your lawyers, and they may not see the problem from your point of view.

"5. Whether you, seller or buyer, retain a lawyer is up to you. It is your decision. The purpose of this notice is to make sure you have some understanding of the transaction, the risks, who represents whom, and what their interests are, when you make that decision. The rules and regulations concerning brokers and title companies prohibit each of them from suggesting that you are better off without a lawyer. If anyone makes that suggestion to you, you should carefully consider whose interest they are serving. The decision whether to hire a lawyer to represent your interests is yours and yours alone."

There is a continuing and compelling need for the protection of consumers in real estate transactions because of the enormous risks. While the measures described above are helpful, they only warn the parties to be represented by an experienced real estate attorney, who will be protecting his client to the maximum.

CHAPTER 4

FOR SALE BY OWNER

In July 1990, *Consumer's Report* published a survey of sellers who sold their homes through brokers. A surprising 20% (one of the lowest overall satisfaction rates among service providers seen by Consumer's Union) reported dissatisfaction with real estate agencies. The usual dissatisfaction rate for service providers is 10%. The most common complaints were that the agent did not earn the commission, the agent put pressure on to sell the house at a lower price too soon, the agent did not show or advertise the house as promised and the seller had problems with the agent during the negotiation stage. About 18% of those surveyed tried to sell their homes themselves. *Should you?*

There's nothing illegal, immoral or fattening about selling your own home, known in the trade as FSBO or "fizzbo" (For Sale By Owner). It's the ultimate do-it-yourself project, and it can be done creatively and profitably. But, just as all worthwhile do-it-yourself tasks such as painting or wallpapering a room require specialized skills, selling your own home may also require skills and experience you do not have. Make no mistake about it, the painter, paperhanger or landscaper to whom you have paid what seemed to be a hefty price have all earned their fees. By the same token, the same can generally be said of real estate agents or brokers. While their primary purpose, of course, is to bring a seller and buyer together, their professional expertise can work for you as a seller in many ways: screening prospective buyers, negotiating price, seeking extra attorney input into a contract, monitoring mortgage financing, inspection, and so forth. So, before you decide to dispense with the real estate agents' professional services and hang out that sign "For Sale By Owner," you should increase your possibility of success by making certain you know what you're doing. You must understand that if you attempt to sell your house yourself, you are buying yourself a part-time job.

THE VULNERABILITY OF FIZZBOS

Homeowners who try to sell without a broker are considered easy pickings by young fledgling real estate salespersons. Older agents usually have many referrals to deal with and don't have the time that new agents have to cultivate FIZZBOS.

A new agent will employ various techniques to obtain the listing:

a. He will learn all he can about the immediate neighborhood by talking to homeowners, shopkeepers, postmen, deliverymen and other people who work in the neighborhood to find out about what improvements are planned, such as new schools, recreation centers and what new businesses are about to relocate there. He will also seek out the identity of those local residents looking for a new home. The agent will then visit the selling homeowner and introduce himself as a residential realty expert and attempt to impress him with his local knowledge to subtly convince the homeowner that he is out of his depth in trying to sell his own home. He will offer to show the house to prospective buyers immediately if the owner would just give a listing for a short period of time.

b.   The agent will prepare sample ads describing the unique qualities of the house, present a good picture of the house and show sample listings of houses in the same price range sold by his agency. The agent will then mention several publications that the owner will surely not be familiar with to persuade him that the professional agent has resources not available to him.

c.   This agent is hungry and has plenty of time. He will be persistent and will not be frustrated if you put him off. He will allow you to become frustrated so that you can turn to him for assistance. By this time you will have more than one of his business cards.

These pressure sales techniques are taught to new agents by super-agent instructors, who are master manipulators. You simply must learn how to resist this kind of pressure so that you can give the process of selling your own home without an agent a fair chance.

Your Best Strategy:

1. Thank the agent for his offer to help. Take his card and send him on his way as quickly as possible, without being impolite.

2. You can learn all you need to about marketing a house, just as the novice agent has recently learned. There are a host of books at your public library or local book store on successful sales strategies and techniques, *most of them written by brokers.*

Keep in mind that it is highly doubtful that you would have chosen this inexperienced real estate agent if you had decided to list your home in the first place.

Here are some basic areas to cover if you are determined to sell without a broker:

PRICE: Determine your price realistically, or you will discourage prospective buyers, or worse yet, cheat yourself. Hire a fee appraiser to estimate the fair market value of your house before you place it on the market. At the very least, visit your local tax assessor to get a feel of what prices similar houses in your area have recently sold for. Take into account those major repairs or replacements you cannot afford or care to undertake. A buyer will expect a credit or some other concession for serious defects or repair items, and who can blame him?

CONTRACT: Visit your friendly real estate attorney and have him prepare a basic contract to have ready in case a potential sale walks through your door. Consult your lawyer before you even place your first ad. What do you do if a red-hot prospect comes in and says: "Let's do a deal?" Without a contract in hand, you could easily lose that deal.

TITLE: Make sure your title is clear by examining the title insurance policy you received when you bought your house.

SURVEY: Have a copy of your survey available to show and explain to a prospective buyer. Understand it yourself.

HOMEOWNER'S WARRANTY: Consider offering a prospective buyer a "homeowner's warranty." There are companies that, for a premium, will guarantee the condition of an existing (resale) dwelling for a given period of time, particularly the major systems, such as electric, plumbing, heating, air conditioning and appliances.

Of course they will inspect your home to ensure it is in good condition before committing themselves and require you to first put everything in good repair.

TIME: Be prepared to give up leisure time on evenings and weekends to show your home to interested (or curious) shoppers.

FACT SHEET: Describe the outstanding features that make your house unique. Include any information you think will be to your benefit such as proximity to schools, quality of school system, location of shopping and entertainment, utility costs, local transportation, number of bedrooms and baths.

HOME IMPROVEMENTS THAT PAY OFF

While improvements are permanent additions that potentially can increase the value of your home, the reality is that few improvements truly increase the resale value of your property by the amount you spend on them. For instance, an in-ground swimming pool may not be as good an investment as it seems, especially in a Northern climate. Do not make the mistake of over improving a house; having a marble Jacuzzi in the most expensive house on the street can actually be a drawback to selling your home.

Start your home improvement plan with minor repairs or replacements. A cracked driveway and dead shrubs will do nothing to enhance the salability of your house. A green, well-kept lawn creates a lasting positive first impression. Regular mowing, trimming and weeding will add that intangible feeling that the owners care about maintaining their property.

While repainting the total exterior of your house should best be left to the professionals, redecorating the interior can entail inexpensive do-it-yourself jobs such as repainting a bathroom, waxing kitchen cabinets, or shampooing the carpets. Why not clean and replace worn or damaged screens, buy a new welcome mat and mailbox, and change unattractive lighting fixtures? Keep colors and styles neutral.

A multi-colored Tiffany-style ceiling fixture may be your favorite, but hardly fits the description of "neutral."

If you can do little else to improve your home, for goodness sake, get rid of all the junk and clutter you've been collecting for years. Discard excess furniture, clean out your closets, attic, basement, garage, and yard. And PLEASE hold your garage sale BEFORE putting that "FOR SALE BY OWNER" sign out on the front lawn.

Finally, "sweeten" your prospects by using potpourri, scented candles, and flowers to please the senses and use baking soda, a great odor neutralizer (it eliminates pet odor). It is sometimes recommended that you have a pot of coffee on the stove, bake bread or brownies or do anything else that would make your home enticing.

BRUCE'S INSIDER TIP: **Keep a permanent file detailing all checks and receipts for improvements. The IRS considers your cost basis for the house to include not only the original purchase price but also money spent on capital improvements. Be knowledgeable about mortgage financing by surveying lenders in your area. Your potential buyers will feel assured that you are a serious seller who has done his homework.**

ADVERTISING: Use local newspapers (daily and weekly), not state or regional. Consider ethnic newspapers, such as Chinese or Indian. Post notices of sale in laundries, on employment bulletin boards, at bowling alleys or in other places people (particularly women) will be looking. Advertise "open houses" the way real estate agents do. Put balloons outside your house on the scheduled date and have plenty of temporary signs showing the way to your home. By the way, be sure to take the temporary signs down immediately after the open house; otherwise, the next time you have an open house, your neighbors may remove the signs before the big day.

Be up-front with your customers. If asked if you've ever had a leaky roof, answer honestly. ("We did, but it's been fixed" will suffice if that is the case.) You can be held accountable for fraud for giving false information. It is not easy to negotiate with buyers face-to-face. Don't overreact emotionally if prospective buyers criticize your home. Be prepared to compromise, particularly after the inspection report.

Who doesn't want to feel that he has negotiated the best deal? So, in setting your price, allow for some fat that can be trimmed. Consider that you will not have to pay a broker 5% or 7% of the purchase price as a commission. However, don't assume that the buyer is unaware of this savings. Therefore, be prepared to reduce your price by at least 2% of your asking price, unless you are desperate. In that case, lower the price even more below your original price. On the other hand, if your house is priced too low, realize that there are vultures out there ready to pounce on such a bargain.

If you've covered the above contingencies by preparing the legal groundwork, investing lots of time and honest effort to improve your home, and learning some negotiating skills, chances are you will, at worst, come out the wiser for it. At best, you'll sell your home at the "right price" to the gratification of both your ego and your bank account.

CHAPTER
5

THE REAL ESTATE CONTRACT OF SALE

While it is not the purpose of this work to instruct the reader how to become a lawyer, it is useful for the principals involved in a real estate sale to become familiar with the most important instrument in the transaction, the "Real Estate Contract of Sale." All of the basic rights of the parties flow from this essential instrument. This agreement represents a "meeting of the minds" between the parties and reduces their unique understanding to writing. In fact, a law in every state called the "Statute of Frauds" requires that a contract for the sale or transfer of real estate must be in writing and that it constitute, at least, a memorandum setting forth the essential terms of the agreement between the parties. Obviously, the purpose for requiring that real estate contracts be in writing is to minimize the risk of misunderstanding and fraud.

What are the essential elements of the contract of sale?

a. The names and marital status of the parties or their representative capacity, if they happen to be a guardian, trustee, executor or attorney-in-fact under a power of attorney. All interested parties must join as sellers. If there is any question of competency, this should be resolved at the inception of the contract.

b. The present address or location of the parties.

c. A description of the property (by street address and by courses and distances or metes and bounds), a reference to a filed map and a reference to the tax lot and block number of the municipality and/or county where located. If possible, a reference to a survey upon which the description was based is helpful (including the date, file number and address and telephone number of the licensed surveyor).

d. WHAT IS INCLUDED WITH THE REAL ESTATE AND DWELLING.

This may not seem to be a very important subject but probably results in more disputes than any other. Sometimes the agent will state in the form contract of sale that all of the items described in the listing agreement are included. Very often the listing does not contain a comprehensive list, often it does not specifically exclude items the seller intends to keep (like a favorite chandelier), and very often there is a misunderstanding as to what are "fixtures" and what are movables or personal property.

Without a specific list, sellers have been known to remove trees, plants, bushes, planters, built-ins, diving boards from swimming pools, washing machine, dryer, dishwasher, electronic garage door opener, garbage disposal, water softener equipment, mirrors, radiator covers, freezer, screens and storm windows and doors.

Buyers are cautioned that this is one way that a seller tries to get even if he feels that the buyer has pushed him too hard on the price.

It is best to do the following:

1. Take pictures of anything you feel may be in question in a "worst case scenario."

2. List everything included or excluded after discussing it with the seller and broker. Make sure that the list becomes a part of the very first version of the contract. Items such as carpets, rugs, drapes, curtains, drapery and curtain hardware, fireplace equipment, TV antennae, fans, and humidifiers, particularly pose problems.

State specifically that these items are included in the same purchase price so that you will not be required to pay a sales tax, if applicable, for the sale of personal property.

e. THE PURCHASE PRICE AND HOW IT IS TO BE PAID

The deposit: Frequently a "good faith" deposit or "earnest money" is given when the parties arrive at some level of understanding as to the sale and purchase of the real estate. At this point, even if a notation is made on the deposit check, such as "deposit for purchase of 123 Smith Street," this is insufficient to satisfy the requirement that the contract of sale must be in writing. Anything less than a "sufficient memorandum" setting forth the essential terms is a "binder," which may or may not be adequate. Accordingly, the safest procedure is to have a contract drawn up by a lawyer or by the agent, subject to the approval of your lawyer before you give a deposit. Of course, the seller or agent will require a deposit in an amount that will be significant enough to deter the buyer from abandoning the deposit if he finds a better deal. In most states the customary amount (except in VA and FHA transactions) is 10% of the purchase price (often in more than one installment).

Who holds the deposit? Usually the agent holds the deposit in the broker's trust account pending the closing of title. If negotiated, and if the deposit is large enough to warrant it, this deposit is placed in an interest-bearing account. At times, the attorney for the seller will insist on holding the deposit in his trust account until closing. The customary arrangement is for the interest to "follow the deposit." For instance, if the deposit is returned because of a defect in title or failure of a contingency, the deposit <u>with interest</u>, is returned to the buyer. Otherwise, the interest goes to the seller at closing.

By negotiation, the interest may be divided between buyer and seller at closing. In a buyer's market, a buyer who insists on the interest will most likely get his way.

An alternative arrangement is to have the buyer assign in escrow a certificate of deposit that has not matured (so that he will not lose interest or be penalized). The advantage is that the certificate remains in the buyer's name and if the deal falls through it saves a lot of paper work.

BRUCE'S INSIDER TIP:

The certificate of deposit method has worked well for me and I recommend it. I have never allowed the interest on the deposit to accrue to the seller's benefit unless it is a very minor amount.

What is a "down payment"? Although often confused with the deposit, this term simply describes the total amount of cash (besides the mortgage financing) put down on the entire transaction by the buyer. It is reasonable to have the buyer represent to the seller that he has sufficient cash (aside from the mortgage applied for) to complete the transaction. It is also legitimate for the seller to insist on proof of buyer's ability to complete the transaction if he gets the financing. A bank reference should suffice as assurance.

The total purchase price is composed of the deposit, usually paid to the broker or seller's attorney on the signing of the contact by the buyer; the proceeds of a mortgage secured by the property given by a lending institution, such as a bank, mortgage or insurance company, a private source, the seller, or assumption by the buyer of the existing mortgage (with permission of the present holder except some FHA or VA mortgages); and the balance of cash paid by the buyer at closing. This balance of cash from buyer is always subject to adjustments, such as municipal assessments for improvements if the work is commenced prior to the date of the contract (or closing), taxes, sewer, water, cost of repairs seller is responsible for, or fuel in tank. Because title will pass to the buyer at this time and the amount due is normally a substantial sum, it is commonly required that this balance be paid in cash or by a certified or bank cashier's check.

CAUTION: In development contracts, builders try to get an "escalator clause" built into the contract of sale, where the purchase price can be increased if the costs of construction or material increase from time of contract to time of closing. In effect, this is a "blank check." If the buyer objects strongly enough, the builder may agree to a cap on the increase. Under no circumstances should a buyer agree to this arrangement without the cap. It should be negotiated <u>out</u> from the inception.

f. THE MORTGAGE CONTINGENCY PROVISION. As previously mentioned, the type of and principal amount of the mortgage, the interest rate (or simply the prevailing rate of interest), the duration of the loan, a limit on "points" or other costs to the buyer, a requirement that the buyer exercise due diligence in pursuing the mortgage application and a time limit to obtain a <u>written</u> mortgage commitment **(in default of which either party can cancel)** are <u>all</u> part of this condition to the contract becoming binding.

In many contracts with builders of new homes, the seller may try to require the buyer to use the lending institution chosen by the seller (who probably has his construction financing with that lender and will likely get some benefit such as a commission). It is always better for the buyer to have his own choice of lenders. In most development contracts, the seller has an option after the contingency period for the buyer to obtain a written commitment, to arrange for the buyer's financing if he can't get his own mortgage. There are many variations, and buyers should be creative and flexible in negotiating these conditions.

g. THE DATE, TIME AND PLACE OF CLOSING OF TITLE. Normally the time of closing is not of the essence. Either the buyer

64

or the seller is entitled to a reasonable postponement, as it is difficult to fix an exact date in the contract of sale. However, as the time approaches for closing, both parties must make definite plans and, depending on the circumstances, either party may make "time of the essence" by his attorney's using these exact words in a notice to the other party and his attorney.

The requirements are technical, and an attorney's services are suggested because if there is a default a lawsuit will surely ensue.

Most builders prevent this type of situation by providing escape clauses in their contracts of sale prohibiting a "time of the essence" condition for a given period of time after the scheduled time for completion and closing in the contract. In addition, in such contracts, delays due to strikes, walkouts, shortage of materials, weather and environmental conditions are regarded as "causes beyond seller's control" and will excuse prompt performance.

 **BRUCE'S INSIDER TIP:**

Never rely on a builder's date for closing a development home. Build in a cushion in your planning and make sure there is an

outside date in the contract when you will have the right to cancel no matter what the builder's hardship is and even if it is beyond his control.

h. TRANSFER OF OWNERSHIP AND QUALITY OF TITLE.

The contract must provide for the seller to transfer ownership of the property by a deed. This is the instrument of transfer of title, which is filed in the central recording place as required by law. There are different types of deeds, such as warranty, bargain and sale with covenant against grantors, bargain and sale, quitclaim and special deeds for representative parties such as trustees, executors and administrators. The quality of title to be conveyed is usually expressed in the nebulous phrase "free and clear of all claims and rights of others" and excepts innocuous rights of way such as those of utility companies and other easements and agreements of record that do not interfere with the present or proposed use of the property and are not violated. Another expression used to describe the quality of title is the more precise term "marketable title." This is defined as the kind of title that a reputable title insurance company doing business in the state where the property is located will insure at <u>regular</u> rates. What is important here is to provide specifically in the contract of sale that if the title is unmarketable or defective, the buyer has the right to cancel and should be entitled to the return of his deposit <u>plus actual search</u>

and survey fees. There is no reason for the innocent buyer to pay these expenses when the title is defective but, incredibly, except in those places where the seller pays for the search, this point is usually absent in form contracts prepared by brokers. It is highly doubtful that the seller's broker will suggest putting it in for the buyer's protection, and the burden to negotiate it into the contract is on the buyer.

i. USE OF PROPERTY. If the property is a residence, the contract should state that it is. There should be a representation by the seller that such use does not violate the zoning ordinance, building code or any other law. The buyer is then given the right to make an inspection, or if required in the municipality, an inspection must be arranged and paid for by the seller to obtain a "certificate of occupancy" upon resale. Some municipalities require this in order to keep track of and upgrade residential properties.

Examine the seller's survey and compare it to the configuration of the actual house. If there is an addition to the house or a new garage not shown on the original survey, the seller should have obtained a building permit and certificate of occupancy. If any violations of law are found, the seller must correct these violations at his expense or the buyer should have the right to cancel the contract. These are essential safeguards and are usually not too well addressed in form contracts.

j. OTHER CONDITIONS AND CONTINGENCIES. As you have seen, many conditions could be imposed as contingencies to a binding contract of sale. These pertain to such things as title, termite, structural and environmental inspections, approvals from governmental agencies and private bodies, and sale by buyer of his present home, and must be spelled out in the contract. As a practical matter what we are really addressing is the protection of the deposit and the assurance of its return if the seller defaults or the condition is not satisfied. This is why the deposit is invariably held in escrow until closing.

k. REPRESENTATIONS:

BY BUYER. The buyer usually represents in the contract that he has sufficient funds, together with the mortgage financing applied for, to complete the transaction. He also represents that he will make a good faith application for the financing and diligently pursue it and cooperate with his chosen lender.

BY SELLER. One of the most important provisions in the contract is a representation of the seller that the plumbing, electrical, heating and if applicable, air conditioning systems and all appliances included in the sale will be in working condition at closing of title. This usually entails a pre-closing inspection by buyer. It must be clearly understood that this representation is independent from the structural inspection (with its procedure whereby the buyer can request repairs and if seller refuses, the contract can be canceled). This representation refers to the condition of the systems and appliances as of the <u>time of closing of title</u>.

l. RISK OF LOSS. Closely related to the condition of the systems is the question of who is responsible for physical deterioration <u>beyond reasonable wear and tear,</u> physical damage, or loss by casualty or otherwise. Since the seller is in possession and control of the property, it is the seller's risk. Contracts frequently provide that the premises shall be delivered by seller "broom clean and in good condition, reasonable wear and tear excepted." The contract must also deal with the possibility of a substantial casualty or total destruction of the subject premises, giving the buyer a right to cancel the contract in any such event.

m. BROKER'S COMMISSION. The contract must provide that the broker will be paid the commission, how much is to be paid and when. The normal arrangement is for the broker to be paid "if, as and when title is passed" to buyer and the balance of the purchase price paid. It is important for the seller to get a representation from buyer that the broker named was the only broker who introduced the buyer to the property. If there was no broker, then each of the parties should represent this to the other in the contract.

n. MISCELLANEOUS. The contract will provide for possession at closing (or other arrangement), no tenancies, no changes in the agreement unless signed by both parties in a subsequent writing, and the form of and address for any notices under the agreement and for the agreement to be binding on all who sign and those who succeed to their rights. (Most builders of development homes prohibit assignment or recording of the contract to avoid buyers' selling the contract for a profit or encumbrances on title in the event of a dispute between the parties.)

The Contract of Sale is the "blueprint" for the entire deal. It is indispensable that everything represented and agreed upon by either of the parties be clearly expressed. The contract of sale protects both parties against ambiguity, misunderstanding, fraud and dispute. Once a closing takes place, all of the provisions, including the representations and warranties (unless expressly reserved) are extinguished. They are <u>merged</u> into the deed and do not survive the transfer of title.

 **BRUCE'S INSIDER TIP:**

The mortgage lender will not even consider the buyer's application unless a fully executed contract of sale accompanies the application. The more comprehensively and

clearly the contract describes the transaction, the more comfortable the lender will be. We have included sample form contracts of sale for real estate in the form section of this book.

CHAPTER
6

GETTING THE RIGHT MORTGAGE

OK, you've found the right house without having to use a buyer's broker, you've seen past the cosmetic repairs made by the seller to market his house, you've had your house inspection and your in-laws approve. Now, how do you finance the purchase?

The key is: **SHOP AROUND**.

WHERE DO YOU START? At your own bank. They know you there, or at least they will be hospitable. Since they have some of your track record, they will probably be more motivated to give you favorable treatment in order to keep your business.

Where else? You can obtain a list of all the lenders in a locality and the types of mortgages they offer, including their current rates, toll-free telephone number, marketing areas, and percentage down requirements, from the same source where *Money Magazine* gets it: HSH Associates, 1200 Route 23, Butler, New Jersey 07405 (201-838-3330).

WHAT IS A MORTGAGE?

A mortgage is a lien or an interest in land created by a written instrument given to secure the payment of a debt or loan. It must be in writing and there must be an underlying debt or obligation. The debt is commonly expressed in a mortgage note or bond.

Surprisingly, only a small percentage of the people who have signed mortgage papers really understand the process. An attorney representing borrowers will explain before the papers are signed that title to the property is being transferred to them, subject to the security lien of the mortgage given to the lender to enforce the debt. Many people erroneously believe that the lender holds the deed until the loan is paid off. In fact, the buyer gets the deed, the lender gets the mortgage.

This mortgage lien is enforceable by the lender upon default of the debtor or mortgagor. The term "default" means breach of the agreement by failure of the debtor to live up to his promises, usually non-payment of principal, interest, or taxes, or failure to maintain insurance on the property given as collateral.

The most immediate and prominent remedy is foreclosure. This involves the commencement of a lawsuit by the creditor-mortgagee resulting in the real property being sold at a public auction to satisfy the balance of principal due, accrued interest, late fees, search fees, attorneys' fees, publication fees and sheriff's fees. The purpose of the action is to collect the debt by terminating the ownership interest of the defaulting debtor. Very often the lienholder will itself bid a nominal amount over the amount of its lien and become the successful bidder. If there is still a balance due after the foreclosure sale, the lender can sue the defaulting mortgagor for the deficit. (There are some states, such as California, where deficiency judgments against homeowners who occupy one-to four-family homes are barred.) If there is a surplus after the foreclosure sale, it goes to the mortgagor.

BRUCE'S INSIDER TIP:

You may be entertaining the thought now that you may be able to "steal" a house at a foreclosure sale. Think carefully; it is not "amateur night." There are professionals out there who know what they are doing and exactly how much they are prepared to bid on a given property. They do not get emotionally involved. You might be carried away and bid over your head or above the real value of the property. Also, the sheriff's sale is subject to certain priority liens, such as real estate taxes, which must be checked in advance of the sale. If you intend to bid at such a sale, you must have cash or a certified check payable to the sheriff (very often, 20% of the bid price). The balance is usually payable within 30 or 60 days or you will lose your deposit. Sometimes, it is a better idea to contact the foreclosing lender and attempt to purchase the property you are interested in after the lender gains ownership.

Basically, mortgages are <u>conventional</u> or <u>insured</u> and are <u>fixed rate</u> or <u>adjustable rate</u>.

A <u>conventional mortgage</u> is financing offered by institutional lenders (banks, savings and loans, mortgage companies) and is not guaranteed or insured. It is usually at a fixed interest rate for a fixed term of 15, 20, 25 or 30 years. The monthly payments remain constant during the term of the loan. The portion of the payment allocated to principal increases while the amount of interest from each payment decreases throughout the period of repayment. In today's economy, there is usually an origination fee ("points") paid by the applicant to obtain a commitment for such a mortgage loan. Each "point" is 1% of the amount borrowed (not the purchase price). As a rule, there is a "due on sale" clause, which does not allow for assumption without the written consent of the lender. That means that if you try to sell the property without paying off the mortgage, the lender can "accelerate" or "call in" the balance (make the entire principal balance of the loan and accrued interest due immediately).

An <u>insured mortgage</u> is one where private mortgage insurance is required by the lender (at a premium). A low down payment typifies this kind of mortgage, providing the borrower is found creditworthy. For example, the conventional insured "MGIC mortgage" (Mortgage Guaranty Insurance Corporation) is one where this private mortgage company collects a premium for providing insurance for the repayment of that portion of the mortgage loan that the lender would not have loaned in the absence of such insurance. The buyer pays the premiums until the principal balance has been reduced to the point where the lender would have made the loan without insurance. In essence, this company is a hired co-signer.

A guaranteed mortgage is one guaranteed by an agency of the federal government, such as a VA (Veterans Administration) or FHA (Federal Housing Authority) mortgage. There is also the FNMA mortgage ("Fannie Mae") guaranteed by the Federal National Mortgage Association, a federally chartered private mortgage company and a FHLMC mortgage (Federal Home Loan Mortgage Corporation).

These agencies usually insure or guaranty to banks and lending companies up to 90% of the principal amount of the loan. These types of mortgages also have a low or no down payment requirement. Such mortgages require that the borrowers reside in the real estate. You cannot finance investment properties with this type of loan. On FHA and VA mortgages, there are very strict limits on what fees the borrower may pay and mandatory appraisals. There is also a very rigorous inspection of the physical condition of the property. All repairs must be made at the expense of the seller. Some VA and FHA mortgages may be assumed <u>without permission of the lender</u> (non-qualifying mortgages issued prior to 1986 for FHA and prior to 1988 for VA).

<u>Assumption of a mortgage can be very hazardous to the seller</u>.

As previously stated, in recent years most mortgages have a "due on sale" provision requiring that the mortgage be paid off if the title to the property is transferred. However, the mortgagee may grant permission to the buyer to assume the mortgage after an application with financial information. Unless the mortgagee releases the seller from the mortgage, the seller remains as a <u>surety</u> (or guarantor) of the obligation. The seller can apply for a release if the buyer presents a satisfactory credit report and executes a "collateral bond." This, of course, is discretionary with the lender. If the seller remains obligated on the assumed mortgage, there is a great danger that the buyer (unless he has a considerable equity invested in the property) will default and leave the seller "holding the bag" by walking away from the property. This means that after a foreclosure, the mortgagee can obtain a personal judgment against the seller. Also, while the assumption remains in effect and until the assumed mortgage is satisfied, the seller must list this mortgage as a contingent liability on any financial statement.

Sellers must give their attorneys detailed information about their outstanding mortgages well in advance of the closing as many mortgages have special requirements as to "payoff."

For instance, in the FHA mortgage loan there is a prepayment penalty if a sufficient advance notice of payoff (usually 30 days prior to a payment date) is not given. On the other hand, there could be a rebate of mortgage insurance premium on prepayment or satisfaction if the "panel" of mortgages of which the given mortgage was part had a low rate of default (but this must be applied for). If you think you are eligible, write to the FHA at the address given below for the U.S. Department of Housing and Urban Development, Washington, D.C., and give your FHA index number, your name and address and the address of the property.

Sellers of homes having FHA mortgages which will be paid off must be aware of special conditions concerning these rebates. Generally speaking, on FHA mortgages you may be entitled to a mortgage insurance premium refund if you acquired your loan after September 1, 1983, paid an up-front mortgage insurance premium at closing and did not default on your mortgage payments. You may be entitled to a share of any excess earnings from the Mutual

Mortgage Insurance Fund if the loan originated <u>before</u> September 1, 1983, if you paid on the loan for more than seven years and if your FHA insurance termination took place before November 5, 1990.

It is interesting to note that when an FHA insured loan is refinanced, the refund from the old premium may be applied toward the upfront premium required for the new mortgage.

The U.S. Department of Housing and Urban Development sponsors a variety of home mortgage programs, such as Rehabilitation Home Mortgages, Graduated Payment Mortgage Plan, Adjustable Rate Mortgage Program, Condominium Mortgage Plan, Home ownership Assistance for Low and Moderate Income Families, Home Equity Conversion Insurance Program (Reverse Mortgage) and others specifically designed to assist senior citizens.

Information regarding the above is readily available from: U.S. Department of Housing and Urban Development, P.O. Box 23699, Washington, D.C. 20026-3699, telephone (703) 235-8117 and Association of Retired Persons, Home Equity Conversion Center, 1909 K Street, N.W., Washington, D.C. 20049, telephone (202) 728-4355.

BRUCE'S INSIDER TIP:

A prospective buyer can place himself in an advantageous negotiating position by <u>pre-qualifying</u> for a mortgage loan even before he has found the house he wishes to purchase. If a buyer can show the seller and broker that there is no necessity for a mortgage contingency in the transaction, it gives him leverage on the price, what items are included and other terms. The seller has the comfort of knowing that he has what is, in effect, an all-cash deal and he can readily do his planning.

<u>Private Financing</u>. Frequently, a relative or friend of the buyer will agree to finance the purchase of a home. The seller, in order to make a deal, will often agree to "take back" a first mortgage from the buyer as part of the purchase price. This can be a good investment on the seller's part and the buyer can benefit greatly by not having to pay an application fee, appraisal fee, credit approval fee and points. He can also save himself the expense of a survey, provided the seller has one that is relatively current. Most of all, the closing can take place quickly. The terms of such financing must be specifically stated in the contract of sale.

Sometimes, a seller will "take back" a second mortgage subject to a first mortgage given to an institutional lender in order to allow the sale to go through or to get a better price. However, care must be exercised since many institutional lenders prohibit "secondary financing." The reason is that a second mortgage reduces the stake of the owner in the property and increases his motivation to abandon the property if things go bad.

Installment Contracts. These are often called "land contracts" and are a form of creative financing in which instead of the seller conveying title to buyer, the seller retains title until the buyer pays a stipulated amount of the purchase price. The buyer then either gets his own financing or seller, at this point, takes back a "purchase money mortgage." This is often done when a buyer has poor credit and cannot initially qualify for a mortgage. In essence, this is a lease-purchase agreement.

Great care must be given in the preparation of such contracts, as the hazards of default by seller, who retains title, are obvious. One way a buyer can partially protect himself is to record the contract or a summary memorandum, which will show up in a title search. The buyer must also make periodic checks of the title to make sure the seller has not placed any additional liens or attempted to sell the property out from under the buyer. The deed, executed at the time of the contract by the seller, should be held in escrow by the seller's lawyer and given to the buyer when the conditions are met.

This type of financing is fraught with perils and should be used only as a last resort.

A Wraparound Mortgage is a form of second or subsequent mortgage financing. The wraparound mortgagee (seller) collects the installments on its purchase money mortgage and on the existing first mortgage from the borrower-buyer and makes the mortgage payment on the existing first mortgage, which is retained in order to keep the favorable rate of interest. A default on the first mortgage is a default on the wraparound mortgage.

Of course, the first mortgagee must agree to this arrangement because there is usually a "due on sale" clause. There are many variations on this theme.

HYBRID MORTGAGES. To meet changing needs, such as tight money situations, high interest rates and instability of money supply, lending institutions, in their ingenuity, have developed novel types of mortgages:

a.   Adjustable or Variable Rate Mortgage: The interest rate fluctuates according to a specific federal index (every one, three, or five years) such as one-year treasury bills at constant maturity, the national mortgage contract rate or 11th district cost of funds.

You should make sure there is a yearly and lifetime <u>cap</u> on increase in the interest rate and (if negotiated) a conversion option (to get a fixed interest rate at prevailing rates after a period of time).

b. <u>Renegotiable Rate Mortgage</u>: There is a fixed schedule of increases or decreases, e.g. changes allowed every three to five years tied to an index of average mortgage rates at the time of renegotiation.

c. <u>Graduated Payment Mortgage</u>: The borrower's income is expected to rise. Monthly payments during the early years are lower than in a conventional mortgage. The payments rise gradually over a period of five to ten years, then level off to an amount higher than with a conventional mortgage.

<u>CAUTION: ONE CONSEQUENCE OF THIS MORTGAGE IS APT TO BE NEGATIVE AMORTIZATION.</u> Instead of your equity growing as you make payments, your equity may be reduced at any given time to compensate for the lower than normal payments during the early years. One variation of this type of mortgage allows for renegotiation of the rate periodically. This type of financing is not recommended unless you are desperate to buy the house or the price is irresistible.

d. Balloon Mortgage: Mortgages that allow for payment of only interest for several years before commencement of amortization or payment of principal and interest as if the mortgage were longer than its actual duration. The installment payments will not retire the mortgage when due, and thus leave a balance or "balloon" amount due. Caution: This mortgage can be dangerous: What if, when the time comes for the balloon payment, the mortgage market is tight or you are out of a job? Refinancing could be difficult.

e. Reverse Mortgage: Instead of the borrower paying the lender, the lender makes periodic installment payments to borrower, the total of which is repayable (with interest) out of the equity when the property is sold or the mortgagor dies. This type of mortgage has an appeal for retired and older mortgagors, who are house-rich but cash-poor. The owner continues to pay taxes and insurance premiums. There are different features, depending on the lender's policies. Some allow the borrower to share in the home's appreciation of value. In looking for the best deal, it is very important to consider the loan's interest rate and closing costs.

f. "Buy-down" Mortgage: If the interest rate is higher than the applicant can reasonably afford, this mortgage allows the applicant or the seller to pay several points in advance in order to allow the borrower to start paying at a lower interest rate. The interest rate would then increase by 1% each year over the next two or three years, depending on how many points were paid in the beginning. This is ideal for individuals whose earnings or cash situation will increase with time. However, "negative amortization" may be a consequence and this should be checked in advance.

There are variations of the buy-down feature in which you deposit money in a non-interest-bearing account, which the lender draws on each month to make up the amount of the monthly payment that you are, at first, unable to meet. There is also the so-called 3-2-1 plan, which reduces the rate for two years at the beginning, 1% each year. In the first year, you would pay 2% less than the mortgage rate, in the second year 1% and in the third year the full rate and continue to pay the full rate for the remaining life of the 30-year loan. The overall cost may be higher than the fixed mortgage, but the reduced rate at the commencement of installments may be worth the extra cost, as it allows you to enter a deal that you otherwise would not be qualified for.

g. <u>Shared-Appreciation Mortgage:</u> This type of mortgage loan can lower monthly payments substantially. In return, the borrower agrees to repay the lender a percentage of the profit when the home is sold. This type of mortgage may be available only in an "up" market. Also, there are risks such as the lender being entitled to repayment after a designated number of years, whether the house is sold or not.

h. Shared-Equity Mortgage: It works like this: Two parties buy a home but only one lives in it, the remaining party acting only as an investor. The occupant pays a fair market rent to his partner who does not live in the house and keeps the proportion of rent that represents his own ownership. The investor partner pays his share of the carrying charges, the monthly mortgage installments and taxes. He splits the deductions with the occupying partner. Eventually they divide the value of the property, including any appreciation in value; usually within a period of three to ten years, the owner-occupant must buy out the investor. Unfortunately, the investor who wants out of such an arrangement is really stuck, as there is no secondary market for such an investment. This is a very poor investment in practice. It is a "get rich quick" idea that is pitched by real estate gurus on late night TV infomercials. This arrangement is, however, useful for parents who assist a grown child to purchase his first home.

A booklet published by the Federal Trade Commission helps prospective buyers understand the myriad types of mortgages and real estate terms. It is called "The Mortgage Money Guide," Consumer Information Center-J, P.O. Box 100, Pueblo, Colorado 81002 (Cost: $1).

Buyers must be acutely aware that the variations are infinite and should get expert advice when exploring the financing aspects of the transaction.

LOCK-IN AGREEMENTS: Once a financing plan is selected, in order to protect the interest rate and other terms of the mortgage commitment, the applicant should protect himself against any changes by entering into such an agreement with the lender for a consideration. Usually the fee is worth it, since the lender will not ordinarily keep the mortgage commitment open for the length of time of the "lock-in" because lenders hedge on the interest rates due to sudden and volatile changes in the money market. For instance, most mortgage commitments state that the actual interest rate for the loan will be fixed just a few days before the mortgage closing. In a lock-in situation, the lender will agree prior to the issuance of the mortgage commitment that it will guarantee for a specific number of days the availability of a specified rate of interest or formula by which the rate will be determined and a fixed number of points, provided the loan is approved and closed within a stated time period. If the lock-in agreement is executed and the loan not approved, the lender must refund the lock-in fee.

A WORD ABOUT NEW CONSTRUCTION AND CONSTRUCTION MORTGAGES.

If you purchase vacant land which you intend to build on, it is assumed that the purchase was subject to soil, percolation and other tests to determine whether a building permit will be issued and whether construction costs will not be prohibitive. This situation must be distinguished from the one previously discussed, where it is a new development and the builder is selling a new home from his subdivision. Here, you own the land and, to finance the construction, unless you are paying all cash, you need to apply to a lender for a construction mortgage loan, which ordinarily will be converted to a permanent mortgage upon completion of the dwelling. Plans and specifications must be agreed upon and an architect chosen, if applicable. Progress payments by the lender will be provided for in the mortgage commitment, and periodic searches of title to ensure the priority of the lender's lien must be made. Some states require that the builder provide a new home warranty but, in any event, one should be obtained.

BRUCE'S INSIDER TIP:

It can be a nightmare being your own general contractor in constructing a new home. It is probably a better idea to enter

into a contract with a builder wherein you sell the land to him and arrange for the construction of the dwelling in a "good and workmanlike manner." The builder will then have to deal with subcontractors and materialmen and you will not have to bother with mechanic's liens and other details. Of course, you will need an expert to check on the quality of construction before you close title. If the builder goes bust, you will not have to contend with a trustee in bankruptcy or a tangled real estate title; however, in such case you will lose the lot and location but not your investment.

THE MODULAR HOME

The basic frame of a modular home is usually pre-constructed off-site, marked by the manufacturer and shipped with instructions for installation on the foundation previously constructed on the owner's site. The advantage is that it may be cheaper than a custom-built home and faster to put up. The materials are usually as good as, and often even better than, those in a standard home. After the basic framed-in shell is in position, subcontractors are used to install the heating, ventilation, air-conditioning, plumbing and electrical systems. The proximity of the factory to the construction site is an important factor, as shipping costs can be substantial.

THE KIT HOME

A kit home is shipped in component parts to the site. It requires much more experience and skill to construct a kit home "from the ground up." Most popular of all kit homes is the log cabin.

BRUCE'S INSIDER TIP:

Advertisers of modular and kit homes use housing and building trade magazines. A good idea is to examine many manufacturers' catalogues. You should also check on the names of contractors who have assembled and installed such homes. Financing is the same as for new construction where you are building a house on a lot you already own.

REMEMBER, EVERYTHING IS NEGOTIABLE!

By now you should see that every aspect of the real estate transaction is negotiable. If you don't <u>ask</u>, you won't get.

Therefore, right from the outset, when dealing with seller's broker, the seller directly, or with a lender about financing, you must be focused and prepared to act to your own advantage. This takes planning, concentration and a keen awareness of the motivation of the other party. You simply cannot naively trust the good faith and honesty of others in business. Although we have adopted consumer measures to counteract the traditional warning "Caveat Emptor" (let the buyer beware), expert advice and knowledge are your only real safeguards against fraud in real estate transactions.

Believe it or not, you can learn the skill of negotiation. There are many excellent books and even courses on the subject. This skill sharpens your thinking when it comes to such issues as the amount of deposit or down payment on a transaction or even no down payment. In applying for a mortgage, negotiations with the lender can get you better terms and result in a substantial savings over the years. Learning this ability to haggle can give you the courage to suggest to a broker that he lower his commission so that the seller can lower the price or pay for some of the repairs out of the commission when the seller is reluctant to do so. After all, a substantial portion of the commission is better than no deal and no commission. Sellers should also learn this essential skill involving give and take.

An excellent and amusing book on the subject is *You Can Negotiate Anything* by Herb Cohen (published by Lyle Stuart Inc.).

BRUCE'S INSIDER TIP:

Many brokers offer to help buyers apply for financing with mortgage brokers or lenders. As a buyer, on first sight you may find "one-stop shopping" attractive. The application for a mortgage is filled out either by the salesperson or by a representative of the mortgage broker or lender <u>at the broker's office</u>. Too often the broker receives a "referral fee" that is not disclosed to the buyer. Be assured that <u>you</u> may be needlessly paying this fee. It is much better for you to shop around for the best mortgage package, which should include the best interest rate and lowest points, credit, appraisal and application fees.

CHAPTER 7

HOUSE INSPECTIONS

THE PRE-PURCHASE HOUSE INSPECTION

How do you protect yourself and your family from the <u>horrors of structural defects, radon, lead, asbestos, water contamination</u> and the like? Obviously, by having a strong **inspection contingency** provision in the contract of sale. As discussed in Chapter 2, this clause should include a comprehensive and specific list of the conditions to be covered, e.g. structural, termite and wood-boring insects, damage from them, environmental (radon, carbon monoxide, asbestos, lead, urea formaldehyde), well, septic, toxic waste, and buried fuel tanks.

For a relatively small fee a buyer can avoid buying "a pig in a poke" by having the house professionally inspected by a reputable engineer or home inspector. Since the buyer places great reliance on the inspection, the inspector should be <u>properly trained and insured</u>. At the very least, the inspection company must have Workers' Compensation, Liability and Errors and Omissions insurance. Unfortunately, very few companies have this coverage and this gives you no recourse in case the inspection was negligently done, accidents occur or the inspector himself is injured. Only Texas licenses inspectors.

The report is of no value to you unless the inspector clearly specifies in writing what must be done to correct any defective conditions and the approximate cost of repair. In order to be in a position where you can negotiate with the owner, you should require the written report within the time limits set forth in the contract. As you have been counseled repeatedly, buying a house is no task for the faint of heart and everything is negotiable.

Where do you find an inspector? It's as easy as "letting your fingers do the walking." The Yellow Pages of your phone directory list inspection services under "building inspection" or "home inspection services."

WHAT ARE "INACCESSIBLE AREAS"?

One tricky way that home inspectors attempt to detract from their potential liability is to designate certain areas as "inaccessible," because either the owner has stored items covering the foundation, roof, eaves, attic, or there are areas covered by sheetrock or other construction. The prospective buyer must attend the inspection, if possible, and insist that such "inaccessible areas" be kept to a minimum. Otherwise, the inspector has an "out" if he fails to detect a substantial defect that you, as the unwitting new owner, will inherit.

The following is a list of specific areas of the home which your home inspector should include in his list of areas to inspect:

1. General Exterior - including visual inspection of roof, gutters, chimney, siding and drainage.

2. Attic - including visual inspection of sheathing, insulation and ventilation.

3. Basement and Foundation - including visual inspection of structure and evidence of water problems.

4. Electrical System - including visual inspection of service line and interior of main panel, and sample testing of outlets, fixtures, and switches.

5. Plumbing System - including visual inspection of supply piping, drain piping and hot water heater and operation of tubs, showers, sinks, toilets and dishwasher.

6. Central Heating - including visual inspection and operation of heating system.

7. Central Cooling - including visual inspection and operation of cooling system (weather permitting).

Depending on what items are contained in the home being purchased, additional testing should be made with regard to the following:

1. Radon and carbon monoxide testing.

2. Wood-boring insect inspection and damage from it.

3. Water analysis for potability (safeness to drink) and pressure.

4. Septic dye test of system and laterals.

5. Lead and asbestos testing.

6. Pool Inspection for cracks and settling, liner problems and inspection of filtration system and motors for efficiency.

HOW TO CHOOSE AN INSPECTION COMPANY

Before you hire a company to perform the all-important pre-purchase home inspection, check its credentials, speak to prior customers, and ask a lot of questions. Some home inspection companies offer a free sample report, inspector biographies and other pertinent information for review. When you hire a company, make sure that it agrees to advise on corrections and give estimates as to the cost of repair. A "no risk guarantee" is offered by some home inspection companies, but this is of no avail unless the company is financially stable. If you are not satisfied with the physical inspection and report, for instance because there are too many "inaccessible areas" or no estimates as to the cost of repairing major defects, you should request a refund of the inspection fee.

Incidentally, even if the seller offers you a homeowner's warranty (as discussed in Chapter 4), this is no substitute for a pre-purchase Home Inspection by a competent home inspection service.

THE CONDITION OF THE PROPERTY: YOUR BEST STRATEGY.

If you are buying a resale, if it is anything other than a "handyman's special," you have a right to reasonably expect that it will be in good repair and that the plumbing, heating, electrical and air conditioning systems (if included) will be in working condition and that the roof and basement will be free of leakage and seepage. Certainly you have a right to receive a structurally safe and environmentally sound dwelling. That is why you are paying for an inspection that is appropriate and adequate to give you a good idea of what you are buying. But that is not enough.

<u>Your must ask the seller and his representative, the broker, many questions.</u>

The seller and the broker have a distinct duty to answer your questions about the past condition of the property, particularly on matters such as past leakage; water or other damage from structural defects, storm, flood, fire or other causes; past infestation; contamination; lead; radon; water potability or septic problems; underground fuel tanks; and whatever else you can think of asking or that you suspect or that you are curious about. <u>However, if you don't ask, the seller and broker ordinarily have no duty to disclose except as to latent (hidden) defects known to them.</u>

Most states require that the broker have the seller fill out a questionnaire disclosing everything necessary for a prospective buyer to know when considering the purchase. If you do not receive a "disclosure statement," then it is a good idea to keep a list of defective and non-functional items and environmental concerns so that you can check off this information against the written findings of the inspector, which are calculated to reveal evidence of past negative conditions. <u>Now is the time to deal with this critical consideration rather than to have to sue later for fraud</u>.

You absolutely must take an active role in purchasing your home. Your attorney, if armed with information you supplied, will pursue your remedies and negotiate for you. It is up to you, however, to decide which items must be taken care of by the seller and if the seller refuses, which items can be compromised and which will result in your canceling the contract.

THE PRE-CLOSING INSPECTION OF NEWLY CONSTRUCTED HOMES

Sellers of new homes as a rule do not permit any inspections other than a pre-closing inspection. So, in most development contracts there won't be a structural or environmental inspection and probably the only inspection (other than the lender's appraisal for mortgage purposes) will be the walk-through or pre-closing inspection of the newly constructed home. You will list the unfinished and non-functional items, and the builder will agree in writing to repair or correct them within a reasonable time. Ordinarily builders will not agree to escrows to secure such corrections.

Off-site improvements are usually covered by a surety bond posted by the builder with the municipality.

PRE-CLOSING INSPECTION OF RESALE HOMES

You will recall that in discussing the contract of sale we referred to the "pre-closing inspection" (as distinguished from the "pre-purchase inspection" of the home by the building inspection service). There are three purposes of the pre-closing inspection: (a) to ensure that all the required repairs have been adequately made; (b) to confirm that all systems are in operating condition; and (c) to confirm that there has been no damage or deterioration beyond ordinary wear and tear.

Remember, the inspection made by your building inspector was done as of a given date. The pre-closing inspection, which is preferably done after the seller has moved (but this is usually impractical), should be performed immediately prior to closing so that any problems can be addressed and resolved when you pay the balance of the purchase price.

Sellers of existing homes are not held to the same standards as builders, but they have a responsibility to reasonably maintain the property between the time of the contract and the time of closing, when they have had exclusive control of the dwelling.

CHAPTER 8

THE SURVEY, ABSTRACT OF TITLE AND TITLE INSURANCE

Certificate OF TITLE

The survey of the premises shows by actual measurement the quantity of land; the courses and distances of its boundary lines; the structures located on the land and their relationship to property lines, streets and party walls; and whether there is a violation of physical restrictions, such as setbacks, on the property. Thus, any building not entirely within the property lines or encroaching upon an adjoining property will be disclosed in the survey.

Since these considerations affect the marketability of titles to real estate, title companies invariably insist that the survey be made by a professional and licensed surveyor and the title insurance policy is issued subject to the facts shown on the survey, or if no survey is made, subject to such conditions as an accurate survey will disclose. **Where There Is Already A Survey Made By A Previous Owner, Depending On The Age, The Title Company And Lender Will Usually Accept The Survey With An _affidavit of no change_** from the seller. This can save the buyer the expense of a survey, usually $200 to $500.

Some states require that appropriate corner markers be set at all property corners unless the prospective owner ordering the survey waives staking in writing.

It is always a good idea for a buyer to have a survey certified to the buyer, his lender, the title insurance company and his attorney. It also helps the buyer to sell the property when the time comes by enabling the buyer to show a prospective buyer the unique physical and other characteristics of the property.

THE TITLE SEARCH

To Determine Whether Title Is Marketable And Insurable, An Abstract Of Title Based Upon An Examination Of All Instruments Of Record In The Central Recording Office Is Made. This is a condensed history of the title to the property and reaches back commonly **60 Years**, the longest possible period of "adverse possession" (where title can be obtained by continuous, open and hostile possession of the land under claim of right.) These searches are usually made by the title company, and an opinion of a title officer in the form of a title commitment or binder is issued to assure the lender and buyer of the marketability of the title and/or priority of the first mortgage lien. The survey is recited in the binder, and a copy attached as part of the report of title. The examination of title requires a high degree of skill and experience, and there are endless types of defects in conveyances and titles. However, most title defects are cleared up with available proofs or an "action to quiet title" is brought in court to do so. Perhaps this is the reason for such a small loss ratio to gross revenues enjoyed by most title guarantee companies.

TITLE INSURANCE

Title companies now do almost all of the title searches in this country. Instead of attorneys engaging abstractors to search title, the title companies hire the abstractors and the title company takes the responsibility for the accuracy of the search. This evolution has allowed for our present stable system of financing of realty. Banks and lenders are now guaranteed by multimillion-dollar title companies that their security (the mortgage) will give them the expected remedies upon default. The search and insurance rates of title companies are regulated by law. Title companies cannot render legal advice or guarantee mortgages; they only guarantee the marketability of title, subject to specified conditions. They also act as "escrow agents" to distribute funds at closing. ***Warning***: **They Do Not Represent Either Seller Or Buyer**.

WHY YOU NEED TITLE INSURANCE

Suppose for a moment that you have closed title and are now safely and happily ensconced in your new home. Suppose further that a mysterious woman appears at your door late at night and claims that she was the real wife of the presumed seller, who actually signed the deed with a woman who claimed to be the person at the door. Well, you think: "I had an attorney and did a search." The bad news is, That Search Will Do You No Good In

This Case. Why? Because the search does not disclose the authenticity of signatures. The attorney for the seller at closing or official who notarized the papers was not under a duty to require the signers of the deed to prove their identities. They only represented that they were the parties named in the deed and that they signed it. All the acknowledgment or notarization recites is that these people appeared, made the above representation and signed the instrument.

It may come as a great surprise that in the eyes of the law the deprived wife in the given circumstances is *more innocent* than you, the buyer, who apparently exercised due diligence and care. The reason: you as buyer, have, at least a reasonable opportunity to make an investigation, while the woman at the door did not. As a practical matter, the title company will buy out the seller-wife. The above scenario, which is not as far-fetched as it might seem, is one good reason for owner's title insurance.

Of course, there are others, such as rights and claims that exist not of record, easements and prescriptive rights. You can be sure that if the lender insists on title insurance as a condition of the loan, there is a compelling necessity for it. Most title companies will charge a nominal fee for an owner's title insurance policy up to the amount of the mortgage plus so much per thousand for the excess over the mortgage up to the purchase price. You can buy only the mortgage title insurance policy, but this is inadvisable. It is a one-time charge and, unlike other insurance, not a *yearly premium*.

When the house is sold, the new purchaser's attorney can order a "continuation search" from the time of the issuance of the former policy, which eases the process.

CHAPTER 9

THE REAL ESTATE SETTLEMENT

PROCEDURES ACT

The story goes that in the early 1970s, Senator William Proxmire of Wisconsin went house-hunting in Maryland. This is what he found: Just about every real estate agent charged the same commission and would not list a house unless the seller agreed to a minimum commission set by the multiple listing service; all surveyors charged the same fee; all attorneys charged the same fee for legal services; and kickbacks to attorneys of part of the title fees and premiums and kickbacks by surveyors to title companies, attorneys, and real estate agents for referrals were rampant.

The result was the Real Estate Settlement Procedures Act (RESPA), which enacted significant reforms to give consumers greater protection from unnecessarily high costs in the settlement process and provide greater and more timely information. This law is generally applicable to all transactions where there is a federally related mortgage loan covering a structure designed to be occupied by one to four families.

RESPA prohibits the splitting of fees and kickbacks other than for actual services performed. It also bars a seller from dictating to a buyer as a condition of sale that he use a particular title company. It also limits the amount of escrow a lender can require of a borrower for taxes, insurance and utilities and requires that lenders give a detailed accounting to borrowers at least once per year. RESPA, which became effective on June 20, 1975, has been hailed as one of the most significant reforms of our era and has been credited with cleaning up a multitude of abuses corruptly embedded in real estate procedures and practices.

For instance, a uniform form of closing statement must be used in applicable transactions throughout the entire country. All types of disclosures must be given to borrowers, including a good faith estimate of costs from the lender, a Disclosure (Truth-In-Lending) Statement as to the interest rate and its effect on installment payments. Most important of all, RESPA provides for serious and heavy fines for those who violate its provisions.

There is also a requirement that mortgage loan servicers notify borrowers in writing of any assignment, sale or transfer of the loan.

CONSUMER FRAUD LAWS

Can brokers offer premiums or prizes to attract buyers? The answer is probably "no" because it distracts prospective purchasers from the terms of the transaction. It "takes their eyes off the ball."

Many states have enacted consumer protection laws to eliminate sharp practices and scams in the marketing of real estate, including interstate sales of vacant lots and timeshares. These laws declare that deception and misrepresentation are unlawful in the advertisement of sales of real estate. Moreover, a growing number of states have adopted "plain language" laws requiring simple language (not legalese) in consumer agreements and disclosure laws requiring sellers and their brokers to reveal certain facts concerning the past condition of the dwelling (particularly defective conditions that are latent and known to seller). Buyers should make it their business to use these laws designed to protect against unfair practices, fraud and deception. **Ask Questions Of The Broker And Seller.** Some of these laws provide for treble damages for violation.

Some states also require lenders to obtain a sworn statement from both buyers and sellers at the closing that they both received advance notice of the number of "points" required to be paid in connection with the mortgage loan.

All states have a Real Estate Commission regulating brokers and real estate salespersons and are vigilant to enforce legal and ethical standards on their licenses.

Constantly Remember! The Traditional Real Estate Agent Must Put The Seller's Interests First. He Owes No Duty To The Buyer Except To Honestly Answer Questions And Disclose Known Latent Defects

CHAPTER 10

HOMEOWNER'S INSURANCE

One of the things you will be required to provide in advance of the closing, assuming that the house is being financed, is the homeowner's policy. This is what is called a multi-peril policy, a fancy way of saying a lot of risks covered under one policy. If you wanted to, you could go out and cherry-pick: that is, buy each individual coverage (fire, theft, liability) separately. That would cost a ton of money. Customarily, the homeowner buys a package policy (one year's premium paid in advance) that covers all of these perils. You'll have to name your lender as a co-insured; and any checks made out with regard to losses on the building will be made out to both of you. That way you can't have a big fire and make off with the proceeds and leave them holding the bag. Check with your agent. There are several homeowners forms; find the one that is right for you. For instance, if you own a condominium unit, there may be blanket insurance held by the condo association, which covers the common areas and the buildings up to the inner walls. In such case, all you need is a condo homeowner's policy, which covers from the inner walls in and the contents of your unit (at a considerable savings in premiums).

Remember that moment of panic the last time you thought your luggage was lost? If you travel at all, you certainly want coverage on your goods while away from home. If you do lose your bags (at carousel roulette) you have a maximum of $1,200 recovery from the airline and even less if you are flying international. So while the prudent traveler never packs valuables in a bag, it does not take long for a couple of suits or dresses to exceed that $1,200. Another timely tip: If your car is stolen, don't you want coverage on personal goods therein? There is a very low limit in the ordinary automobile insurance policy. Your insurance agent will not know your needs unless you tell him clearly.

It is important to know that all the lender requires is fire insurance with extended coverage (covering windstorm damage, explosions, etc.) so that the property can be repaired or restored. The lender is concerned only with its own security.

Let's say you have a designer sofa that is seven years old and very serviceable, but it burns up in a fire. Believe it or not, its fair-market value is probably only 10% or 15% of its original cost or replacement value. Therefore, a fair-market value homeowner's policy (though less expensive) will not give you enough money to replace the sofa, but a replacement value policy will. A replacement value policy makes sense in a building as well.

Suppose you buy a previously owned home. Perhaps it's 75 to 80 years old, Victorian and gorgeous. You were able to buy it for $100,000; however, to replace it in today's world might cost double that.

If this home were to burn down and you had only a fair-market policy in place, you'd get only the $100,000, not nearly enough to rebuild your home.

In deciding what the monetary limits of your homeowner's policy should be, you must, at a minimum, cover the principal amount of the mortgage. Unless your fire is a lot hotter than most, the land is not going to burn. Therefore, you need not carry fire insurance for the full purchase price of your home. If you overinsure your home, this can come back to haunt you if you later appeal your tax assessment, as this is a reflection of your own opinion of the value.

Because there is a low monetary limit on jewelry, cameras, china, furs, stamp and coin collections, objects of art and the like, in a standard policy you should consider increasing the coverage for such items. The insurance company will usually require estimates or receipts upon which to base the value. This type of rider to the policy is called a "floater."

Most lenders demand an escrow of several months' insurance premiums at closing and one-twelfth of the annual premium each month with your installment of principal, interest and real estate taxes. At the end of one year the lender will have enough in the escrow account to renew the insurance policy, and you will not have to come up with a large sum to pay the renewal premium.

Some lenders, in recent years, will allow the mortgagor to renew his own policy and provide proof of coverage and payment of premium.

BRUCE'S INSIDER TIP:

You should always deal with an insurance agent who you know or will get to know, not directly with a large anonymous company. If you have a loss, you want someone who will "go to bat for you" with the big, bad insurance company. You want to be able to say: "You've earned commissions all those years, now it's my turn." Always opt for replacement value. If you have a loss, you do not want to find that you are only getting a small percentage of the replacement cost because of depreciation.

By all means, save receipts for large and expensive items and take pictures or videotapes of your most expensive possessions so that in the event of a loss you have proof of

ownership. Often, after a loss, the insurance adjuster will blithely say: "Well, if you show me receipts, we could settle this claim." Well, you've gotta be kidding me. How many people have receipts for everything they have purchased?

On one occasion, my car was stolen when my son was on his way to college with everything but the kitchen sink in the car. The only reason why the sink wasn't there was that he couldn't find a wrench to detach it from the house. When the adjuster asked for the receipts, I could only chuckle. But he was adamant. I got together with the adjuster and his boss and I said: "Tell you what we will do, gentlemen. We will go to your home right now and if you can show me receipts for everything in your home, I will drop my claim altogether." Well, clearly, I knew they couldn't, and they knew they couldn't. Now we were talking the same language and we settled the matter.

Take a larger deductible to save premiums. Be judicious about making claims since the insurance company can refuse to renew your policy or sometimes cancel it for a high incidence of claims. If you do have a large claim and your agent cannot help you settle it with the insurance company, consider using a public adjuster. They are professionals, who charge 10%-15% of the claim, but usually make up their fees in the settlement because they know how to deal with insurance company adjusters. Make sure you have adequate "additional living expense" coverage, as you may have to live in a motel, mobile home or rented quarters if you must leave your home while it is being rebuilt or repaired.

Consider "umbrella insurance," which is an excess liability policy with coverage of $1 million or more, which coverage comes into effect after your homeowner's and automobile limits are exhausted.

LIFE AND DISABILITY INSURANCE OFFERED BY LENDERS

Lenders offer reducing term life insurance to homeowners to cover their mortgages in the event of death, and disability policies to cover mortgage payments during periods of total disability. These are, for the most part, bad deals. The premiums are invariably higher than term insurance you can get elsewhere. Try savings bank life insurance for term insurance and try to get disability insurance through an affinity group you already belong to or can join, such as AAA or AARP. By all means, ask a lot of questions and shop around.

CHAPTER

11

FINDING A COMPETENT LAWYER
FOR A REASONABLE FEE

If you have gotten the impression from prior chapters that it is imperative that both buyers and sellers engage an attorney *right from the beginning*, you are right. While you're at it, make it an experienced *real estate attorney.* Remember, you are choosing a specialist to handle a special job.

There should be no pussyfooting about it. Real estate is technical, intricate and complex legal stuff and you can easily lose a lot dealing with people who are motivated by profit, not humanity or principle. You need an effective legal representative. How do you find the right lawyer? The strong likelihood is that you won't find him through the Yellow Pages. Surely, there are people you deal with whose business judgment you respect. Ask them who they have engaged to represent them. For instance, ask your insurance agent, your banker, your landlord, a teacher, a business associate or fellow worker, or call the city, county or state bar association and ask them to recommend an attorney experienced in residential real estate closings.

The next step is to make an appointment to discuss your representation and discuss a fee if you wish to hire this lawyer. Yes, you are going to interview your attorney, and you are looking for the right man or woman who has the skill and experience to do the job. You are not looking to choose a friend or companion. You are not trying to beat a murder rap.

No matter what a good real estate attorney will cost you, no attorney or a bad attorney will cost you a lot more.

WHAT SHOULD YOU LOOK FOR?

1. Can you communicate with this person or are you dealing with a "know-it-all" who doesn't listen? This is all the comfort level you are seeking. There are approximately 860,000 lawyers in the United States, but only 1.5% or around 13,400 in 24 categories are regarded as *The Best Lawyers in America* (1995-1996 edition). It is doubtful that you will need such high-priced talent. Try referring to *Martindale-Hubbel Law Directory* to find a real estate attorney in your area (available in most public libraries).

2. Ask the attorney about his experience with the kind of transaction you are involved in. Get the names of present and past clients and contact some of them.

3. You are asking the attorney to represent you in the deal, not to make the deal. Attorneys should not offer business advice as to the advisability of the transaction itself on the merits.

4. Trust your "people skills" in judging the competence of the lawyer. Ask your questions, particularly about the fee, and don't assume anything. Make sure you are not being charged for the

brief interview. Ask whether the attorney would consider a "package fee" if you are buying a home and also selling your present home. In any event, try not to have the fee based on an hourly rate. Most real estate lawyers will agree to charge a "flat fee" and you will feel secure that you have "capped" the fee and won't have to worry about the "meter running." You will be very surprised how welcome your candor will be to this lawyer. If it isn't, get out of there fast.

5. Ask whether the attorney will be handling the matter himself or whether an associate or paralegal will be handling it under his supervision. Pin down the question of ultimate responsibility for the proper professional services you are entitled to. Meet the associate and see whether you are comfortable with the arrangement.

6. If you hire the lawyer, get it in writing. Spell out what services will be performed on your behalf and what is excluded from the flat fee. Get into the good habit of keeping records.

CHARTING A COURSE THROUGH THE ICEBERGS

Your lawyer will first look over the listing agreement with the broker, if you are a seller, and explain it to you and point out the pitfalls. For example, it may be desirable to require a minimum number of showings, open houses or advertisements to be placed by the broker; if that number isn't met, you will have the right to cancel the listing. Your lawyer will collect all of your title papers and make sure that there is adequate proof of ownership. He will then determine who must sign a contract to properly convey title and ascertain what liens affect the premises. He will explain the community property laws if applicable in your state, the homestead laws, if applicable, and the rules pertaining to joint ownership. He will give you an outline of how the tax laws may affect this transaction. He will, of course, analyze the contract of sale, explain it to you and suggest amendments to protect you.

If you are a buyer, he will review and analyze the contract and prepare an amendment modifying the language so that it contains the conditions and changes to protect you. Of course, all of the items on your "laundry list" will find their way into your amendment to the contract.

Ultimately, there will be a meeting of the minds on the language in the contract. Once the process gets under way, there is usually a great deal of cooperation and harmony in proceeding to closing.

CHAPTER

12

THE CLOSING OF TITLE

OK, you've heard from the lawyer and he's told you how much you need to close the deal. The arrangements have been made with the bank for certified or bank checks payable to you (the safest way) for the balance of the down payment and closing costs. Your lawyer told you to bring along some personal checks just in case. You have planned this day for a long time. You have made the arrangements for homeowner's insurance with your own insurance agent. (Remember: better to know him and not deal with a large company that doesn't know you and won't take your part in the event of a loss.) You will bring a copy of the policy and paid bill for the lender and flood insurance, if required. Oh, yes, you've already placed the utilities in your own name. You've also double-checked the date with the mover.

The lender's attorney or legal department has reviewed or prepared the necessary instruments to cover the mortgage loan, and the sellers and their attorney will meet you at your attorney's office to "close title." The closing checks have been cut. Before the closing, you will make your pre-closing inspection. You're so proud of yourself, you've even made out change-of-address cards and can't wait to move in. All contingencies have been met. All systems are "GO."

Wait A Second! What If All The Contingencies Have *Not* Been Satisfied?

It doesn't happen that often, but occasionally a seller will refuse to deliver the premises "broom clean" or to make agreed repairs, or will remove items included in the sale. The one effective weapon is not to close. Of course, additional expenses will be incurred, particularly those associated with preparing the mortgage papers, but it's worth it. The party who is at fault will end up paying these expenses. Usually these matters are resolved without a lawsuit and everyone goes on with the closing.

ADJUSTMENTS AT CLOSING

All liens, mortgages, charges against both parties, filing fees and credits will be itemized on the closing statement. It is essential that both parties keep a fully executed copy of this statement, as it will be needed for tax purposes.

Both buyer and seller must be alert and focused, and it is essential that they understand the method and reason for each charge and deduction. Many mistakes are buried at closings. Here are the ripest areas for error:

a. The payoff of mortgages. Make sure if you are a seller that you have carefully examined the mortgage payoff letter(s) to ensure that you are given credit for the escrow balance and all installments, particularly the last one you paid. If the closing attorney is to cancel the mortgage of record when it is returned by the lender, you should not pay the lender a cancellation charge. Make sure that the closing attorney or escrow agent sends the payoff check to your lender by overnight mail. The cost is usually less than the per diem rate of interest and you will be charged interest for only one day (not for the number of days it ordinarily takes for the check to be mailed and received).

b. There are various ways of figuring the tax proration. The only fair method is to calculate the total taxes for the year and then arrive at a per diem rate. This is multiplied by the number of days in the year that have elapsed. This gives us the amount the seller is responsible for. We then subtract what the seller has paid in taxes. The difference is the adjustment (either in favor of or against the seller). This method applies only to calendar year quarterly tax payments.

c. Watch out for extraneous fees the lender may add on, such as photo fee, warehousing fee, processing fee, document preparation, or review. If a given fee was not revealed to you in the mortgage application or mortgage commitment, you should fight not to pay it. You were entitled to full disclosure and should not hesitate to tell a representative of the lender that if he insists on the hidden charge, you will report this to the banking commission or other appropriate law enforcement body.

d. Make sure that your old mortgagee has your new address. You may be entitled to an adjustment when the lender audits your account. In fact, if the loan you paid off at closing was a non-qualified FHA loan, you should now apply for a rebate of the premium paid for mortgage insurance premium (dependent on the favorable experience of the FHA with loans in your "panel").

e. Often overlooked adjustments are: escrow balance of taxes held by mortgagee, maintenance and capital replacement escrows held by condominium associations, fuel oil left in the tank and prepaid burglar alarm central station charges.

OCCUPANCY PROBLEMS AT CLOSING

It does happen: The mover doesn't show up. Can you imagine the seller's embarrassment when his mover has the wrong date? The sellers are at the lawyer's office and their teen-age son calls to say that the buyer's movers are outside the house and their own mover hasn't arrived. After a few calls, it is obvious that nothing could be done for a few days or even a week. What does everyone do?

Since the seller's mover (or sellers, for not confirming the date with the mover) goofed up, the sellers must be inconvenienced and pay the expenses of such a fiasco. Their furniture will be moved into the garage or other available area (even storage, if necessary) by the buyer's movers, who will be paid for this additional work by sellers. Sellers will have to stay with relatives or at a hotel until they can move. In the meantime, the closing will take place *with an adequate sum out of the seller's proceeds of sale held in escrow until they are moved out.*

OTHER ESCROW ARRANGEMENTS

By agreement the parties can provide for the seller to remain in possession after closing at a daily occupancy rate. This is frequently done when a mortgage commitment is about to run out and the buyers wish to retain a favorable interest rate or the sellers cannot move until some later date and the buyers still have a place to live. A fixed sum is held in escrow until the premises are vacated. The party in possession agrees to pay all utilities, aside from the daily charge for occupancy, and indemnifies the new owner against any claims. Of course, he must also agree to keep his insurance in effect until he moves out.

Sometimes it is necessary for the buyers to occupy the premises prior to the closing. If convenient for the sellers, an occupancy agreement with an escrow deposit can be entered into, but this should be avoided because the buyers will frequently find things wrong with the home that they have previously failed to discover. Even though they have acknowledged the good condition of the property in the occupancy agreement, as a practical matter they can delay closing unless the seller has repaired the faulty condition or agreed to make an allowance at closing.

Whatever the scenario, the closing attorney holds in escrow a sufficient amount (either by deposit by buyers or from the proceeds of sale to sellers) to cover the cost of recovery of possession if there is a default by either occupying party.

ESCROWS FOR REPAIRS

If repairs are required as a result of the pre-closing inspection and there is not sufficient time to make them prior to closing, or if the repairs made were inadequate, unless the lack of repairs will make the dwelling uninhabitable a sufficient amount of money can be held by buyer's attorney in escrow to cover the cost of repair, or the parties can settle on a sum, give the credit to buyer at closing and end the matter.

IRS TAX INFORMATION RETURNS

It is almost incredible that it has only been since 1987 that the IRS has required that sales of real estate must be reported (on one-to-four-unit residential real estate). One wonders how the IRS knew about real estate transactions and the profits from them before that time. At closing the sellers must give their Social Security numbers, sign a form (1099S or B), which contains their new address and the sales price for the residential unit being sold. A copy of this form is filed with the IRS and sent to sellers by the closing attorney prior to January 31st of the following year.

The 1099 form is <u>not</u> required where seller is a corporation, or for refinances, gifts, foreclosures, abandonments or involuntary conversions.

WHAT TYPE OF DEED SHOULD A SELLER GIVE?

If you are the seller, **never** give a warranty deed even if it is the custom in your area to do so. The time to be aware of this is at the time you sign the contract. Spell out in the contract that you will give a bargain and sale deed with covenant against grantor's acts. Such a deed contains your representation only to your immediate purchaser that you have not done anything to disturb the free and clear nature of the title. This should be more than sufficient for any buyer or his title company.

The reason for not giving a warranty deed: You are not a title company. One who gives a warranty deed guarantees good title not only to the immediate grantee (buyer) but also to remote grantees.

Someone four or five times removed in the chain of title can sue you in the future. Why should this hang over any seller's head?

Preparation for Closing

A careful seller's attorney will advise seller of the time and place of closing, what paid bills to bring to the closing, to arrange for the utility readings and transfer of the accounts to buyer, to bring the keys and such other details that must be settled at closing.

A careful buyer's attorney will obtain the mortgage payoff statement(s), verify bridge and equity loan balances and arrange for payment of other liens, order a run-down from the title company and advise seller's attorney of the number and types of checks the buyer will deliver to complete the transaction. Buyer's attorney will have his clients in earlier than the closing of title for the closing of the mortgage. Buyer's attorney will prepare and fax a copy of the proposed closing statement to seller's attorney, as buyer's attorney will control the payment of liens and placement of the new first mortgage as a paramount lien. Buyer's attorney will arrange for the broker to turn over the deposit so that he can deposit it together with the mortgage proceeds and balance of funds from buyer and then prepare trust account checks to pay seller, the title company, brokers' commissions and record the deed and mortgage.

DELIVERY OF PAPERS AND RECORDING

The buyers pay their funds to the sellers, the mortgage papers are signed, the deed signed and delivered, everyone shakes hands and wishes each other well and the keys are finally turned over to the new owners. Of course, the sellers have left all of the instruction booklets for the appliances and must explain the idiosyncrasies of the burglar alarm system one more time.

Buyer's attorney will forward the original deed and mortgage to the county recording office and will send the recorded instruments to his clients in due time. He will also send his final report to the title company so that the appropriate title policies can be generated. The parties will be given copies of all pertinent papers and told to open files for them. The Buyers will be advised to keep records of all capital improvements and repairs so that they can be accounted for later on for tax purposes.

Invariably there are mutual wishes of luck and good health exchanged. Hopefully, everyone will live happily ever after.

CHAPTER

13

AFTER THE CLOSING

The first purchase for your new home should be a new *file cabinet*. At the closing of title, you received a number of papers and instruments. These are essential records that you must preserve and have available in the future. This is a great time to start good habits like keeping significant records.

Aside from all the personal records you had *before* the closing, you now have a sheath of papers *from* the closing. These consist of, at least, copies of the deed, mortgage note and mortgage, payment book or temporary coupons for mortgage installments, the closing statement (of the purchase or, if you sold, the sale), the survey, the builder's warranty (if a new home), the appliance instruction books, your homeowner's and, if applicable, flood insurance policies, and the Regulation Z Mortgage Disclosure Statement. Within weeks after the closing, your attorney (if you are the buyer) will send you the recorded deed and owner's title insurance policy. These are your records of home ownership and must be available when you need them for tax, insurance and other important purposes. They must be kept until your home is sold.

If you have purchased a new home, you should try to obtain the plans and specifications and keep the sales brochures just in case they become important in the event of a future dispute with the builder or need to remodel or repair your home.

You should also start a file for receipts for major equipment and furniture purchases and capital improvements. While you're at it, you should make an inventory of furnishings and belongings for insurance purposes. There are many computer programs already programmed to help you do this. Better yet, take still pictures or videotapes of every room in the house and refresh them every two years. Please remember to keep these records and film off the premises in case of fire or explosion. In the event of such a casualty, this will be strong proof of your ownership of these items.

Current tax returns should be kept in your file for three years and older returns for six years. Credit card numbers should all be listed with emergency numbers for the credit card companies in the event of a loss or theft. Have a separate file folder for your insurance policies. Also, have a file for service contracts. Warranties should be filed and kept separately. Your original recorded deed, your will and personal records, such as your marriage certificate, judgment of divorce, birth certificate, military record, life insurance policies, vehicle titles, retirement account records, passport and Social Security card, should be kept in a safe-deposit box. Common sense and good judgment should dictate what should be kept and for how long.

Just some information concerning your mortgage to tuck away until you need it: **If you are concerned about whether your bank or**

143

mortgage company has calculated the change in your adjustable mortgage rate correctly, is holding an excessive amount of tax or insurance escrow, or whether you have paid in enough equity in the property to dispense with private mortgage insurance, you can obtain a private audit from <u>America Homeowners Association: (703) 892-4663, Consumer Loan Advocates: (708) 615-0024, or Loantech: (800) 888-6781.</u>

<u>BE IT EVER SO - SAFE, THERE'S NO PLACE LIKE HOME</u>

Change the tumblers on your locks; install dead-bolts. Study the layout of the house and observe the exterior as if you were a burglar "casing the joint." Is the dwelling partially hidden by shrubbery? Is the lighting adequate? Should an alarm system be considered?

Are there hazards to pedestrians, such as tree roots, potholes and walkway irregularities? Are there water hazards? Should a fence be installed?

Develop an evacuation plan, particularly if there is more than one floor in the dwelling. Explain and post it for all family members. Have a prearranged meeting place outside of the house. Purchase an escape ladder. Install fire extinguishers. Smoke detectors? Carbon monoxide detectors?

HOME SWEET ENERGY-EFFICIENT HOME

Undoubtedly, your utility company has a home energy audit program. This will require an inspection and recommendations for improvements and an analysis of the operation cost and proposed savings from the installation of these improvements. Some utility companies even offer low or no-interest loans to make these suggested improvements. Some of the most common suggestions for improvements are: caulking windows and doors, weatherstripping, insulation upgrades in attic, walls, windows and doors, pipes and water heater, low-flow showerheads, faucet aerators, installation of an electronic thermostat, attic ventilating fan, reflective film, door sweeps, thermal windows, reduction of temperature setting on hot water heater, heat recirculators on fireplace, repair of leaks and replacement of filters. Don't overdo it. Bear in mind that the more you seal your home with insulation, the more of a risk you run of radon accumulation. So, keep a reasonable balance of ventilation, as well.

If you keep accurate records, plan for potential hazards, maintain your home in good repair and conserve energy, you will not only save money in the long run, but you will enhance the market value of your home when it is time to sell (with your lawyer at your side.)

EPILOGUE

We trust that you and <u>your lawyer</u> will use at least some of the facts, insights and information contained in this book. We hope that you will profit by it in your real estate ventures and make your "American Dream" come true.

FORMS

Rather than interrupt the flow of the text by interspersing forms of real estate instruments, all the forms will be presented in one place for reference purposes.

INDEX OF FORMS

1. Buyer Agency Contract and Agency Disclosure (short form-Utah)
2. Buyer Agency Contract and Agency Disclosure (long form-Utah)
3. Listing Contract and Agency Disclosure (Exclusive Right to Sell-Utah)
4. Real Estate Broker's Purchase Contract (Utah)
5. One To Four Family Residential Earnest Money Contract (All Cash, Assumption, Third Party Conventional or Seller Financing Resale-Texas)
6. One To Four Family Residential Earnest Money Contract Resale (FHA Insured or VA Guaranteed Financing - Texas)
7. Uniform Residential Appraisal Report (Freddie Mac-Fannie Mae)
8. New Jersey Contract for Sale of Real Estate (All-State Legal Supply Co.)
9. Sample of Amendment to N.J. Contract of Sale (containing contingencies in favor of Buyer)

10. Seller's Disclosure Statement (Florida)

11. N.J. Bargain and Sale Deed with Covenant as to Grantor's Acts (All-State Legal Supply Co.)

12. N.J. Mortgage Note (All-State Legal Supply Co.)

13. N.J. Mortgage (All-State Legal Supply Co.)

14. HUD-1 Uniform Settlement Statement (All-State Legal Supply Co.)

15. Home Inspection Report (HouseMaster of America)

16. Title Insurance Policy (Lawyers Title Insurance Corp)

17. Metes And Bounds Description

18. Survey

BUYER AGENCY CONTRACT AND AGENCY DISCLOSURE SHORT FORM-UTAH

BUYER AGENCY CONTRACT & AGENCY DISCLOSURE
(Short Form)
THIS IS A LEGALLY BINDING AGREEMENT - READ CAREFULLY BEFORE SIGNING

THIS AGREEMENT, is entered into on this _____ day of _____ , 19 _____ , by and between _____ (the "Company"); and the prospective buyer/tenant, _____ (the "Buyer".)

1. AGENCY RELATIONSHIP. The Buyer hereby agrees that the Company, including _____ as agent for the Company (the "Agent") will act as exclusive agent for the Buyer and will assist Buyer in negotiating for the ☐ purchase ☐ lease, ☐ exchange ☐ option of real property described as: _____ (the "Property"). As the Buyer's agent, they will act consistent with their fiduciary duties to the Buyer of loyalty, full disclosure, confidentiality, and reasonable care. This Agreement begins on the date first shown above, and ends on the earlier of: (a) Buyer's closing of the Property; (b) notice to the Company that buyer no longer desires to negotiate the acquisition of the Property; or (c) written notice of cancellation sent by either party to the other.

2. BUYER DUTIES/REPRESENTATIONS. The Buyer represents to the Company that, as of the date of this Agreement the buyer has not entered into any other agreements with another brokerage or real estate agent to represent the buyer. The Buyer will: (a) **IN ALL COMMUNICATIONS WITH OTHER REAL ESTATE AGENTS, NOTIFY THOSE AGENTS THAT THE BUYER HAS ENTERED INTO THIS AGREEMENT WITH THE COMPANY;** (b) furnish the Agent with relevant personal and financial information to facilitate the Buyer's ability to acquire the Property; and (c) exercise care and diligence in evaluating the physical and legal condition of the property selected by the Buyer.

3. COMPANY REPRESENTATIONS REGARDING PROPERTY. Neither the Company or the Agent will make any representations or warranties regarding the physical or legal condition of any property selected by the Buyer. **THE COMPANY AND THE AGENT STRONGLY RECOMMEND THAT IN CONNECTION WITH ANY OFFER TO ACQUIRE A PROPERTY, THE BUYER RETAIN THE PROFESSIONAL SERVICES OF LEGAL AND/OR TAX ADVISORS, PROPERTY INSPECTORS, SURVEYORS, AND OTHER PROFESSIONALS TO SATISFY THE BUYER AS TO ANY AND ALL ASPECTS OF THE PHYSICAL AND LEGAL CONDITION OF THE PROPERTY SELECTED BY THE BUYER.**
(_____) (_____) **Buyer's Initials**

4. COMPENSATION. The commission paid to the Company by Owner of the Property or the listing brokerage shall satisfy the Buyer's obligation to the Company for the Company's service to the Buyer.

5. ENTIRE AGREEMENT. This Agreement contains the entire agreement between the parties relating to the subject matter of this Agreement. This Agreement shall not be modified or amended except in writing signed by both parties.

IN WITNESS WHEREOF, the undersigned have set their hands as of the date first above written.

Company

by: _____
(Authorized Agent)

_____
(Company)

_____
(Address/Phone)

Buyer

_____
(Name)

_____
(Address/Phone)

_____
(Name)

_____
(Address/Phone)

RECEIPT

The undersigned acknowledges receipt of a copy of this document bearing all signatures.

Buyer _____ Date _____   Buyer _____ Date _____

Buyer Agency Agreement (Short Form) 6/10/93

WHITE: Broker   CANARY: Agent   PINK: Buyer

BUYER AGENCY CONTRACT AND AGENCY DISCLOSURE LONG FORM-UTAH

BUYER AGENCY CONTRACT & AGENCY DISCLOSURE
THIS IS A LEGALLY BINDING AGREEMENT - READ CAREFULLY BEFORE SIGNING

THIS AGREEMENT, is entered into on this _____ day of _____ , 19 _____ , by and between _____ (the "Company"); and the prospective buyer/tenant, _____ (the "Buyer".)

1. TIME PERIOD. The Buyer hereby retains the Company, including _____ as agent for the Company (the "Agent") to act as ☐ Exclusive ☐ Non-Exclusive Agent of the Buyer, to locate and/or negotiate for the ☐ purchase ☐ lease, ☐ exchange ☐ option of real property (collectively referred to below as "acquiring" a property). This Agreement begins on the date first shown above, and ends on the earlier of: _____ or closing of a property acquisition. If this Agreement is Exclusive, Buyer may not, during the term of this Agreement, enter into another Buyer representation agreement with another agent or brokerage.

2. BUYER DUTIES/REPRESENTATIONS. The Buyer represents to the Company that, as of the date of this Agreement, the Buyer has not entered into any other agreements with another brokerage or real estate agent to represent the Buyer. The Buyer will: (a) **IN ALL COMMUNICATIONS WITH OTHER REAL ESTATE AGENTS, NOTIFY THOSE AGENTS THAT THE BUYER HAS ENTERED INTO THIS AGREEMENT WITH THE COMPANY;** (b) furnish the Agent with relevant personal and financial information to facilitate the Buyer's ability to acquire a property; (c) exercise care and diligence in evaluating the physical and legal condition of the property selected by the Buyer; and (d) disclose to the Agent all properties in which the Buyer is either negotiating to acquire or has a present interest in acquiring. Those properties are listed as follows _____

The properties listed above ☐ are ☐ are **NOT** subject to the compensation terms in Section 5.

3. EQUAL HOUSING OPPORTUNITY. All properties will be presented in compliance with federal, state and local fair housing laws.

4. COMPANY REPRESENTATIONS REGARDING PROPERTY. Except as provided in section 6 below, neither the Company nor the Agent will make any representations or warranties regarding the physical or legal condition of any property selected by the Buyer. **THE COMPANY AND THE AGENT STRONGLY RECOMMEND THAT IN CONNECTION WITH ANY OFFER TO ACQUIRE A PROPERTY, THE BUYER RETAIN THE PROFESSIONAL SERVICES OF LEGAL AND/OR TAX ADVISORS, PROPERTY INSPECTORS, SURVEYORS, AND OTHER PROFESSIONALS TO SATISFY THE BUYER AS TO ANY AND ALL ASPECTS OF THE PHYSICAL AND LEGAL CONDITION OF THE PROPERTY SELECTED BY THE BUYER.** (_____) (_____) **Buyer's Initials**

5. COMPENSATION. The Buyer agrees to pay the Company if during the term of the Agreement, or within (_____) days after termination of this Agreement, the Buyer, or any other person acting in the Buyer's behalf, acquires any real property shown by the Agent to the Buyer during the term of this Agreement. If the property is listed with a brokerage, the selling commission paid to the Company by the listing brokerage shall satisfy the Buyer's obligations to the Company. If the property is not listed with a brokerage, the Company's compensation shall be paid by the Buyer in the amount of: $ _____ or _____ % of the purchase/lease price of the property. In either event, the compensation shall be paid at closing.

6. AGENCY RELATIONSHIPS. The Company and the Agent agree to act as agent for the Buyer and will work diligently to locate a property acceptable to the Buyer, and to assist the Buyer in negotiating the acquisition of a property. As the Buyer's agent, they will act consistent with their fiduciary duties to the Buyer of loyalty, full disclosure, confidentiality, and reasonable care. The Buyer does however, understand that the Company and the Agent, may now, or in the future, agree to act as agent for a Seller who may wish to negotiate on the sale or lease of the Seller's property. Then the Company and Agent would be acting as a **Limited Agent** representing both the Buyer and the Seller at the same time. **Limited agency** is allowed under Utah law only with the **informed consent** of the Buyer and the Seller. For consent to be informed, the **Buyer must understand that:**

　　6.1 Conflicting Duties. With limited agency, conflicting duties of disclosure, loyalty and confidentiality to each party will arise.

　　6.2 Duty of Neutrality. To resolve these conflicting duties, the Limited Agent will be bound by a further duty of **neutrality.** Being neutral, the Limited Agent will not disclose to either party information likely to weaken the bargaining position of the other. However, the Limited Agent will disclose to both parties material information known to the Limited Agent regarding a defect in the Property and the ability of the other to fulfill all obligations under this agreement;

　　6.3 Conditions for Buyer's Consent. If the Buyer consents to limited agency, the consent is conditioned upon the Limited Agent (i) having obtained from the Seller informed consent to the limited agency; and (ii) informing the Buyer of the limited agency when the Buyer first expresses an interest in the Seller's property.

ACCORDINGLY, THE BUYER UNDERSTANDS THAT BY SIGNING THIS AGREEMENT, THE BUYER CONSENTS TO A LIMITED AGENCY AS DESCRIBED ABOVE. (_____) (_____) **Buyer's Initials**

　　6.4 No Subagency. With the exception of the Agent, the Buyer does not authorize any other salesagent or associate brokers affiliated with the Company nor any real estate agents affiliated with any other brokerage to act as agent for the Buyer. In the event neither the Principal/Branch Broker nor the Agent are available, Buyer authorizes the Principal/Branch Broker for the Company to appoint a temporary subagent.

7. SPECIAL TERMS AND CONDITIONS. Attach Addendum if applicable.

8. DISPUTE RESOLUTION/ATTORNEY'S FEES. Should any dispute arise out of this Agreement, the parties agree that the dispute shall be submitted to mediation in accordance with the Utah Real Estate Buyer/Seller Mediation Rules of the American Arbitration Association. Each party agrees to bear its own costs of mediation. If mediation fails and legal action is commenced, the party prevailing in such action shall be entitled, in addition to any other relief, to court costs and actual attorney fees reasonably incurred in such action. Nothing in this section shall prohibit any party from seeking emergency equitable relief pending mediation. By marking this box ☐ , and adding their initials, the Buyer (_____) (_____), agrees that mediation under this section is not mandatory, but is optional upon agreement of all parties.

9. TERMINATION. Either party may cancel this Agreement at any time by providing written notice to the other party at the address shown below.

10. ENTIRE AGREEMENT. This Agreement contains the entire agreement between the parties relating to the subject matter of this Agreement. This Agreement shall not be modified or amended except in writing signed by both parties.

IN WITNESS WHEREOF, the undersigned have set their hands as of the date first above written.

Company	Buyer
by: _____	_____
(Authorized Agent)	(Name)
_____	_____
(Company)	(Address/Phone)
_____	_____
(Address/Phone)	(Name)
	_____
	(Address/Phone)

RECEIPT

The undersigned acknowledges receipt of a copy of this document bearing all signatures.

Buyer _____ Date _____　　Buyer _____ Date _____

Buyer Agency Agreement (Long Form) 6/10/93

LISTING
CONTRACT AND
AGENCT
DISCLOSURE

EXCLUSIVE RIGHT TO SELL-UTAH

LISTING CONTRACT & AGENCY DISCLOSURE
Exclusive Right to Sell
Form A
THIS IS A LEGALLY BINDING AGREEMENT - READ CAREFULLY BEFORE SIGNING

THIS AGREEMENT, is entered into on this _____ day of _____ , 19 _____ , between _____ (the "Seller") and _____ (the "Company").

1. TERM OF LISTING The Seller hereby grants the Company, including _____ as agent for the Company (the "Agent") starting on the date of execution of this Agreement, and ending at 5:00 p.m. (Mountain Time) on the _____ day of _____ , 19 _____ (the "Listing Period"), the Exclusive Right to Sell, Lease, or Exchange certain real property owned by the Seller, described as: _____ _____ (the "Property"), at the price and terms stated on Form B or at such other price and terms to which the Seller may agree in writing. The Agent hereby agrees to use reasonable efforts to find a buyer or tenant ("buyer") for the Property.

2. COMPANY FEE If, during the Listing Period, the Agent, the Company, any other real estate agent or the Seller locates a party who is ready, able and willing to buy, lease or exchange (collectively referred to "acquire") the Property, or any part thereof, at said price and terms, or any other price or terms to which the Seller may agree in writing, the Seller agrees to pay the Company a commission of $ _____ or _____ % of such sale, lease, or exchange price which commission, unless otherwise agreed in writing, shall be due and payable on the date of closing of the acquisition of the Property. If the buyer is ready, willing, and able to close, and the Seller refuses to close, after having contracted with the buyer to do so, the Seller shall be obligated to pay the Company a fee based on the above formula.

3. EXTENSION PERIOD If within _____ months after expiration, the Property is acquired by any party to whom the Property was offered or shown by the Company, the Agent, the Seller, or any other real estate agent during the Listing Period, the Seller agrees to pay the Company the commission stated in Section 2 if the Seller is not obligated to pay a commission on such acquisition to another brokerage pursuant to another valid sales agency contract entered into after the expiration date of this Agreement.

4. EQUAL HOUSING OPPORTUNITY All properties will be presented in compliance with federal, state and local fair housing laws.

5. SELLER WARRANTIES The Seller warrants that it has marketable title and an established right to sell, lease or exchange the Property. The Seller agrees to execute the necessary documents of conveyance and to prorate general taxes, insurance, rents, interest and other expenses affecting the Property to the agreed date of possession. The Seller further agrees to furnish the buyer at closing good and marketable title with a policy of title insurance in the amount of the purchase price and in the name of the buyer. In the event the acquisition includes personal property, the Seller agrees to sign proper conveyance documents which shall contain acceptable evidence of title or right to sell, lease, or exchange the personal property.

6. AGENCY RELATIONSHIPS. The Company and the agent agree to act as agent for the Seller and will work diligently to locate a buyer for the Property. As the Seller's agent, they will act consistent with their fiduciary duties to the Seller of loyalty, full disclosure, confidentiality, and reasonable care. The Seller understands however, that the Company and the Agent may now, or in the future, agree to act as agent for a buyer who may wish to negotiate a purchase of the Property. Then the Company and the Agent would be acting as a **Limited Agent** representing both the Seller and the prospective buyer at the same time. Limited agency is allowed under Utah law only with the informed consent of the Seller and the prospective buyer. For consent to be informed, the Seller must understand that:

    6.1 Conflicting Duties. With limited agency, conflicting duties of disclosure, loyalty and confidentiality to each party will arise;

    6.2 Duty of Neutrality. To resolve these conflicting duties, the Limited Agent will be bound by a further duty of neutrality. Being neutral, the Limited Agent will show no preference to either party in their mutual dealings. Also, the Limited Agent will not disclose to either party information likely to weaken the bargaining position of the other. However, the Limited Agent will disclose to both parties material information known to the Limited Agent regarding a defect in the Property and the ability of the other to fulfill all obligations under their agreement; and

    6.3 Conditions for Seller's Consent. If the Seller consents to limited agency, the consent is conditioned upon the Limited Agent (i) having obtained from the prospective buyer, informed consent to such limited agency (ii) having notified the Seller of the prospective buyers informed consent to such limited agency upon first contact with the Seller.

ACCORDINGLY, THE SELLER CONSENTS TO LIMITED AGENCY AS DESCRIBED ABOVE (_____ **) (** _____ **) Seller's Initials**

    6.4 Subagency. The Seller further understands that other salesagents and associate brokers affiliated with the Company, and other brokerages, may act as subagent of the Seller in finding a buyer for the Property, but only if they are authorized to do so by the Seller. A subagent is treated under the law as the Seller's agent, and the Seller may be liable for the acts and omissions of a subagent, one who, for example, misrepresents the Property. Accordingly, the Seller authorizes the following to act as subagents for the Seller.

☐ Agent and Principal/Branch Broker ☐ All agents affiliated with Company ☐ all other brokerages

In the event neither the Principal/Branch Broker nor the Agent are available, Seller authorizes the Principal/Branch Broker for the Company to appoint a temporary subagent.

    6.5 Commission Sharing. The Company is authorized to share the commission listed in section 2, with another brokerage.

7. SELLER DISCLOSURES. The Seller agrees in connection with this Agreement to provide to the Company a disclosure statement regarding the Seller's knowledge of the Property. The disclosure statement must be signed by the Seller.

8. DISPUTE RESOLUTION/ATTORNEY'S FEES Should any dispute arise out of this Agreement, the parties agree that the dispute shall be submitted to mediation in accordance with the Utah Real Estate Buyer/Seller Mediation Rules of the American Arbitration Association. Each party agrees to bear its own costs of mediation. If mediation fails and legal action is commenced, the party prevailing in such action shall be entitled, in addition to any other relief, to court costs and actual attorney fees reasonably incurred in such action. Nothing in this section shall prohibit any party from seeking emergency equitable relief pending mediation. By marking this box ☐, and adding their initials the Seller (_____) (_____), agrees that mediation under this section is not mandatory, but is optional upon agreement of all parties.

9. INFORMATION RELEASE The Company is authorized to obtain financial information from any mortgagee or other party holding a lien or interest on the Property.

10. MULTIPLE LISTING SERVICE The Company is authorized and instructed to offer this Property through the Salt Lake Board of REALTORS® Multiple Listing Service. The Company is further authorized to disclose after closing the terms of sale and final sales price of the Property.

11. KEY BOX/OPEN HOUSE The Company ☐ is ☐ is not authorized to have a key to the Property. The Company ☐ is ☐ is not authorized and instructed to have a key box installed on the Property. The Company ☐ is ☐ is not authorized to hold "Open Houses" at the Property. The Seller accepts full responsibility for any loss or damage that might result from "Open Houses" and/or the use of the key/key box from any source whatsoever and agrees to hold the Company, the Agent and the Salt Lake Board of REALTORS® and its Multiple Listing Service harmless from any and all liability as a result of holding "Open Houses" and/or having the key to or key box installed on the Property.

12. SIGNAGE The Company is authorized to place an appropriate sign on the Property.

13. FORM B Provisions of Form B (Property Description Form) are by this reference made part of this contract.

14. ENTIRE AGREEMENT This Agreement may not be changed, modified or altered, except by prior written consent of the parties hereto.

IN WITNESS WHEREOF, the undersigned agree to the above terms and acknowledges receipt of a copy of this Agreement.

Company   **Seller**

by _____   _____
   (Authorized Agent)   (Name)   (Address/Phone)

_____   _____
(Company)   (Address/Phone)   (Name)   (Address/Phone)

_____
(Principal Broker - insert name)

Listing Agreement 9/1/93

REAL ESTATE BROKER'S PURCHASE CONTRACT- UTAH

REAL ESTATE PURCHASE CONTRACT

This is a legally binding Contract. Utah State Law requires that licensed real estate agents use this form, but the Buyer and the Seller may legally agree in writing to alter or delete provisions of this form. If you desire legal or tax advice, consult your attorney or tax advisor.

EARNEST MONEY RECEIPT

The Buyer _____ offers to purchase the **Property** described below and delivers to Brokerage, as **Earnest Money Deposit $** _____ in the form of _____ to be deposited within three business days after **Acceptance** of this offer to purchase by all parties.

_____ Received by _____ on _____ (Date)
Brokerage   Phone Number

OFFER TO PURCHASE

1. PROPERTY: _____

City _____ County _____ , Utah.

1.1 Included Items. Unless excluded herein, this sale shall include all fixtures presently attached to the **Property:** plumbing, heating, air-conditioning and venting fixtures and equipment, water heater, built-in appliances, light fixtures and bulbs, bathroom fixtures, curtains and draperies and rods, window and door screens, storm doors, window blinds, awnings, installed television antenna, satellite dishes and system, wall-to-wall carpets, automatic garage door opener and transmitter(s), fencing, trees and shrubs. The following personal property shall also be included in this sale and conveyed under separate Bill of Sale with warranties as to title: _____
_____

1.2 Excluded Items. The following items are excluded from this sale _____

2. PURCHASE PRICE AND FINANCING. Buyer agrees to pay for the **Property** as follows:

$ _____   **Earnest Money Deposit**

$ _____   **Existing Loan:** Buyer agrees to assume and pay an existing loan in this approximate amount presently payable at $ _____ per month including principal, interest (presently at _____ % per annum), ☐ real estate taxes, ☐ property insurance premium and ☐ mortgage insurance premium. Buyer agrees to pay any transfer and assumption fees. Seller ☐ shall ☐ shall not be released from liability on said loan. Any net differences between the approximate balance of the loan shown above and the actual balance at **Closing** shall be adjusted in ☐ Cash ☐ Other _____.

$ _____   **Proceeds from New Loan:** Buyer reserves the right to apply for any of the following loans under the terms described below. ☐ Conventional ☐ FHA ☐ VA ☐ Other _____. Seller agrees to pay $ _____ toward Discount Points and Buyer's other loan and closing costs, to be allocated at Buyer's discretion.
☐ For a fixed rate loan: Amortized and payable over _____ years, interest shall not exceed _____ % per annum; monthly principal and interest payment shall not exceed $ _____ , or
☐ For an Adjustable Rate Mortgage (ARM): Amortized and payable over _____ years; initial interest rate shall not exceed _____ % per annum; initial monthly principal and interest payments shall not exceed $ _____ . Maximum Life Time interest rate shall not exceed _____ % per annum.

$ _____   **Seller Financing:** (See attached Seller Financing Addendum)

$ _____   **Other:** _____

$ _____   **Balance of Purchase Price in Cash at Closing**

$ _____   **Total Purchase Price**

2.1 **Existing/New Loan Application.** Buyer agrees to make application for a loan specified above within _____ calendar days **(Application Date)** after **Acceptance**. Buyer will have made **Loan Application** only when Buyer has: (a) completed, signed, and delivered to the Lender the initial loan application and documentation required by the Lender; and (b) paid all loan application fees as required by the Lender. Buyer will continue to provide the Lender with any additional documentation as required by the Lender. If, within seven calendar days after receipt of written request from Seller, Buyer fails to provide to Seller written evidence that Buyer has made **Loan Application** by the **Application Date**, then Seller may, prior to the **Qualification Date** below, cancel this **Contract** by providing written notice to Buyer. The Brokerage, upon receipt of a copy of such written notice, shall release to Seller, and Seller agrees to accept as Seller's exclusive remedy, the **Earnest Money Deposit** without the requirement of any further written authorization from Buyer.

2.2 **Qualification.** Buyer and the **Property** must qualify for a loan for which application has been made under section 2.1 within _____ calendar days **(Qualification Date)** after **Acceptance**. The **Property** is deemed qualified if, on or before the **Qualification Date**, the **Property**, in its current condition and for the Buyer's intended use, has appraised at a value not less than the Total Purchase Price. Buyer is deemed qualified if, on or before the **Qualification Date**, the Lender verifies in writing that Buyer has been approved as of the verification date.

2.3 **Qualification Contingency.** If Seller has not previously voided this **Contract** as provided in Section 2.1, and either the **Property** or Buyer has failed to qualify on or before the **Qualification Date**, either party may cancel this **Contract** by providing written notice to the other party within three calendar days after the **Qualification Date**, otherwise Buyer and the **Property** are deemed qualified. The Brokerage, upon receipt of a copy of such written notice, shall return to Buyer the **Earnest Money Deposit** without the requirement of any further written authorization of Seller.

3. CLOSING. This transaction shall be closed on or before _____, 19, _____ **Closing** shall occur when: (a) Buyer and Seller have signed and delivered to each other (or to the escrow/title company), all documents required by this **Contract**, by the Lender, by written escrow instructions and by applicable law; and (b) the monies required to be paid under these documents, have been delivered to the escrow/title company in the form of cashier's check, collected or cleared funds. Seller and Buyer shall each pay one-half (1/2) of the escrow **Closing** fee, unless otherwise agreed by the parties in writing. Taxes and assessments for the current year, rents, and interest on assumed obligations shall be prorated as set forth in this Section. Unearned deposits on tenancies shall be transferred to Buyer at **Closing**. Prorations set forth in this Section, shall be made as of ☐ date of **Closing** ☐ date of possession ☐ other _____.

4. POSSESSION. Unless otherwise agreed in writing by the parties, Seller shall deliver possession to Buyer within _____ hours after **Closing**.

5. CONFIRMATION OF AGENCY DISCLOSURE. At the signing of this **Contract** the listing agent _____ represents ☐ Seller ☐ Buyer, and the selling agent _____ represents ☐ Seller ☐ Buyer. Buyer and Seller confirm that prior to signing this **Contract** written disclosure of the agency relationship(s) was provided to him/her. ( ) Buyer's Initials ( ) Seller's Initials.

6. TITLE TO PROPERTY AND TITLE INSURANCE. (a) Seller has, or shall have at **Closing**, fee title to the **Property** and agrees to convey such title to Buyer by general warranty deed, free of financial encumbrances as warranted under Section 10.6; (b) Seller agrees to pay for and furnish Buyer at **Closing** with a current standard form owner's policy of title insurance in the amount of the **Total Purchase Price**; (c) the title policy shall conform with Seller's obligations under subsections (a) and (b) above. Unless otherwise agreed under subsection 8.4, the commitment shall conform with the title insurance commitment provided under Section 7.

7. SELLER DISCLOSURES. No later than _____ calendar days after **Acceptance**, Seller will deliver to Buyer the following Seller Disclosures: (a) a Seller property condition disclosure for the **Property**, signed and dated by Seller; (b) a commitment for the policy of title insurance required under Section 6, to be issued by the title insurance company chosen by Seller, including copies of all documents listed as Exceptions on the Commitment; (c) a copy of all loan documents relating to any loan now existing which will encumber the **Property** after **Closing**; and (d) a copy of all leases affecting the **Property** not expiring prior to **Closing**. Seller agrees to pay any title commitment cancellation charge under subsection (b).

8. GENERAL CONTINGENCIES. In addition to **Qualification** under Section 2.2 this offer is: (a) subject to Buyer's approval of the content of each of the items referenced in Section 7 above; and (b) ☐ is ☐ is not subject to Buyer's approval of an inspection of the **Property**. The inspection shall be paid for by Buyer and shall be conducted by an individual/company of Buyer's choice. Seller agrees to fully cooperate with such inspection and a walk-through inspection under Section 11 and to make the **Property** available for the same.

8.1 Buyer shall have _____ calendar days after **Acceptance** in which to review the content of Seller Disclosures, and, if the inspection contingency applies, to complete and evaluate the inspection of the Property, and to determine, if, in Buyer's sole discretion, the content of all Seller Disclosures (including the Property Inspection) is acceptable.

8.2 If Buyer does not deliver a written objection to Seller regarding a Seller Disclosure or the Property Inspection within the time provided in subsection 8.1 above, that document or inspection will be deemed approved or waived by Buyer.

Page 1 of 2 pages   **Seller's Initials (**) Date _____   **Buyer's Initials (**) Date _____

8.3 If Buyer objects, Buyer and Seller shall have seven calendar days after receipt of the objections to resolve Buyer's objections. Seller may, but shall not be required to, resolve Buyer's objections. If Buyer's objections are not resolved within the seven calendar days, Buyer may void this **Contract** by providing written notice to Seller within the same seven calendar days. The Brokerage, upon receipt of a copy of Buyer's written notice, shall return to Buyer the **Earnest Money Deposit** without the requirement of any further written authorization from Seller. If this **Contract** is not voided by Buyer, Buyer's objection is deemed to have been waived. However, this waiver does not affect those items warranted in Section 11.

8.4 Resolution of Buyer's objections under Section 8.3 shall be in writing and shall be specifically enforceable as covenants of this **Contract**.

9. SPECIAL CONTINGENCIES. This offer is made subject to: _____

The terms of attached Addendum # _____ are incorporated into this **Contract** by this reference.

10. SELLER'S LIMITED WARRANTIES. Seller's warranties to Buyer regarding the condition of the **Property** are limited to the following:

10.1 When seller delivers possession of the **Property** to Buyer, it will be broom-clean and free of debris and personal belongings;

10.2 Seller will deliver possession of the **Property** to Buyer with the plumbing, plumbed fixtures, heating, cooling, ventilating, electrical and sprinkler systems, appliances and fireplaces in working order;

10.3 Seller will deliver possession of the **Property** to Buyer with the roof and foundation free of leaks known to Seller;

10.4 Seller will deliver possession of the **Property** to Buyer with any private well or septic tank serving the **Property** in working order and in compliance with governmental regulations;

10.5 Seller will be responsible for repairing any of Seller's moving-related damage to the **Property**;

10.6 At **Closing**, Seller will bring current all financial obligations encumbering the **Property** which are assumed in writing by Buyer and will discharge all such obligations which Buyer has not so assumed; and

10.7 As of **Closing**, Seller has no knowledge of any claim or notice of an environmental, building or zoning code violation regarding the **Property** which has not been resolved.

11. VERIFICATION OF WARRANTED AND INCLUDED ITEMS. Before **Closing**, Buyer may conduct a "walk-through" inspection of the **Property** to determine whether or not items warranted by Seller in Section 10.1, 10.2, 10.3 and 10.4 are in the warranted condition and to verify items included in Section 1.1 are presently on the **Property**. If any item is not in the warranted condition, Seller will correct, repair or replace it as necessary or, with the consent of Buyer, escrow an amount at **Closing** to provide for such repair or replacement. The Buyer's failure to conduct a "walk-through" inspection, or to claim during the "walk-through" inspection that the **Property** does not include all items referenced in Section 1.1, or is not in the condition warranted in Section 10, shall not constitute a waiver by Buyer of Buyer's rights under Section 1.1 or of the warranties contained in Section 10.

12. CHANGES DURING TRANSACTION. Seller agrees that no changes in any existing leases shall be made, no new leases entered into, and no substantial alterations or improvements to the **Property** shall be made or undertaken without the written consent of the Buyer.

13. AUTHORITY OF SIGNERS. If Buyer or Seller is a corporation, partnership, trust, estate or other entity, the person executing this **Contract** on its behalf warrants his or her authority to do so and to bind Buyer or Seller.

14. COMPLETE CONTRACT. This instrument together with its addenda, any attached exhibits, and Seller Disclosures constitute the entire **Contract** between the parties and supersedes and replaces any and all prior negotiations, representations, warranties, understandings or contracts between the parties. This **Contract** cannot be changed except by written agreement of the parties.

15. DISPUTE RESOLUTION. The parties agree that any dispute or claim relating to this **Contract**, including but not limited to the disposition of the **Earnest Money Deposit**, the breach or termination of this **Contract**, or the services relating to this transaction, shall first be submitted to mediation in accordance with the Utah Real Estate Buyer/Seller Mediation Rules of the American Arbitration Association. Disputes shall include representations made by the parties, any Broker or other person or entity in connection with the sale, purchase, financing, condition or other aspect of the **Property** to which this **Contract** pertains, including without limitation, allegations of concealment, misrepresentation, negligence and/or fraud. Each party agrees to bear its own costs of mediation. Any agreement signed by the parties pursuant to the mediation shall be binding. If mediation fails, the procedures applicable and remedies available under this **Contract** shall apply. Nothing in this Section 15 shall prohibit any party from seeking emergency equitable relief pending mediation. By marking this box ☐, and adding their initials, the Buyer ( ), and the Seller ( ), agree that mediation under this Section 15 is not mandatory, but is optional upon agreement of all parties.

16. DEFAULT. If Buyer defaults, Seller may elect to either retain the **Earnest Money Deposit** as liquidated damages or to return the **Earnest Money Deposit** and sue Buyer to enforce Seller's rights. If Seller defaults, in addition to return of the **Earnest Money Deposit**, Buyer may elect to either accept from Seller as liquidated damages, a sum equal to the **Earnest Money Deposit**, or to sue Seller for specific performance and/or damages. If Buyer elects to accept the liquidated damages, Seller agrees to pay the liquidated damages to Buyer upon demand. Where a Section of this **Contract** provides a specific remedy the parties intend that the remedy shall be exclusive regardless of rights which might otherwise be available under common law.

17. ATTORNEY'S FEES. In any action arising out of this **Contract**, the prevailing party shall be entitled to costs and reasonable attorney's fees.

18. DISPOSITION OF EARNEST MONEY. The **Earnest Money Deposit** shall not be released unless it is authorized by: (a) Section 2, Section 8.3 or Section 15; (b) separate written agreement of the parties; or (c) court order.

19. ABROGATION. Except for express warranties made in this **Contract**, the provisions of this **Contract** shall not apply after **Closing**.

20. RISK OF LOSS. All risk of loss or damage to the **Property** shall be borne by Seller until **Closing**.

21. TIME IS OF THE ESSENCE. Time is of the essence regarding the dates set forth in this transaction. Extensions must be agreed to in writing by all parties. Performance under each Section of this **Contract** which references a date shall be required absolutely by **5:00 PM Mountain Time** on the stated date.

22. FACSIMILE (FAX) DOCUMENTS. Facsimile transmission of any signed original document, and retransmission of any signed facsimile transmission, shall be the same as delivery of an original. If the transaction involves multiple Buyers or Sellers, facsimile transmissions may be executed in counterparts.

23. ACCEPTANCE. Acceptance occurs when Seller or Buyer, responding to an offer or counteroffer of the other: (a) signs the offer or counter where noted to indicate acceptance; and (b) communicates to the other party or the other party's agent that the offer or counteroffer has been signed as required.

24. OFFER AND TIME FOR ACCEPTANCE. Buyer offers to purchase the **Property** on the above terms and conditions. If Seller does not accept this offer by _____ ☐ AM ☐ PM Mountain Time _____ 19 _____ , this offer shall lapse; and the Brokerage shall return the **Earnest Money Deposit** to Buyer.

_____   _____   _____   _____
(Buyer's Signature)   (Offer Date)   (Buyer's Signature)   (Offer Date)

The above date shall be the **Offer Reference Date**.

_____   _____   _____   _____
(Notice Address)   (Phone)   (Notice Address)   (Phone)

ACCEPTANCE/REJECTION/COUNTER OFFER

CHECK ONE:

☐ **Acceptance of Offer to Purchase:** Seller **Accepts** the foregoing offer on the terms and conditions specified above.

_____   _____   _____   _____   _____   _____
(Seller's Signature)   (Date)   (Time)   (Seller's Signature)   (Date)   (Time)

_____   _____
(Notice Address)   (Notice Address)

☐ **Rejection:** Seller **Rejects** the foregoing offer. _____ (Seller's initials) _____ (Date) _____ (Time)

☐ **Counter Offer:** Seller presents for Buyer's **Acceptance** the terms of Buyer's offer subject to the exceptions or modifications as specified in the attached **Counter Offer #** _____ .

Page 2 of 2 pages   **Seller's Initials (**) Date _____   **Buyer's Initials (**) Date _____

THIS FORM APPROVED BY THE UTAH REAL ESTATE COMMISSION AND THE OFFICE OF THE UTAH ATTORNEY GENERAL, JUNE, 1993

ONE TO FOUR FAMILY RESIDENTIAL EARNEST MONEY CONTRACT

ALL CASH, ASSUMPTION, THIRD PARTY CONVENTIONAL OR SELLER FINANCING RESALE-TEXAS

ONE TO FOUR FAMILY RESIDENTIAL EARNEST MONEY CONTRACT (RESALE)
ALL CASH, ASSUMPTION, THIRD PARTY CONVENTIONAL OR SELLER FINANCING
PROMULGATED BY THE TEXAS REAL ESTATE COMMISSION (TREC)
NOTICE: Not For Use For Condominium Transactions

1. **PARTIES:** _____ (Seller) agrees to sell and convey to _____ (Buyer) and Buyer agrees to buy from Seller the property described below.

2. **PROPERTY:** Lot _____, Block _____, _____ Addition, City of _____, _____ County, Texas, known as _____ (Address), or as described on attached exhibit, together with the following items, if any: curtains and rods, draperies and rods, valances, blinds, window shades, screens, shutters, awnings, wall-to-wall carpeting, mirrors fixed in place, ceiling fans, attic fans, mail boxes, television antennae and satellite dish with controls, permanently installed heating and air conditioning units and equipment, window air conditioning units, built-in security and fire detection equipment, lighting and plumbing fixtures, water softener, built-in kitchen equipment, garage door openers with controls, built-in cleaning equipment, all swimming pool equipment, shrubbery, permanently installed outdoor cooking equipment, built-in fireplace screens and all other property owned by Seller and attached to the above described real property except the following property which is not included:_____

_____

_____.

All property sold by this contract is called the "Property."   The Property ☐ is ☐ is not subject to mandatory membership in an owners' association and its assessments and requirements.

3. **SALES PRICE:**
   A. Cash portion of Sales Price payable by Buyer . . . . $_____
   B. Sum of all financing described below (excluding any private mortgage insurance [PMI] premium) . $_____
   C. Sales Price (Sum of A and B) . . . . $_____

4. **FINANCING:** The portion of Sales Price not payable in cash shall be paid as follows: (Check applicable boxes below)
   ☐ A. **ASSUMPTION:**
   ☐ (1)   Buyer shall assume the unpaid principal balance of a first lien promissory note payable to _____
   _____ which unpaid balance at closing will be $_____ . The total current monthly payment including principal, interest and reserve deposits is $_____ . Buyer's initial payment shall be the first payment due after closing.
   ☐ (2)   Buyer shall assume the unpaid principal balance of a second lien promissory note payable to _____
   _____ which unpaid balance at closing will be $_____ . The total current monthly payment including principal, interest and reserve deposits is $_____ . Buyer's initial payment shall be the first payment due after closing.

   Buyer's assumption of an existing note includes all obligations imposed by the deed of trust securing the note.

   If the unpaid balance(s) of any assumed loan(s) as of the Closing Date varies from the loan balance(s) stated above, the ☐ cash payable at closing ☐ sales price shall be adjusted by the amount of any variance; provided, if the total principal balance of all assumed loans varies in an amount greater than $350.00 at closing, either party may terminate this contract and the Earnest Money shall be refunded to Buyer unless either party elects to eliminate the excess in the variance by an appropriate adjustment at closing. If the noteholder requires (a) payment of an assumption fee in excess of $_____ in A(1) above or $_____ in A(2) above and Seller declines to pay such excess, or (b) an increase in the interest rate to more than _____ % in A(1) above, or _____ % in A(2) above, or (c) any other modification of the loan documents, Buyer may terminate this contract and the Earnest Money shall be refunded to Buyer. A vendor's lien and deed of trust to secure assumption shall be required which shall automatically be released on execution and delivery of a release by noteholder. If Seller is released from liability on any assumed note, the vendor's lien and deed of trust to secure assumption shall not be required.

   NOTICE TO BUYER: The monthly payments, interest rates or other terms of some loans may be adjusted by the lender at or after closing. If you are concerned about the possibility of future adjustments, do not sign the contract without examining the notes and deeds of trust.

   NOTICE TO SELLER: Your liability to pay the note assumed by Buyer will continue unless you obtain a release of liability from the lender. If you are concerned about future liability, you should use the TREC Release of Liability Addendum.

   ☐ B. **THIRD PARTY FINANCING:**
   ☐ (1)   A third party first lien note of $_____ (excluding any financed PMI premium), due in full in _____ year(s), with interest not to exceed _____ % per annum for the first _____ year(s) of the loan. The loan shall be ☐ with ☐ without PMI.

Initialed for identification by Buyer_____ and Seller_____

TREC NO. 20-2

One to Four Family Residential Earnest Money Contract Concerning_____Page Two   10-25-93

(Address of Property)

☐ (2)   A third party second lien note of $_____ , due in full in _____ year(s), with interest not to exceed _____ % per annum for the first _____ year(s) of the loan.

☐ C. TEXAS VETERANS' HOUSING ASSISTANCE PROGRAM LOAN:
A Texas Veterans' Housing Assistance Program Loan (the Program Loan) of $_____ for a period of at least _____ years at the interest rate established by the Texas Veterans' Land Board at the time of closing.

☐ D. SELLER FINANCING: A promissory note from Buyer to Seller of $_____, bearing _____% interest per annum, secured by vendor's and deed of trust liens, in accordance with the terms and conditions set forth in the attached TREC Seller Financing Addendum. If an owner policy of title insurance is furnished, Buyer shall furnish Seller with a mortgagee policy of title insurance.

☐ E. CREDIT APPROVAL ON ASSUMPTION OR SELLER FINANCING: Within _____ days after the effective date of this contract, Buyer shall deliver to Seller ☐ credit report ☐ verification of employment, including salary ☐ verification of funds on deposit in financial institutions ☐ current financial statement to establish Buyer's creditworthiness for assumption approval or seller financing and ☐ _____.
If Buyer's documentation is not delivered within the specified time, Seller may terminate this contract by notice to Buyer within 5 days after expiration of the time for delivery, and the Earnest Money shall be paid to Seller. If this contract is not so terminated, Seller shall be deemed to have accepted Buyer's credit. If the documentation is timely delivered, and Seller determines in Seller's sole discretion that Buyer's credit is unacceptable, Seller may terminate this contract by notice to Buyer within 5 days after expiration of the time for delivery and the Earnest Money shall be refunded to Buyer. If Seller does not so terminate this contract, Seller shall be deemed to have accepted Buyer's credit. Buyer hereby authorizes any credit reporting agency to furnish to Seller at Buyer's sole expense copies of Buyer's credit reports.

Within _____ days after the effective date of this contract Buyer shall apply for all third party financing or noteholder's approval of any assumption and shall make every reasonable effort to obtain financing or assumption approval. Financing or assumption approval shall be deemed to have been obtained when the lender determines that Buyer has satisfied all of lender's financial conditions (those items relating to Buyer's ability to qualify for assumption approval or a loan). If financing (including any financed PMI premium) or assumption approval is not obtained within _____ days after the effective date hereof, this contract shall terminate and the Earnest Money shall be refunded to Buyer. Each note to be executed hereunder shall be secured by vendor's and deed of trust liens.

5. **EARNEST MONEY:** Buyer shall deposit $_____ as Earnest Money with _____
_____at_____
(Address), as Escrow Agent, upon execution of this contract by both parties. ☐ Additional Earnest Money of $_____shall be deposited by Buyer with Escrow Agent on or before _____, 19_____. If Buyer fails to deposit the Earnest Money as required by this contract, Buyer shall be in default.

6. **TITLE POLICY AND SURVEY:**
☐ A. TITLE POLICY: Seller shall furnish to Buyer at Seller's expense an Owner Policy of Title Insurance (the Title Policy) issued by _____ (the Title Company) in the amount of the Sales Price, dated at or after closing, insuring Buyer against loss under the provisions of the Title Policy, subject to the promulgated exclusions (including existing building and zoning ordinances) and the following exceptions:
   (1)   Restrictive covenants common to the platted subdivision in which the Property is located.
   (2)   The standard printed exception for standby fees, taxes and assessments.
   (3)   Liens created as part of the financing described in Paragraph 4.
   (4)   Utility easements created by the dedication deed or plat of the subdivision in which the Property is located.
   (5)   Reservations or exceptions otherwise permitted by this contract or as may be approved by Buyer in writing.
   (6)   The standard printed exception as to discrepancies, conflicts, shortages in area or boundary lines,encroachments or protrusions, or overlapping improvements.
   (7)   The standard printed exception as to marital rights.
   (8)   The standard printed exception as to waters, tidelands, beaches, streams, and related matters.
Within 20 days after the Title Company receives a copy of this contract, Seller shall furnish to Buyer a commitment for Title Insurance (the Commitment) and, at Buyer's expense, legible copies of restrictive covenants and documents evidencing exceptions in the Commitment other than the standard printed exceptions. Seller authorizes the Title Company to mail or hand deliver the Commitment and related documents to Buyer at Buyer's address shown below. If the Commitment is not delivered to Buyer within the specified time, the time for delivery shall be automatically extended up to 15 days. Buyer shall have 5 days after the receipt of the Commitment to object in writing to matters disclosed in the Commitment. Buyer may object to existing building and zoning ordinances and items 6(A)(1) through (8) above if Buyer determines that any such ordinance or items prohibits the following use or activity: _____
_____
_____.

☐   B. SURVEY REQUIRED: (Check one box only)

  ☐ (1)   Within _____ days after Buyer's receipt of a survey plat furnished to a third-party lender at Buyer's expense, Buyer may object in writing to any matter shown on the plat which constitutes a defect or encumbrance to title.

  ☐ (2)   Within _____ days after the effective date of this contract, Buyer may object in writing to any matter which constitutes a defect or encumbrance to title shown on a survey plat obtained by Buyer at Buyer's expense.

The survey shall be made by a Registered Professional Land Surveyor acceptable to the title company and any lender. The plat shall: (a) identify the Property by metes and bounds or platted lot description; (b) show that the survey was made and staked on the ground with corners permanently marked; (c) set forth the dimensions of the property; (d) show the location of all improvements, highways, streets, roads, railroads, rivers, creeks or other waterways, fences, easements and rights of way on the Property ; (e) show any discrepancies or conflicts in boundaries, any visible encroachments, and any portion of the Property lying within the 100 year floodplain as shown on the current Federal Emergency Management Agency map; and (f) contain the surveyor's certificate that the survey as shown by the plat is true and correct. Utility easements created by the dedication deed and plat of the subdivision in which the Property is located shall not be a basis for objection.

Buyer's failure to object under Paragraph 6A or 6B within the time allowed shall constitute a waiver of Buyer's right to object; except that the requirements in Schedule C of the Commitment shall not be deemed to have been waived. If objections are made by Buyer or any third party lender, Seller shall cure the objections within 15 days from the date Seller receives them and the Closing Date shall be extended as necessary. If objections are not cured by the extended Closing Date, this contract shall terminate and the Earnest Money shall be refunded to Buyer unless Buyer elects to waive the objections.

NOTICE TO SELLER AND BUYER:

(1)   Broker advises Buyer to have an Abstract covering the Property examined by an attorney of Buyer's selection, or Buyer should be furnished with or obtain a Title Policy. If a Title Policy is furnished, the Commitment should be promptly reviewed by an attorney of Buyer's choice due to the time limitations on Buyer's right to object.

(2)   If the Property is situated in a utility or other statutorily created district providing water, sewer, drainage, or flood control facilities and services, Chapter 50 of the Texas Water Code requires Seller to deliver and Buyer to sign the statutory notice relating to the tax rate, bonded indebtedness, or standby fee of the district prior to final execution of this contract.

(3)   Buyer is advised that the presence of wetlands, toxic substances including lead-base paint or asbestos and wastes or other environmental hazards or the presence of a threatened or endangered species or its habitat may affect Buyer's intended use of the Property. If Buyer is concerned about these matters, an addendum either promulgated by TREC or required by the parties should be used.

(4)   If the Property adjoins and shares a common boundary with the tidally influenced submerged lands of the state, Section 33.135, Texas Natural Resources Code, requires a notice regarding coastal area property to be included in the contract. An addendum either promulgated by TREC or required by the parties should be used.

7. PROPERTY CONDITION.

  A. SELLER'S DISCLOSURE OF PROPERTY CONDITION (the "Notice")(Section 5.008 Property Code)(check one box only):

    ☐ (1)   Buyer has received the Notice.

    ☐ (2)   Buyer has not received the Notice. Within _____ days after the effective date of this contract, Seller shall deliver the notice to Buyer. If Seller fails to deliver the Notice within the time allowed, Buyer may terminate this contract within three days after the time for delivery of the Notice. If Seller timely delivers the Notice, Buyer may terminate this contract for any reason within seven days after Buyer receives the Notice.

  B. REQUIRED REPAIRS OR INSPECTIONS. (Check one box only):

    ☐ (1)   Buyer accepts the Property in its present condition. Buyer shall pay for any repairs designated by a lender.

    ☐ (2)   Buyer requires the completion of any repairs designated by a lender and the following repairs: _____
_____.

    ☐ (3)   Buyer requires the completion of any repairs designated by a lender and any repairs designated by Buyer pursuant to the attached Property Condition Addendum. Buyer shall pay for inspections, reinspections, reports and certificates.

  C. PAYMENT FOR TREATMENT OR REPAIRS. Subject to the limitations set out below, Seller shall pay for any treatment or repairs required by the contract, any lender and any Property Condition Addendum. Seller is not obligated to pay more than $ _____ for treatment and repairs resulting from termites or other wood-destroying insects or to pay more than $ _____ for all other repairs. Seller shall also pay for turning utilities on for inspections and reinspections.

  D. BUYER'S CHOICES. After Seller receives all inspection reports and repair designations made by Buyer or any lender pursuant to 7B(2) or 7B(3), Seller shall notify Buyer within 7 days (1) of the costs of all required treatment and repairs and (2) whether Seller will pay the costs that exceed the amounts in 7C. If Seller notifies Buyer that Seller will not pay the excess costs, Buyer may (1) pay the excess costs (2) accept the Property with the costs of treatment and repairs not to exceed the amounts in 7C (if permitted by any lender), or (3) terminate this contract and the Earnest Money shall be refunded to Buyer. Buyer shall notify Seller of Buyer's choice within 5 days after Buyer is notified Seller will not pay the excess costs.

If Seller does not notify Buyer, Buyer shall notify Seller of Buyer's choice from the three alternatives provided above within 12 days after Seller receives all inspection reports and repair designations from Buyer and any lender. *If Buyer does not notify Seller of Buyer's choice within the specified time, Buyer shall accept the Property with the costs of treatment and repairs limited to the amounts stated in 7C.*

If the total cost of required treatment and repairs exceeds 5% of the Sales Price and Seller agrees to pay the total cost, Buyer may (1) accept the property with all required treatment and repairs, or (2) terminate this contract and the Earnest Money shall be refunded to Buyer. Buyer shall notify Seller of Buyer's choice within 5 days after Seller notifies Buyer that Seller will pay all costs of treatment and repair. *If Buyer does not notify Seller of Buyer's choice within the specified time Buyer shall accept the Property with all required treatment and repairs.*

E. COMPLETION OF TREATMENT OR REPAIRS. Seller shall complete required or agreed treatment and repairs prior to the Closing Date. If Seller fails to complete any required or agreed treatment or repairs, Buyer may do so; Seller shall be liable for the cost up to the maximum agreed amount which shall be deducted from the sales proceeds or collected from Seller at closing if necessary. Buyer may also exercise applicable remedies provided in Paragraph 15.

8. **BROKERS' REPRESENTATION AND FEES:**_____

(Listing Broker) represents ☐ Seller only ☐ Seller and Buyer.

Any other broker represents:

☐ Seller as Listing Broker's subagent;

☐ Buyer only as Buyer's agent.

Brokers' fees shall be paid as specified by separate written agreements.

9. **CLOSING:** The closing of the sale shall be on or before _____, 19_____, or within 7 days after objections to title and survey have been cured, whichever date is later (the Closing Date); *however, if financing or assumption approval has been obtained pursuant to Paragraph 4, the Closing Date shall be extended up to 15 days only if necessary to comply with lender's closing requirements* (for example, survey, insurance policies, property repairs, closing documents). If either party fails to close this sale by the Closing Date, the non-defaulting party shall be entitled to exercise the remedies contained in Paragraph 15. At closing Seller shall furnish tax statements or certificates showing no delinquent taxes, and a General Warranty Deed conveying good and indefeasible title showing no additional exceptions to those permitted in Paragraph 6.

10. **POSSESSION:** Seller shall deliver possession of the Property to Buyer on _____in its present or required repaired condition, subject to the dollar limitations of Paragraph 7, ordinary wear and tear excepted. Any possession by Buyer prior to closing or by Seller after closing that is not authorized by a temporary lease form promulgated by TREC or required by the Parties shall establish a landlord-tenant at sufferance relationship between the parties. *Consult your insurance agent prior to change of possession as insurance coverage may be limited or terminated.*

11. **SPECIAL PROVISIONS:** [Insert only factual statements and business details applicable to this sale. A licensee shall not add to a promulgated earnest money contract form factual statements or business details for which a contract addendum, lease or other form has been promulgated by TREC for mandatory use. 22 TAC §537.11 (d).]

12. **SALES EXPENSES:** The following expenses shall be paid at or prior to closing:

A. Appraisal fees shall be paid by _____.

B. The total of loan discount and buydown fees (including any Texas Veterans' Housing Assistance Program Participation Fee) shall not exceed _____% of the loan of which Seller shall pay the first _____% of the loan and Buyer shall pay the remainder.

C. Seller's Expenses: Releases of existing liens, including prepayment penalties and recording fees; release of Seller's loan liability; tax statements or certificates; preparation of deed; one-half of escrow fee; and other expenses stipulated to be paid by Seller under other provisions of this contract.

D. Buyer's Expenses: Loan application, origination and commitment fees; loan assumption costs; preparation and recording of deed of trust to secure assumption; lender required expenses incident to new loan(s): (for example, PMI premium, preparation of loan documents, survey, recording fees, tax service and research fees, warehouse or underwriting fees, copies of restrictions and easements, amortization schedule, premiums for mortgagee title policies and endorsements required by lender, credit reports, photos; required premiums for flood and hazard insurance; required reserve deposit for insurance premiums and ad valorem taxes; interest on all monthly installment payment notes from date of disbursements to one month prior to dates of first monthly payments; customary Program Loan costs for Buyer; one-half of escrow fee; and other expenses stipulated to be paid by Buyer under other provisions of this contract.

E. PMI premium not to exceed _____ shall be paid by Buyer, and ☐ paid in cash at closing ☐ added to the amount of the loan or ☐ paid as follows: _____
_____.

F. If any sales expense exceeds the amount stated in this contract to be paid by either party, either party may terminate this contract unless either party agrees to pay such excess. In no event shall Buyer pay charges and fees expressly prohibited by the Texas Veteran's Housing Assistance Program or other government loan program regulations.

13. **PRORATIONS:**   Flood and hazard insurance premiums (excluding mortgage insurance), taxes for the current year, interest, maintenance fees, assessments and rents shall be prorated through the Closing Date. However, if a loan is assumed and the lender maintains an escrow account for the payment of taxes and insurance, the above items ☐ shall ☐ shall not be prorated. Whether or not prorations are made, the escrow account shall be transferred to Buyer without any deficiency.   If prorations are made Buyer shall reimburse Seller for the amount in the transferred account. If prorations are not made, the escrow account shall be transferred to Buyer without reimbursement to Seller. If a transfer is permitted by the insurance carrier, the insurance policy in force ☐ shall ☐ shall not be transferred to Buyer. If the insurance policy in force is not transferred, Buyer shall pay the premium for a new policy.

14. **CASUALTY LOSS:** If any part of the Property is damaged or destroyed by fire or other casualty loss, Seller shall restore the Property to its previous condition as soon as reasonably possible, but in any event by the Closing Date. If Seller is unable to do so without fault, Buyer may either (a) terminate this contract and the Earnest Money shall be refunded to Buyer (b) extend the time for performance up to 15 days and the Closing Date shall be extended as necessary or (c) accept the Property in its damaged condition and accept an assignment of insurance proceeds.   Provisions of the Texas Property Code to the contrary shall not apply.

15. **DEFAULT:** If Buyer fails to comply with this contract, Buyer shall be in default, and Seller may either (a) enforce specific performance, seek such other relief as may be provided by law, or both, or (b) terminate this contract and receive the Earnest Money as liquidated damages, thereby releasing both parties from this contract. If Seller is unable without fault to make any non-casualty repairs or deliver the Commitment within the time allowed, Buyer may either terminate this contract and receive the Earnest Money as the sole remedy or extend the time for performance up to 15 days and the Closing Date shall be extended as necessary. If Seller fails to comply with this contract for any other reason, Seller shall be in default and Buyer may either (a) enforce specific performance, seek such other relief as may be provided by law, or both, or (b) terminate this contract and receive the Earnest Money, thereby releasing both parties from this contract.

16. **ATTORNEY'S FEES:** If Buyer, Seller, Listing Broker, Other Broker or Escrow Agent is a prevailing party in any legal proceeding brought under or with relation to this contract, such party shall be entitled to recover from the non-prevailing party all costs of such proceeding and reasonable attorney's fees.

17. **ESCROW:** The Earnest Money is deposited with Escrow Agent with the understanding that Escrow Agent is not (a) a party to this contract and does not have any liability for the performance or non-performance of any party to this contract, (b) liable for interest on the Earnest Money or (c) liable for any loss of Earnest Money caused by the failure of any financial institution in which the Earnest Money has been deposited unless the financial institution is acting as Escrow Agent. If either party makes demand for the payment of the Earnest Money, Escrow Agent has the right to require from all parties and brokers a written release of liability of Escrow Agent for disbursement of the Earnest Money. Any refund or disbursement of Earnest Money under this contract shall be reduced by the amount of unpaid expenses incurred on behalf of the party receiving the Earnest Money, and Escrow Agent shall pay the same to the creditors entitled thereto. At closing, the Earnest Money shall be applied first to any cash down payment, then to Buyer's closing costs and any excess refunded to Buyer. Demands and notices required by this paragraph shall be in writing and delivered by hand delivery or by certified mail, return receipt requested.

18. **REPRESENTATIONS:** Seller represents that as of the Closing Date (a) there will be no liens, assessments, Uniform Commercial Code or other security interests against the Property which will not be satisfied out of the Sales Price unless securing payment of any loans assumed by Buyer and (b) assumed loans will be without default. If any representation in this contract is untrue on the Closing Date, this contract may be terminated by Buyer and the Earnest Money shall be refunded to Buyer. All representations contained in this contract and an agreement for mediation shall survive closing.

19. **NOTICES:** All notices shall be in writing and effective when mailed to or hand-delivered at the addresses shown below.

20. **FEDERAL TAX REQUIREMENT:** If Seller is a "foreign person", as defined by applicable law, or if Seller fails to deliver an affidavit that Seller is not a "foreign person", then Buyer shall withhold from the sales proceeds an amount sufficient to comply with applicable tax law and deliver the same to the Internal Revenue Service together with appropriate tax forms. IRS regulations require filing written reports if cash in excess of specified amounts is received in the transaction.

21. **DISPUTE RESOLUTION:** It is the policy of the State of Texas to encourage the peaceable resolution of disputes through alternative dispute resolution procedures. The parties are encouraged to use an addendum approved by TREC to submit to

One to Four Family Residential Earnest Money Contract Concerning_____Page Six   10-25-93

(Address of Property)

mediation disputes which cannot be resolved in good faith through informal discussion.

22. **AGREEMENT OF PARTIES:**   This contract contains the entire agreement of the parties and cannot be changed except by their written agreement. Addenda which are a part of this contract are (list): _____

_____.

23. **CONSULT YOUR ATTORNEY:** Brokers cannot give legal advice. This is intended to be a legally binding contract. READ IT CAREFULLY. If you do not understand the effect of this contract, consult your attorney BEFORE signing.

Buyer's   Seller's
Attorney:_____   Attorney:_____
EXECUTED in multiple originals the _____day of _____, 19_____ *(THE EFFECTIVE DATE).*
(BROKER: FILL IN THE DATE OF FINAL ACCEPTANCE AND THE PARTIES' ADDRESSES.)

_____   _____
Buyer   Seller

_____   _____
Buyer   Seller

_____   _____
Buyer's Address   Phone No.   Seller's Address   Phone No.

> The form of this contract has been approved by the Texas Real Estate Commission. Such approval relates to this contract form only. No representation is made as to the legal validity or adequacy of any provision in any specific transaction. It is not suitable for complex transactions. Extensive riders or additions are not to be used. (10-93) TREC NO. 20-2. This form replaces TREC NO. 20-1.

AGREEMENT BETWEEN BROKERS

Listing Broker agrees to pay _____, Other Broker, a fee of _____ of the total sales price when the Listing Broker's fee is received. Escrow Agent is authorized and directed to pay Other Broker from Listing Broker's fee at closing.

_____   _____
Other Broker   License No.   Listing Broker   License No.

By:_____   By:_____

_____   _____
Other Broker's Address   Phone No.   Listing Broker's Address   Phone No.

RECEIPT

Receipt of ☐ Contract and ☐ $_____ Earnest Money in the form of _____

_____
is acknowledged.
Escrow Agent: _____   By:_____

Date:_____, 19____.   _____
                                                    Address

                                                    City   Texas   Zip Code

№   457   TREC NO. 20-2

ONE TO FOUR FAMILY RESIDENTIAL EARNEST MONEY CONTRACT RESALE

FHA INSURED OR VA GUARANTEED FINANCING-TEXAS

ONE TO FOUR FAMILY RESIDENTIAL EARNEST MONEY CONTRACT (RESALE)

FHA INSURED OR VA GUARANTEED FINANCING

PROMULGATED BY THE TEXAS REAL ESTATE COMMISSION (TREC)
Notice: Not For Use For Condominium Transactions

1. **PARTIES:** _____ (Seller) agrees to sell and convey to _____ (Buyer) and Buyer agrees to buy from Seller the Property described below.

2. **Property:** Lot _____, Block _____, _____ Addition, City of _____, _____ County, Texas, known as _____ (Address), or as described on attached exhibit, together with the following items, if any: curtains and rods, draperies and rods, valances, blinds, window shades, screens, shutters, awnings, wall-to-wall carpeting, mirrors fixed in place, ceiling fans, attic fans, mail boxes, television antennae and satellite dish with controls, permanently installed heating and air conditioning units and equipment, window air conditioning units, built-in security and fire detection equipment, lighting and plumbing fixtures, water softener, built-in kitchen equipment, garage door openers with controls, built-in cleaning equipment, all swimming pool equipment, shrubbery, permanently installed outdoor cooking equipment, built-in fireplace screens and all other Property owned by Seller and attached to the above described real Property except the following Property which is not included:_____

_____.

   All Property sold by this contract is called the "Property." The Property ☐ is ☐ is not subject to mandatory membership in an owners' association and its assessments and requirements.

3. **SALES PRICE:**
   A.   Cash portion of the Sales Price payable by Buyer. . . . .$_____
   B.   Sum of all financing described below excluding VA Funding Fee or FHA Mortgage
        Insurance Premium (MIP) . . . .$_____
   C.   Sales Price (Sum of A and B). . . . .$_____

4. **FINANCING:** The portion of the Sales Price not payable in cash shall be paid as follows: (Check applicable boxes below)
   ☐ A.   **FHA INSURED FINANCING:**
   This contract is subject to approval for Buyer of a Section _____ FHA Insured Loan (the Loan) of not less than $_____ (excluding any financed MIP), amortizable monthly for not less than _____ years, with interest not to exceed _____% per annum for the first _____ year(s) of the Loan.
   As required by HUD-FHA, if FHA valuation is unknown, "It is expressly agreed that, notwithstanding any other provisions of this contract, the purchaser (Buyer) shall not be obligated to complete the purchase of the Property described herein or to incur any penalty by forfeiture of earnest money deposits or otherwise unless the purchaser (Buyer) has been given in accordance with HUD/FHA or VA requirements a written statement issued by the Federal Housing Commissioner, Department of Veterans Affairs, or a Direct Endorsement Lender setting forth the appraised value of the Property of not less than $_____. The purchaser (Buyer) shall have the privilege and option of proceeding with consummation of the contract without regard to the amount of the appraised valuation. The appraised valuation is arrived at to determine the maximum mortgage the Department of Housing and Urban Development will insure. HUD does not warrant the value or the condition of the Property. The purchaser should satisfy himself/herself that the price and the condition of the Property are acceptable."
   If the FHA appraised value of the Property (excluding closing costs and MIP) is less than the Sales Price (3C above), Seller may reduce the Sales Price to an amount equal to the FHA appraised value (excluding closing costs and MIP) and the parties to the sale shall close the sale at such lower Sales Price with appropriate adjustments to 3A and 3B above.
   NOTICE TO BUYER: For housing built before 1978, HUD requires Buyer to sign a notice relating to lead paint prior to signing this contract.
   ☐ B.   **VA GUARANTEED FINANCING:**
   This contract is subject to approval for Buyer of a VA guaranteed loan (the Loan) of not less than $_____ (excluding any financed Funding Fee), amortizable monthly for not less than _____ years, with interest not to exceed _____% per annum for the first _____ year(s) of the loan.
   VA NOTICE TO BUYER: "It is expressly agreed that, notwithstanding any other provisions of this contract, the Buyer shall not incur any penalty by forfeiture of earnest money or otherwise or be obligated to complete the purchase of the Property described herein, if the contract purchase price or cost exceeds the reasonable value of the Property established by the Department of Veterans Affairs. The Buyer shall, however, have the privilege and option of proceeding with the consummation of this contract without regard to the amount of the reasonable value established by the Department of Veterans Affairs."

Initialed for identification by Buyer_____ and Seller_____   № 444   TREC NO. 21-2

If Buyer elects to complete the purchase at an amount in excess of the reasonable value established by VA, Buyer shall pay such excess amount in cash from a source which Buyer agrees to disclose to the VA and which Buyer represents will not be from borrowed funds except as approved by VA. If VA reasonable value of the Property is less than the Sales Price (3C above), Seller may reduce the Sales Price to an amount equal to the VA reasonable value and the parties to the sale shall close at such lower Sales Price with appropriate adjustments to 3A and 3B above.

☐ C. TEXAS VETERANS' HOUSING ASSISTANCE PROGRAM LOAN:

A Texas Veterans' Housing Assistance Program Loan (the Program Loan) of $_____ for a period of at least _____ years at the interest rate established by the Texas Veterans' Land Board at the time of closing. Within _____ days after the effective date of this contract Buyer shall apply for all loan(s) and shall make every reasonable effort to obtain financing. Financing shall be deemed to have been approved when the lender has determined that Buyer has satisfied all of lender's financial conditions (those items relating to Buyer's ability to qualify for a loan). If financing (including any financed MIP or Funding Fee) is not obtained within _____ days after the effective date hereof, this contract shall terminate and the Earnest Money shall be refunded to Buyer. NOTE: Describe special terms of any non-fixed rate loan in Paragraph 11.

5. **EARNEST MONEY:** Buyer shall deposit $_____ as Earnest Money with _____
_____ at _____
(Address), as Escrow Agent, upon execution of this contract by both parties. ☐ Additional Earnest Money of $_____ shall be deposited by Buyer with Escrow Agent on or before _____, 19_____. If Buyer fails to deposit the Earnest Money as required by this contract, Buyer shall be in default.

6. **TITLE POLICY AND SURVEY:**

☐ A. TITLE POLICY: Seller shall furnish to Buyer at Seller's expense an Owner Policy of Title Insurance (the Title Policy) issued by _____ (the Title Company) in the amount of the Sales Price, dated at or after closing, insuring Buyer against loss under the provisions of the Title Policy, subject to the promulgated exclusions (including existing building and zoning ordinances) and the following exceptions:

(1)   Restrictive covenants common to the platted subdivision in which the Property is located.
(2)   The standard printed exception for standby fees, taxes and assessments.
(3)   Liens created as part of the financing described in Paragraph 4.
(4)   Utility easements created by the dedication deed or plat of the subdivision in which the Property is located.
(5)   Reservations or exceptions otherwise permitted by this contract or as may be approved by Buyer in writing.
(6)   The standard printed exception as to discrepancies, conflicts, shortages in area or boundary lines, encroachments or protrusions, or overlapping improvements.
(7)   The standard printed exception as to marital rights.
(8)   The standard printed exception as to waters, tidelands, beaches, streams, and related matters.

Within 20 days after the Title Company receives a copy of this contract, Seller shall furnish to Buyer a commitment for Title Insurance (the Commitment) and, at Buyer's expense, legible copies of restrictive covenants and documents evidencing exceptions in the Commitment other than the standard printed exceptions. Seller authorizes the Title Company to mail or hand deliver the Commitment and related documents to Buyer at Buyer's address shown below. If the Commitment is not delivered to Buyer within the specified time, the time for delivery shall be automatically extended up to 15 days. Buyer shall have 5 days after the receipt of the Commitment to object in writing to matters disclosed in the Commitment. Buyer may object to existing building and zoning ordinances and items 6(A)(1) through (8) above if Buyer determines that any such ordinance or items prohibits the following use or activity: _____
_____
_____.

☐ B. SURVEY REQUIRED: (Check one box only)

☐ (1)   Within _____ days after Buyer's receipt of a survey plat furnished to a third-party lender at Buyer's expense, Buyer may object in writing to any matter shown on the plat which constitutes a defect or encumbrance to title.
☐ (2)   Within _____ days after the effective date of this contract, Buyer may object in writing to any matter which constitutes a defect or encumbrance to title shown on a survey plat obtained by Buyer at Buyer's expense.

The survey shall be made by a Registered Professional Land Surveyor acceptable to the title company and any lender. The plat shall: (a) identify the Property by metes and bounds or platted lot description; (b) show that the survey was made and staked on the ground with corners permanently marked; (c) set forth the dimensions of the Property; (d) show the location of all improvements, highways, streets, roads, railroads, rivers, creeks or other waterways, fences, easements and rights of way on the Property ; (e) show any discrepancies or conflicts in boundaries, any visible encroachments, and any portion of the Property lying within the 100 year floodplain as shown on the current Federal Emergency Management Agency map; and (f) contain the surveyor's certificate that the survey as shown by the plat is true and correct. Utility easements created by the dedication deed and plat of the subdivision in which the Property is located shall not be a basis for objection.

Buyer's failure to object under Paragraph 6A or 6B within the time allowed shall constitute a waiver of Buyer's right to object; except that the requirements in Schedule C of the Commitment shall not be deemed to have been waived. If objections are made by Buyer or any third party lender, Seller shall cure the objections within 15 days from the date Seller receives them and the Closing Date shall be extended as necessary. If objections are not cured by the extended Closing Date, this contract shall terminate and the Earnest Money shall be refunded to Buyer unless Buyer elects to waive the objections.

NOTICE TO SELLER AND BUYER:

(1)   Broker advises Buyer to have an Abstract covering the Property examined by an attorney of Buyer's selection, or Buyer should be furnished with or obtain a Title Policy. If a Title Policy is furnished, the Commitment should be promptly reviewed by an attorney of Buyer's choice due to the time limitations on Buyer's right to object.

(2)   If the Property is situated in a utility or other statutorily created district providing water, sewer, drainage, or flood control facilities and services, Chapter 50 of the Texas Water Code requires Seller to deliver and Buyer to sign the statutory notice relating to the tax rate, bonded indebtedness, or standby fee of the district prior to final execution of this contract.

(3)   Buyer is advised that the presence of wetlands, toxic substances including lead-base paint or asbestos and wastes or other environmental hazards or the presence of a threatened or endangered species or its habitat may affect Buyer's intended use of the Property. If Buyer is concerned about these matters, an addendum either promulgated by TREC or required by the parties should be used.

(4)   If the Property adjoins and shares a common boundary with the tidally influenced submerged lands of the state, Section 33.135, Texas Natural Resources Code, requires a notice regarding coastal area property to be included in the contract. An addendum either promulgated by TREC or required by the parties should be used.

7. PROPERTY CONDITION.

A. SELLER'S DISCLOSURE OF PROPERTY CONDITION (the "Notice")(Section 5.008 Property Code)(check one box only):
   ☐ (1)   Buyer has received the Notice.
   ☐ (2)   Buyer has not received the Notice. Within _____ days after the effective date of this contract, Seller shall deliver the Notice to Buyer. If Seller fails to deliver the Notice within the time allowed, Buyer may terminate this contract within three days after the time for delivery of the Notice. If Seller timely delivers the Notice, Buyer may terminate this contract for any reason within seven days after Buyer receives the Notice.

B. REQUIRED REPAIRS OR INSPECTIONS. (Check one box only):
   ☐ (1)   Buyer requires the completion of any repairs designated by a lender and the following repairs: _____
   _____.
   ☐ (2)   Buyer requires the completion of any repairs designated by a lender and any repairs designated by Buyer pursuant to the attached Property Condition Addendum. Buyer shall pay for inspections, reinspections, reports and certificates.

C. PAYMENT FOR TREATMENT OR REPAIRS. Subject to the limitations set out below, Seller shall pay for any treatment or repairs required by the contract, any lender and any Property Condition Addendum. Seller is not obligated to pay more than $ _____ for treatment and repairs resulting from termites or other wood-destroying insects or to pay more than $ _____ for all other repairs. Seller shall also pay for turning utilities on for inspections and reinspections.

D. BUYER'S CHOICES. After Seller receives all inspection reports and repair designations made by Buyer or any lender pursuant to 7B(1) or 7B(2), Seller shall notify Buyer within 7 days (1) of the costs of all required treatment and repairs and (2) whether Seller will pay the costs that exceed the amounts in 7C. If Seller notifies Buyer that Seller will not pay the excess costs, Buyer may (1) pay the excess costs (2) accept the Property with the costs of treatment and repairs not to exceed the amounts in 7C (if permitted by any lender), or (3) terminate this contract and the Earnest Money shall be refunded to Buyer. Buyer shall notify Seller of Buyer's choice within 5 days after Buyer is notified Seller will not pay the excess costs.

If Seller does not notify Buyer, Buyer shall notify Seller of Buyer's choice from the three alternatives provided above within 12 days after Seller receives all inspection reports and repair designations from Buyer and any lender. *If Buyer does not notify Seller of Buyer's choice within the specified time, Buyer shall accept the Property with the costs of treatment and repairs limited to the amounts stated in 7C.*

If the total cost of required treatment and repairs exceeds 5% of the Sales Price and Seller agrees to pay the total cost, Buyer may (1) accept the Property with all required treatment and repairs, or (2) terminate this contract and the Earnest Money shall be refunded to Buyer. Buyer shall notify Seller of Buyer's choice within 5 days after Seller notifies Buyer that Seller will pay all costs of treatment and repair. *If Buyer does not notify Seller of Buyer's choice within the specified time Buyer shall accept the Property with all required treatment and repairs.*

E. COMPLETION OF TREATMENT OR REPAIRS. Seller shall complete required or agreed treatment and repairs prior to the Closing Date. If Seller fails to complete any required or agreed treatment or repairs, Buyer may do so; Seller shall be liable for the cost up to the maximum agreed amount which shall be deducted from the sales proceeds or collected from Seller at closing if necessary. Buyer may also exercise applicable remedies provided in Paragraph 15.

8. **BROKERS' REPRESENTATION AND FEES:**_____

(Listing Broker) represents ☐ Seller only ☐ Seller and Buyer.

Any other broker represents:

☐ Seller as Listing Broker's subagent;

☐ Buyer only as Buyer's agent.

Brokers' fees shall be paid as specified by separate written agreements.

9. **CLOSING:** The closing of the sale shall be on or before _____, 19_____, or within 7 days after objections to title and survey have been cured, whichever date is later (the Closing Date); *however, if financing has been obtained pursuant to Paragraph 4,* the Closing Date shall be extended up to 15 days only if necessary to comply with lender's closing requirements (for example, survey, insurance policies, Property repairs, closing documents). If either party fails to close this sale by the Closing Date, the nondefaulting party shall be entitled to exercise the remedies contained in Paragraph 15. At closing Seller shall furnish tax statements or certificates showing no delinquent taxes and a General Warranty Deed conveying good and indefeasible title showing no additional exceptions to those permitted in Paragraph 6.

10. **POSSESSION:** Seller shall deliver possession of the Property to Buyer on _____ _____ in its present or required repaired condition, subject to the dollar limitations of Paragraph 7, ordinary wear and tear excepted. Any possession by Buyer prior to closing or by Seller after closing that is not authorized by a temporary lease form promulgated by TREC or required by the Parties shall establish a landlord-tenant at sufferance relationship between the Parties. *Consult your insurance agent prior to change of possession as insurance coverage may be limited or terminated.*

11. **SPECIAL PROVISIONS:** [Insert only factual statements and business details applicable to this sale. A licensee shall not add to a promulgated earnest money contract form factual statements or business details for which a contract addendum, lease or other form has been promulgated by TREC for mandatory use. 22 TAC §537.11 (d).]

12. **SALES EXPENSES:** The following expenses shall be paid at or prior to closing:

A. Appraisal fees shall be paid by _____.

B. The total of the loan discount and buydown fees (including any Texas Veterans' Housing Assistance Program Participation Fee) shall not exceed _____% of the loan of which Seller shall pay the first _____% of the loan and Buyer shall pay the remainder.

C. Seller's Expenses: Releases of existing liens, including prepayment penalties and recording fees; tax statements or certificates; preparation of deed; one-half of escrow fee; expenses FHA or VA prohibits Buyer to pay (for example, preparation of loan documents, copies of restrictions, photos, excess cost of survey, remaining one-half of escrow fee); tax service and research fees; and other expenses stipulated to be paid by Seller under other provisions of this contract.

D. Buyer's Expenses: Interest on the note(s) from date of disbursement to 1 month prior to dates of first monthly payments, expenses stipulated to be paid by Buyer under other provisions of this contract; any customary Texas Veterans' Housing Assistance Program Loan costs for Buyer; and premiums for mortgagee title policy and endorsements required by lender.

   (1)   FHA Buyer: All prepaid items required by applicable HUD-FHA or other regulations (for example, required premiums for flood and hazard insurance, reserve deposits for other insurance, ad valorem taxes and special governmental assessments); expenses incident to any loan (for example, preparation of loan documents, survey, recording fees, copies of restrictions and easements, amortization schedule, loan origination fee, credit reports, photos, loan related inspection fee); and one-half of escrow fee.

   (2)   VA Buyer: All prepaid items (for example, required premiums for flood and hazard insurance, reserve deposits for other insurance, ad valorem taxes and special governmental assessments); expenses incident to any loan (for example, credit reports, recording fees, loan origination fee, that portion of survey cost VA Buyer may pay by VA Regulation,

loan related inspection fees).

    E. The VA Loan Funding Fee or FHA Mortgage Insurance Premium (MIP) not to exceed _____ shall be paid by Buyer, and ☐ paid in cash at closing ☐ added to the amount of the loan or ☐ paid as follows: _____
_____.

    F. If any sales expense exceeds the amount stated in this contract to be paid by either party, either party may terminate this contract unless either party agrees to pay such excess. In no event shall Buyer pay charges and fees expressly prohibited by FHA, VA or other government loan program regulations.

13. **PRORATIONS:** Flood and hazard insurance premiums (excluding mortgage insurance), taxes for the current year, interest, maintenance fees, assessments and rents shall be prorated through the Closing Date. Buyer shall be obligated to pay taxes for the current year.

14. **CASUALTY LOSS:** If any part of the Property is damaged or destroyed by fire or other casualty loss, Seller shall restore the Property to its previous condition as soon as reasonably possible, but in any event by the Closing Date. If Seller is unable to do so without fault, Buyer may either (a) terminate this contract and the Earnest Money shall be refunded to Buyer (b) extend the time for performance up to 15 days and the Closing Date shall be extended as necessary or (c) accept the Property in its damaged condition and accept an assignment of insurance proceeds. Provisions of the Texas Property Code to the contrary shall not apply.

15. **DEFAULT:** If Buyer fails to comply with this contract, Buyer shall be in default, and Seller may either (a) enforce specific performance, seek such other relief as may be provided by law, or both, or (b) terminate this contract and receive the Earnest Money as liquidated damages, thereby releasing both parties from this contract. If Seller is unable without fault to make any non-casualty repairs or deliver the Commitment within the time allowed, Buyer may either terminate this contract and receive the Earnest Money as the sole remedy or extend the time for performance up to 15 days and the Closing Date shall be extended as necessary. If Seller fails to comply with this contract for any other reason, Seller shall be in default and Buyer may either (a) enforce specific performance, seek such other relief as may be provided by law, or both, or (b) terminate this contract and receive the Earnest Money, thereby releasing both parties from this contract.

16. **ATTORNEY'S FEES:** If Buyer, Seller, Listing Broker, Other Broker or Escrow Agent is a prevailing party in any legal proceeding brought under or with relation to this contract, such party shall be entitled to recover from the non-prevailing party all costs of such proceeding and reasonable attorney's fees.

17. **ESCROW:** The Earnest Money is deposited with Escrow Agent with the understanding that Escrow Agent is not (a) a party to this contract and does not have any liability for the performance or non-performance of any party to this contract, (b) liable for interest on the Earnest Money or (c) liable for any loss of Earnest Money caused by the failure of any financial institution in which the Earnest Money has been deposited unless the financial institution is acting as Escrow Agent. If either party makes demand for the payment of the Earnest Money, Escrow Agent has the right to require from all parties and brokers a written release of liability of Escrow Agent for disbursement of the Earnest Money. Any refund or disbursement of Earnest Money under this contract shall be reduced by the amount of unpaid expenses incurred on behalf of the party receiving the Earnest Money, and Escrow Agent shall pay the same to the creditors entitled thereto. At closing, the Earnest Money shall be applied first to any cash down payment, then to Buyer's closing costs and any excess refunded to Buyer. Demands and notices required by this paragraph shall be in writing and delivered by hand delivery or by certified mail, return receipt requested.

18. **REPRESENTATIONS:** Seller represents that as of the Closing Date there will be no liens, assessments, Uniform Commercial Code or other security interests against any of the Property which will not be satisfied out of the Sales Price. If any representation in this contract is untrue on the Closing Date, this contract may be terminated by Buyer and the Earnest Money shall be refunded to Buyer. All representations contained in this contract and an agreement for mediation shall survive closing.

19. **NOTICES:** All notices shall be in writing and effective when mailed to or hand-delivered at the addresses shown below.

20. **FEDERAL TAX REQUIREMENT:** If Seller is a "foreign person", as defined by applicable law, or if Seller fails to deliver an affidavit that Seller is not a "foreign person", then Buyer shall withhold from the sales proceeds an amount sufficient to comply with applicable tax law and deliver the same to the Internal Revenue Service together with appropriate tax forms. IRS regulations require filing written reports if cash in excess of specified amounts is received in the transaction.

21. **DISPUTE RESOLUTION:** It is the policy of the State of Texas to encourage the peaceable resolution of disputes through alternative dispute resolution procedures. The parties are encouraged to use an addendum approved by TREC to submit to mediation disputes which cannot be resolved in good faith through informal discussion.

22. **AGREEMENT OF PARTIES:** This contract contains the entire agreement of the parties and cannot be changed except by their written agreement. Addenda which are a part of this contract are (list):_____
_____
_____.

23. **CONSULT YOUR ATTORNEY:** Brokers cannot give legal advice. This is intended to be a legally binding contract. READ IT CAREFULLY. If you do not understand the effect of this contract, consult your attorney BEFORE signing.

FHA or VA Residential Earnest Money Contract Concerning_____Page Six 10-25-93

(Address of Property)

Buyer's   Seller's
Attorney:_____   Attorney:_____

EXECUTED in multiple originals the _____day of _____, 19_____ (THE EFFECTIVE DATE).
(BROKER: FILL IN THE DATE OF FINAL ACCEPTANCE AND THE PARTIES' ADDRESSES.)

_____   _____
Buyer   Seller

_____   _____
Buyer   Seller

_____   _____
Buyer's Address   Phone No.   Seller's Address   Phone No.

> The form of this contract has been approved by the Texas Real Estate Commission. Such approval relates to this contract form only. No representation is made as to the legal validity or adequacy of any provision in any specific transaction. It is not suitable for complex transactions. Extensive riders or additions are not to be used. (10-93) TREC NO. 21-2. This form replaces TREC NO. 21-1.

AGREEMENT BETWEEN BROKERS

Listing Broker agrees to pay _____, Other
Broker, a fee of _____ of the total sales price when the Listing Broker's fee is received. Escrow Agent is authorized and directed to pay Other Broker from Listing Broker's fee at closing.

_____   _____
Other Broker   License No.   Listing Broker   License No.

By:_____   By:_____

_____   _____
Other Broker's Address   Phone No.   Listing Broker's Address   Phone No.

RECEIPT

Receipt of ☐ Contract and ☐ $_____ Earnest Money in the form of _____
_____
is acknowledged.

Escrow Agent: _____   By:_____

Date: _____, 19_____.   _____
                                                  Address

                                                  _____
                                                  City   State   Zip Code

UNIFORM RESIDENTIAL APPRAISAL REPORT- FREDDIE MAC FANNIE MAE

☐ ☐
Property Description   **UNIFORM RESIDENTIAL APPRAISAL REPORT** File No. ___

SUBJECT

| Property Address | | City | | State | Zip Code |

Legal Description ___ County ___

Assessor's Parcel No. ___ Tax Year ___ R.E. Taxes $ ___ Special Assessments $ ___

Borrower ___ Current Owner ___ Occupant: ☐ Owner ☐ Tenant ☐ Vacant

Property rights appraised ☐ Fee Simple ☐ Leasehold Project Type ☐ PUD ☐ Condominium (HUD/VA only) HOA$ ___ /Mo.

Neighborhood or Project Name ___ Map Reference ___ Census Tract ___

Sale Price $ ___ Date of Sale ___ Description and $ amount of loan charges/conscessions to be paid by seller ___

Lender/Client ___ Address ___

Appraiser ___ Address ___

NEIGHBORHOOD

Location	☐ Urban	☐ Suburban	☐ Rural	**Predominant occupancy**	**Single family housing** PRICE $(000) / AGE (yrs)	**Present land use %**	**Land use change**
Built up	☐ Over 75%	☐ 25-75%	☐ Under 25%			One family ___	☐ Not likely ☐ Likely
Growth rate	☐ Rapid	☐ Stable	☐ Slow	☐ Owner	Low	2-4 family ___	☐ In process
Property values	☐ Increasing	☐ Stable	☐ Declining	☐ Tenant	High	Multi-family ___	To: ___
Demand/supply	☐ Shortage	☐ In balance	☐ Over supply	☐ Vacant (0-5%)	Predominant	Commercial ___	
Marketing time	☐ Under 3 mos.	☐ 3-6 mos.	☐ Over 6 mos.	☐ Vacant (over 5%)			

Note: Race and the racial composition of the neighborhood are not appraisal factors.

Neighborhood boundaries and characteristics: ___

Factors that affect the marketability of the properties in the neighborhood (proximity to employment and amenities, employment stability, appeal to market, etc.): ___

Market conditions in the subject neighborhood (including support for the above conclusions related to the trend of property values, demand/supply, and marketing time - - such as data on competitive properties for sale in the neighborhood, description of the prevalence of sales and financing concessions, etc.). ___

PUD

Project Information for PUDs (If applicable) - - Is the developer/builder in control of the Home Owners' Association (HOA)? ☐ Yes ☐ No

Approximate total number of units in the subject project ___ Approximate total number of units for sale in the subject project ___

Describe common elements and recreational facilities: ___

SITE

Dimensions ___ | Topography ___

Site area ___ Corner Lot ☐ Yes ☐ No | Size ___

Specific zoning classification and description ___ | Shape ___

Zoning compliance ☐ Legal ☐ Legal nonconforming (Grandfathered use) ☐ Illegal ☐ No zoning | Drainage ___

Highest & best use as improved: ☐ Present use ☐ Other use (explain) ___ | View ___

Utilities	Public	Other	Off-site Improvements	Type	Public	Private	Landscaping ___
Electricity	☐		Street		☐	☐	Driveway Surface ___
Gas	☐		Curb/gutter		☐	☐	Apparent easements ___
Water	☐		Sidewalk		☐	☐	FEMA Special Flood Hazard Area ☐ Yes ☐ No
Sanitary sewer	☐		Street lights		☐	☐	FEMA Zone ___ Map Date ___
Storm sewer	☐		Alley		☐	☐	FEMA Map No. ___

Comments (apparent adverse easements, encroachments, special assessments, slide areas, illegal or legal nonconforming zoning use, etc.): ___

DESCRIPTION OF IMPROVEMENTS

GENERAL DESCRIPTION	EXTERIOR DESCRIPTION	FOUNDATION	BASEMENT	INSULATION
No. of Units ___	Foundation ___	Slab ___	Area Sq. Ft. ___	Roof ___ ☐
No. of Stories ___	Exterior Walls ___	Crawl Space ___	% Finished ___	Ceiling ___ ☐
Type (Det./Att.) ___	Roof Surface ___	Basement ___	Ceiling ___	Walls ___ ☐
Design (Style) ___	Gutters & Dwnspts. ___	Sump Pump ___	Walls ___	Floor ___ ☐
Existing/Proposed ___	Window Type ___	Dampness ___	Floor ___	None ___ ☐
Age (Yrs.) ___	Storm/Screens ___	Settlement ___	Outside Entry ___	Unknown ___ ☐
Effective Age (Yrs.) ___	Manufactured House ___	Infestation ___		

ROOMS	Foyer	Living	Dining	Kitchen	Den	Family Rm.	Rec. Rm.	Bedrooms	# Baths	Laundry	Other	Area Sq. Ft.
Basement												
Level 1												
Level 2												

Finished area **above** grade contains: ___ Rooms; ___ Bedroom(s); ___ Bath(s); ___ Square Feet of Gross Living Area

INTERIOR	Materials/Condition	HEATING	KITCHEN EQUIP.	ATTIC	AMENITIES	CAR STORAGE:
Floors		Type ___	Refrigerator ☐	None ☐	Fireplace(s) # ___ ☐	None ☐
Walls		Fuel ___	Range/Oven ☐	Stairs ☐	Patio ___ ☐	Garage ___ # of cars
Trim/Finish		Condition ___	Disposal ☐	Drop Stair ☐	Deck ___ ☐	Attached ___
Bath Floor		COOLING	Dishwasher ☐	Scuttle ☐	Porch ___ ☐	Detached ___
Bath Wainscot		Central ___	Fan/Hood ☐	Floor ☐	Fence ___ ☐	Built-In ___
Doors		Other ___	Microwave ☐	Heated ☐	Pool ___ ☐	Carport ___
		Condition ___	Washer/Dryer ☐	Finished ☐		Driveway ___

COMMENTS

Additional features (special energy efficient items, etc.): ___

Condition of the improvements, depreciation (physical, functional, and external), repairs needed, quality of construction, remodeling/additions, etc.: ___

Adverse environmental conditions (such as, but not limited to, hazardous wastes, toxic substances, etc.) present in the improvements, on the site, or in the immediate vicinity of the subject property.: ___

UNIFORM RESIDENTIAL APPRAISAL REPORT   File No. _____

COST APPROACH

ESTIMATED SITE VALUE . . . . = $ _____
ESTIMATED REPRODUCTION COST-NEW-OF IMPROVEMENTS:

Dwelling _____ Sq. Ft @ $ _____ = $ _____
_____ Sq. Ft @ $ _____ = _____
_____ = _____
Garage/Carport _____ Sq. Ft @ $ _____ = _____
Total Estimated Cost New. . . . . = $ _____
Less   Physical   Functional   External
Depreciation _____ = $ _____
Depreciated Value of Improvements. . . . . = $ _____
"As-is" Value of Site Improvements . . . . = $ _____
INDICATED VALUE BY COST APPROACH. . . . . = $ _____

Comments on Cost Approach (such as, source of cost estimate, site value, square foot calculation and for HUD, VA and FmHA, the estimated remaining economic life of the property): _____
_____
_____
_____
_____
_____
_____

SALES COMPARISON ANALYSIS

ITEM	SUBJECT	COMPARABLE NO. 1		COMPARABLE NO. 2		COMPARABLE NO. 3	
Address							
Proximity to Subject							
Sales Price	$	$		$		$	
Price/Gross Liv. Area	$	$		$		$	
Data and/or Verification Source							
VALUE ADJUSTMENTS	DESCRIPTION	DESCRIPTION	+ (−) $ Adjustment	DESCRIPTION	+ (−) $ Adjustment	DESCRIPTION	+ (−) $ Adjustment
Sales or Financing Concessions							
Date of Sale/Time							
Location							
Leasehold/Fee Simple							
Site							
View							
Design and Appeal							
Quality of Construction							
Age							
Condition							
Above Grade Room Count	Total / Bdrms / Baths	Total / Bdrms / Baths		Total / Bdrms / Baths		Total / Bdrms / Baths	
Gross Living Area	Sq. Ft.	Sq. Ft.		Sq. Ft.		Sq. Ft.	
Basement & Finished Rooms Below Grade							
Functional Utility							
Heating/Cooling							
Energy Efficient Items							
Garage/Carport							
Porch, Patio, Deck, Fireplace(s), etc.							
Fence, Pool, etc.							
Net Adj. (total)		+ □ − □ $		+ □ − □ $		+ □ − □ $	
Adjusted Sales Price of Comparable		$		$		$	

Comments on Sales Comparison (including the subject property's compatibility to the neighborhood, etc.): _____
_____
_____
_____
_____

ITEM	SUBJECT	COMPARABLE NO. 1	COMPARABLE NO. 2	COMPARABLE NO. 3
Date, Price and Data Source for prior sales within year of appraisal				

Analysis of any current agreement of sale, option, or listing of the subject property and analysis of any prior sales of subject and comparables within one year of the date of appraisal:
_____

INDICATED VALUE BY SALES COMPARISON APPROACH. . . . . $ _____
INDICATED VALUE BY INCOME APPROACH (If Applicable) Estimated Market Rent $ _____ /Mo. x Gross Rent Multiplier _____ = $ _____

RECONCILIATION

This appraisal is made □ "as is" □ subject to the repairs, alterations, inspections or conditions listed below □ subject to completion per plans and specifications.
Conditions of Appraisal: _____

Final Reconciliation: _____
_____

The purpose of this appraisal is to estimate the market value of the real property that is the subject of this report, based on the above conditions and the certification, contingent and limiting conditions, and market value definition that are stated in the attached Freddie Mac Form 439/Fannie Mae Form 1004B (Revised _____).
I (WE) ESTIMATE THE MARKET VALUE, AS DEFINED, OF THE REAL PROPERTY THAT IS THE SUBJECT OF THIS REPORT, AS OF _____
(WHICH IS THE DATE OF INSPECTION AND THE EFFECTIVE DATE OF THIS REPORT) TO BE $ _____

APPRAISER:	SUPERVISORY APPRAISER (ONLY IF REQUIRED):	
Signature _____	Signature _____	□ Did □ Did Not
Name _____	Name _____	Inspect Property
Date Report Signed _____	Date Report Signed _____	
State Certification # _____ State	State Certification # _____ State	
Or State License # _____ State	Or State License # _____ State	

NEW JERSEY CONTRACT FOR SALE OF REAL ESTATE

ALL-STATE LEGAL SUPPLY CO.

CONTRACT FOR SALE OF REAL ESTATE

Prepared by: (Print signer's name below signature)

....

This Contract for Sale is made on   , 19

BETWEEN

whose address is

referred to as the Seller,

AND

whose address is

referred to as the Buyer.

The words "Buyer" and "Seller" include all Buyers and all Sellers listed above.

1. Purchase Agreement. The Seller agrees to sell and the Buyer agrees to buy the property described in this contract.

2. Property. The property to be sold consists of: (a) the land and all the buildings, other improvements and fixtures on the land; (b) all of the Seller's rights relating to the land; and (c) all personal property specifically included in this contract. The real property to be sold is commonly known as
in the   of   in the County of
, and State of New Jersey. It is shown on the municipal tax map as lot
in block   . This property is more fully described in the attached Schedule A.

3. Purchase Price. The purchase price is $

4. Payment of Purchase Price. The Buyer will pay the purchase price as follows:

Previously paid by the Buyer (initial deposit) $

Upon signing of this contract (balance of deposit) $

Amount of mortgage (paragraph 6) $

By assuming the obligation to pay the present mortgage according to its terms. This mortgage shall be in good standing at the closing. Either party may cancel this contract if the Lender does not permit the Buyer to assume the mortgage (estimated balance due). $

By the Seller taking back a note and mortgage for   years at
     % interest with monthly payments based on a   year
payment schedule. The Buyer will pay the Seller's attorney $
for the preparation of the necessary documents. The Buyer will also pay all recording costs and provide the Seller with an adequate affidavit of title. $

Balance to be paid at closing of title, in cash or by certified or bank cashier's check (subject to adjustment at closing) $

5. Deposit Moneys. All deposit moneys will be held in trust by
until

6. Mortgage Contingency. The Buyer agrees to make a good faith effort to obtain a first mortgage loan upon the terms listed below. The Buyer has until   , 19   , to obtain a commitment from a lender for this mortgage loan or to agree to buy the property without this loan. If this is not done before this deadline, and any agreed upon extensions, either party may cancel this contract.

Type of Mortgage: ☐ conventional,   ☐ FHA,   ☐VA,   ☐ other ....
Amount of Loan: $ Interest Rate: %
Length of Mortgage: years with monthly payments based on a   year payment schedule.
Points: The Buyer agrees to pay   points for a total of $
           The Seller agrees to pay   points for a total of $

7. Time and Place of Closing. The closing date cannot be made final at this time. The Buyer and Seller agree to make   , 19   , the estimated date for the closing. Both parties will fully cooperate so the closing can take place on or before the estimated date. The closing will be held at

8. Transfer of Ownership. At the closing, the Seller will transfer ownership of the property to the Buyer. The Seller will give the Buyer a properly executed deed and an adequate affidavit of title. If the Seller is a corporation, it will also deliver a corporate resolution authorizing the sale.

9. Type of Deed. A deed is a written document used to transfer ownership of property. In this sale, the Seller agrees to provide and the Buyer agrees to accept a deed known as bargain and sale with covenants against grantors' acts.

10. Personal Property and Fixtures. Many items of property become so attached to a building or other real property that they become a part of it. These items are called fixtures. They include such items as fireplaces, patios and built-in shelving. All fixtures are INCLUDED in this sale unless they are listed below as being EXCLUDED.

(a) The following items are INCLUDED in this sale: gas and electric fixtures, chandeliers, wall-to-wall carpeting, linoleum, mats and matting in halls, screens, shades, awnings, storm windows and doors, T.V. antenna, water pump, sump pump, water softeners.

(b) The following items are EXCLUDED from this sale:

11. Physical Condition of the Property. This property is being sold ''as is''. The Seller does not make any claims or promises about the condition or value of any of the property included in this sale. The Buyer has inspected the property and relies on this inspection and any rights which may be provided for elsewhere in this contract. The Seller agrees to maintain the grounds, buildings and improvements subject to ordinary wear and tear.

12. Inspection of the Property. The Seller agrees to permit the Buyer to inspect the property at any reasonable time before the closing. The Seller will permit access for all inspections provided for in this contract.

13. Building and Zoning Laws. The Buyer intends to use the property as a   family home. The Seller states that this use does not violate any applicable zoning ordinance, building code or other law. The Seller will obtain and pay for all inspections required by law. This includes any municipal ''certificate of occupancy''. If the Seller fails to correct any violations of law, at the Seller's own expense, the Buyer may cancel this contract.

14. Flood Area. The federal and state governments have designated certain areas as ''flood areas''. This means they are more likely to have floods than other areas. If this property is in a ''flood area'' the Buyer may cancel this contract within 30 days of the signing of this contract by all parties.

15. Property Lines. The Seller states that all buildings, driveways and other improvements on the property are within its boundary lines. Also, no improvements on adjoining properties extend across the boundary lines of this property.

16. Ownership. The Seller agrees to transfer and the Buyer agrees to accept ownership of the property free of all claims and rights of others, except for:

(a) the rights of utility companies to maintain pipes, poles, cables and wires over, on and under the street, the part of the property next to the street or running to any house or other improvement on the property;

(b) recorded agreements which limit the use of the property, unless the agreements: (1) are presently violated; (2) provide that the property would be forfeited if they were violated, or (3) unreasonably limit the normal use of the property; and

(c) all items included in Schedule A as part of the description of the property.

In addition to the above, the ownership of the Buyer must be insurable at regular rates by any title insurance company authorized to do business in New Jersey subject only to the above exceptions.

17. Correcting Defects. If the property does not comply with paragraphs 15 or 16 of this contract, the Seller will be notified and given 30 days to make it comply. If the property still does not comply after that date, the Buyer may cancel this contract or give the Seller more time to comply.

18. Termite Inspection. The Buyer is permitted to have the property inspected by a reputable termite inspection company to determine if there is any damage or infestation caused by termites or other wood-destroying insects. If the Buyer chooses to have this inspection, the inspection must be completed and the Seller notified of the results within 10 days of the signing of this contract by all parties. The Buyer will pay for this inspection. If infestation or damage is found, the Seller will be given 10 days to agree to exterminate all infestation and repair all damage before the closing. If the Seller refuses or fails (within the 10-day period) to agree to exterminate all infestation and repair all damage before the closing, the Buyer may cancel this contract.

19. Risk of Loss. The Seller is responsible for any damage to the property, except for normal wear and tear, until the closing. If there is damage, the Buyer can proceed with the closing and either:

(a) require that the Seller repair the damage before the closing; or

(b) deduct from the purchase price a fair and reasonable estimate of the cost to repair the property.

In addition, either party may cancel this contract if the cost of repair is more than 10% of the purchase price.

20. Cancellation of Contract. If this contract is legally and rightfully cancelled, the Buyer can get back the deposit and the parties will be free of liability to each other. However, if the contract is cancelled in accordance with paragraphs 13, 14, 17, 18 or 19 of this contract, the Seller will pay the Buyer for all title and survey costs.

21. Assessments for Municipal Improvements. Certain municipal improvements such as sidewalks and sewers may result in the municipality charging property owners to pay for the improvement. All unpaid charges (assessments) against the property for work completed before the closing will be paid by the Seller at or before the closing. If the improvement is not completed before the closing, then only the Buyer will be responsible. If the improvement is completed, but the amount of the charge (assessment) is not determined, the Seller will pay an estimated amount at the closing. When the amount of the charge is finally determined, the Seller will pay any deficiency to the Buyer (if the estimate proves to have been too low), or the Buyer will return any excess to the Seller (if the estimate proves to have been too high).

22. Adjustments at Closing. The Buyer and Seller agree to adjust the following expenses as of the closing date: rents, municipal water charges, sewer charges, taxes, interest on any mortgage to be assumed and insurance premiums. If the property is heated by fuel oil, the Buyer will buy the fuel oil in the tank at the closing date. The price will be the current price at that time as calculated by the supplier. The Buyer or the Seller may require that any person with a claim or right affecting the property be paid off from the proceeds of this sale.

23. Possession. At the closing the Buyer will be given possession of the property. No tenant will have any right to the property unless otherwise agreed in this contract.

24. Complete Agreement. This contract is the entire and only agreement between the Buyer and the Seller. This contract replaces and cancels any previous agreements between the Buyer and the Seller. This contract can only be changed by an agreement in writing signed by both Buyer and Seller. The Seller states that the Seller has not made any other contract to sell the property to anyone else.

25. Parties Liable. This contract is binding upon all parties who sign it and all who succeed to their rights and responsibilities.

26. Notices. All notices under this contract must be in writing. The notices must be delivered personally or mailed by certified mail, return receipt requested, to the other party at the address written in this contract, or to that party's attorney.

27. Realtor's Commission. The Seller agrees to pay the REALTOR(S) a commission for services rendered in procuring this sale as follows:

....

           Name of REALTOR   Commission

....

Address   Tel. #

....

           Name of REALTOR   Commission

....

Address   Tel. #

This commission will not be earned until the title is transferred and the purchase price is paid. This commission will be paid at the closing.

SIGNED AND AGREED TO BY:

Witnessed or Attested by: Date Signed:

....(Seal)

                                             BUYER

....(Seal)

As to Buyer(s)   BUYER

....(Seal)

                                             SELLER

....(Seal)

As to Seller(s)   SELLER

STATE OF NEW JERSEY, COUNTY OF   SS.:
    I CERTIFY that on   , 19   ,

                                                       personally came before me
and acknowledged under oath, to my satisfaction, that this person (or if more than one, each person):
    (a) is named in and personally signed this document; and
    (b) signed, sealed and delivered this document as his or her act and deed.

                                        ....
                                                (Print name and title below signature)

STATE OF NEW JERSEY, COUNTY OF   SS.:
    I CERTIFY that on   , 19   ,

personally came before me, and this person acknowledged under oath, to my satisfaction, that:
    (a) this person is the   secretary of
                                             the corporation named in this document;
    (b) this person is the attesting witness to the signing of this document by the proper corporate officer who is
                             the   President of the corporation;
    (c) this document was signed and delivered by the corporation as its voluntary act duly authorized by a
        proper resolution of its Board of Directors;
    (d) this person knows the proper seal of the corporation which was affixed to this document; and
    (e) this person signed this proof to attest to the truth of these facts.

Signed and sworn to before me on   ....
                , 19   (Print name of attesting witness below signature)

....

CONTRACT
FOR SALE OF REAL ESTATE

Between

                               Seller,

And

                               Buyer.

Dated: *, 19*

Record and return to:

SAMPLE OF AMENDMENT TO N.J. CONTRACT OF SALE

CONTAINING CONTINGENCIES IN FAVOR OF BUYER

AMENDMENT TO CONTRACT OF SALE

BETWEEN:

Sellers

and

Buyer

To the extent that this Amendment may vary, alter, modify or contradict the provisions of the Contract of Sale dated   , 19   , the provisions of this Amendment shall control. The words "Buyer" and "Seller" herein include all Buyers and Sellers listed above. All time periods shall commence as of the date of execution of this Amendment.

---

1. All deposit monies paid hereunder are to be held by attorney for Seller, in an interest bearing trust account, until closing of title. Accrued interest shall be equally divided between the Buyer and Seller at the time of closing. Should title to the property not close, accrued interest shall follow the deposit. For the purpose of said interest bearing trust account, the social security number of Buyer is: and of the Seller:

    It is agreed that Seller's attorney shall act as escrow agent only and shall not incur or assume any liability in that capacity. In the event there is a dispute concerning the escrowed funds, the escrow agents, at their sole discretion, may pay any of these monies into a Court of competent jurisdiction until the dispute is resolved by judicial determination or otherwise.

2. The Deed to be delivered at the time of closing shall be a Bargain & Sale Deed with covenant against grantors.

3. The balance of the purchase price at closing may be paid by attorney Trust Account check of Buyer's attorney.

4. In the event that Buyer's bank or mortgage company or any municipal authority requires a Certificate of Occupancy, well, water or septic certification in connection with the financing to be arranged for the purchase or the purchase transaction itself, then Seller shall, at their own cost and expense, deliver same in time for a submittal to the bank or mortgage company so that closing can take place as provided in the Contract of Sale. Seller will undertake any required repairs to obtain the necessary approvals at their own expense.

5. The premises shall be free of tenancies, leases and occupancies of any kind and in broom clean condition at time of delivery of possession and Deed at closing of title.

6. Seller shall pay Buyer's attorney a mortgage cancellation fee of $35.00 for each mortgage to be cancelled of record at the time of closing. Any mortgages not held by a financial lending institution shall be delivered by Seller to Buyer at closing of title, duly endorsed for cancellation.

7. If Buyer voids this Contract as a result of defective title which Seller cannot cure, all deposit money with interest shall be forthwith returned to Buyer upon demand of Buyer or her attorney and Sellers shall reimburse Buyer for actual search and survey expenses not exceeding $500.00.

8. Physical inspection of premises. The Buyer is permitted to have the property inspected by an engineer, builder or home inspector to determine the presence of structural defects or environmental conditions and to determine that all electrical, plumbing, heating, sewer/septic and air conditioning systems are in working order and need no major replacements or repairs. If the Buyer chooses to have this inspection, this inspection must be completed within 15 days of the date of the execution of this Amendment; otherwise, the Buyer waives her rights under this Section. The Buyer will pay for this inspection. If structural defects or adverse environmental conditions are found, or if all of the aforesaid systems and any appliances included with this sale are not in working order or are in need of major replacements or repairs, the Buyer will provide the Seller with a copy of a written report and the Seller will be given 7 calendar days to notify the Buyer whether or not the Seller agrees at their own cost and expense to correct the structural defects, remove the adverse environmental conditions, put the aforementioned systems in working order and make all needed major replacements or repairs, or the Buyer may cancel this Contract. The Buyer, however, at her option may waive the results of the inspection in writing and this Contract shall become binding. Any agreed upon repairs will be completed prior to the closing.

9. Radon Inspection. Performance by Buyer is subject to Buyer obtaining an inspection of any residential structures on the property for the presence of Radon Gas. Buyer will pay for this inspection and complete it and notify Seller of its results within twenty-one (21) days of the execution of this Amendment. If the test reveals the presence of more than 4 pci/1 of Radon, Buyer will provide Sellers with a copy of the written report and Seller shall have ten (10) days to notify Buyer whether Seller will reduce the concentration of Radon to 4 pci/1 or less. If Seller does not agree to so reduce the concentration of Radon, Buyer may cancel the agreement and Seller shall refund the down payment (with interest if the funds are held in an interest bearing account) and this agreement shall terminate. It is understood and agreed that the Buyer shall also be permitted to conduct an inspection of the wells on the premises for the presence of Radon Gas.

10. The Buyer shall have the right, at Buyer's expense, to have the well water tested by a licensed professional or licensed testing service. If such test reveals that the water supply is not potable or that the supply is insufficient, the Buyers shall deliver a copy of the

written report to Sellers. If the Seller shall be unwilling to undertake all corrective measures necessary to render the water potable or provide sufficient flow, the Buyer shall have the right to terminate this Contract. Said inspection shall be completed within fifteen (15) days of the execution of this Amendment.

11. The Termite Inspection shall be completed within fifteen (15) days of the date of execution of this Amendment.

12. <u>Underground Storage Tanks</u>. Seller represents that there are no underground fuel storage tanks on the premises to be conveyed as defined in NJSA 58:10A-22 and that in the event such underground storage tanks exist, Seller has complied with the statutory requirements set forth in the Act, including but not limited to registration of the facility and the installation of the appropriate monitoring systems.

13. Seller agrees to maintain premises including the lawn and landscaping pending closing of title.

14. The "risk of loss" provision of the Contract of Sale shall be amended to state that in the event the subject premises suffers damages exceeding 10% of the purchase price, either party may declare this Contract null and void, save and except the Seller's obligation to return all deposit monies paid hereunder.

15. Seller represents that the plumbing, heating, electrical and air conditioning, if any, systems and all appliances included in this sale, shall be in operating condition at time of closing.

16. It is expressly understood and agreed that title to the land and premises in question are not derived from any Martin Act proceedings or any act for the sale of land for nonpayment of municipal taxes or assessments or color of title possession.

17. In the event that any Home Equity loan affects the property being purchased, the Seller represents that they will immediately close the account as of the day of closing and not make any additional withdrawals against any line of credit feature of such loan subsequent to this Amendment to the Contract being executed by all parties.

18. The Federal and State Governments have designated certain areas as "flood hazard areas". This means they are more likely to have floods than other areas. If the subject property is located within a "flood hazard area", the Buyer may cancel this Contract within thirty (30) days of the execution of this Amendment by all parties, and in that event, neither party will have any further liability to the other, save and except Seller's obligation to refund the deposit monies paid hereunder to the Buyer.

WITNESS: DATE:

_____   _____   _____
                                                    , Seller

_____   _____   _____
                                                     , Seller

_____   _____   _____
                                                    , Buyer

-------------------   ---------   ---------------------------
                                                    , Buyer

SELLER'S
DISCLOSURE
STATEMENT

SELLER'S DISCLOSURE STATEMENT

1. Seller(s) Name(s):

   Property Address

   Is each individual named above a U.S. Citizen or resident alien? Yes ☐ No ☐

   Approximate Age of Property: Date Purchased:

2. **NOTICE TO SELLER**

   Each Seller is obligated to disclose to a buyer all known facts that materially and adversely affect the value of the property being sold and that are not readily observable. This disclosure statement is designed to assist Seller in complying with disclosure requirements and to assist Buyer in evaluating the property being considered. The listing real estate broker, the selling real estate broker and their respective agents will also rely upon this information when they evaluate, market and present Seller's property to prospective buyers.

3. **NOTICE TO BUYER**

   This is a disclosure of Seller's knowledge of the condition of the property as of the date signed by Seller and is not a substitute for any inspections or warranties that Buyer may wish to obtain. It is not a warranty of any kind by Seller or a warranty or representation by the listing broker, the selling broker, or their agents.

4. **OCCUPANCY**

   Does Seller currently occupy this property? Yes ☑ No ☐ If not, how long has it been since Seller occupied the property? _____

5. **LAND (SOILS, DRAINAGE AND BOUNDARIES)**

   (a) Is there any fill or expansive soil on the property? Yes ☐ No ☐ Unknown ☑

   (b) Do you know of any sliding, settling, earth movement, upheaval or earth stability problems that have occurred on the property or in the immediate neighborhood? Yes ☐ No ☑

   (c) Is the property located in an earthquake zone? Yes ☐ No ☑ Unknown ☐

   (d) Is the property located in a flood zone or wetlands area? Yes ☑ No ☐ Unknown ☐

   (e) Do you know of any past or present drainage or flood problems affecting the property or adjacent properties? Yes ☐ No ☑

   (f) Do you know of any encroachments, boundary line disputes, or easements affecting the property? Yes ☐ No ☑

   If any of your answers in this section are "Yes," explain in detail:_____
   _____

6. **ROOF**

   (a) Age: _____ years.

   (b) Has the roof ever leaked during your ownership? Yes ☐ No ☑

   (c) Has the roof been replaced or repaired during your ownership? Yes ☐ No ☑

   (d) Do you know of any problems with the roof or rain gutters? Yes ☐ No ☑

   If any of your answers in this section are "Yes," explain in detail: _____
   _____

7. **TERMITES, DRYROT, PESTS**

   (a) Do you have any knowledge of termites, dryrot, or pests on or affecting the property? Yes ☐ No ☑

   (b) Do you have any knowledge of any damage to the property caused by termites, dryrot, or pests? Yes ☐ No ☑

   (c) Is your property currently under warranty or other coverage by a licensed pest control company? Yes ☐ No ☑

   (d) Do you know of any termite / pest control reports or treatments for the property in the last five years? Yes ☐ No ☑

   If any of your answers in this section are "Yes," explain in detail: _____
   _____

8. **STRUCTURAL ITEMS**

   (a) Are you aware of any past or present movement, shifting, deterioration, or other problems with walls or foundations? Yes ☐ No ☑

   (b) Are you aware of any past or present cracks or flaws in the walls or foundations? Yes ☐ No ☑

   (c) Are you aware of any past or present water leakage in the house? Yes ☐ No ☑

   (d) Are you aware of any past or present problems with driveways, walkways, patios, or retaining walls on the property? Yes ☐ No ☑

   (e) Have there been any repairs or other attempts to control the cause or effect of any problem described above? Yes ☑ No

   If any of your answers in this section are "Yes," explain in detail. When describing repairs or control efforts, describe the location, extent, date, and name of the person who did the repair or control effort:_____
   _____

9. **BASEMENTS AND CRAWL SPACES (Complete only if applicable)**

   (a) Does the property have a sump pump? Yes ☐ No ☑

   (b) Has there ever been any water leakage, accumulation, or dampness within the basement or crawlspace? Yes ☐ No ☑

   If "Yes," describe in detail: _____

   (c) Have there been any repairs or other attempts to control any water or dampness problem in the basement or crawlspace? Yes ☐ No ☑

   If "Yes," describe the location, extent, date, and name of the person who did the repair or control effort: _____
   _____

10. **ADDITIONS/REMODELS**

    (a) Have you made any additions, structural changes, or other alterations to the property? Yes ☐ No ☑

    If "Yes", did you obtain all necessary permits and approvals and was all work in compliance with building codes? Yes ☐ No ☐. If your answer is "No," explain: _____

    (b) Did any former owners of the property make any additions, structural changes, or other alterations to the property? Yes ☐ No ☑ Unknown ☐. If "Yes", was all work done with all necessary permits and approvals in compliance with building codes? Yes ☐ No ☐ Unknown ☐. If your answer is "No," explain: _____
    _____

11. **PLUMBING-RELATED ITEMS**
    (a) What is your drinking water source: Public _X_ Private System ____ Well on Property ____
    (b) If your drinking water is from a well, when was your water last checked for safety and what was the result of the test? _____
    (c) Do you have a water softener? Yes ☐ No ☒ Leased ☐ Owned ☐
    (d) What is the type of sewage system: Public Sewer _X_ Private Sewer ____ Septic Tank ____ Cesspool ____
    (e) Is there a sewage pump? Yes ☐ No ☐
    (f) When was the septic tank or cesspool last serviced? _____
    (g) Do you know of any leaks, backups, or other problems relating to any of the plumbing, water, and sewage-related items? Yes ☐ No ☒
        If your answer is "Yes," explain in detail: _____

12. **HEATING AND AIR CONDITIONING**
    (a) Air Conditioning _X_ Central Electric ____Central Gas ___Window _X_(#) Units Included in Sale
    (b) Heating _X_ Electric ____Fuel Oil ___Natural Gas ___Other:_____
    (c) Water Heating _X_ Electric ____Gas ___Solar
    Are you aware of any problems regarding these items? Yes ☐ No ☒. If "Yes," explain in detail: _____
    _____

13. **ELECTRICAL SYSTEM**
    Are you aware of any problems or conditions that affect the value or desirability of the electrical system? Yes ☐ No ☒.
    If "Yes," explain in detail: _____

14. **OTHER EQUIPMENT AND APPLIANCES BEING SOLD**
    Mark the items included in the sale of your property:

    _X_ Electric Garage Door Opener ___Number of Transmitters ___Security Alarm System (___Owned ___Leased)
    ___ Smoke Detectors ___How Many? _X_ Lawn Sprinklers _X_ Automatic Timer
    _X_ Swimming Pool ___Pool Heater ___Spa/Hot Tub ___Pool/Spa Equipment (list):_____
    _X_ Refrigerator _X_ Stove ___Microwave Oven _X_ Washer _X_ Dryer _X_ Dishwasher ___Trash Compactor
    _X_ Intercom _X_ Ceiling Fans ___Other:_____
    Are any of these in need of repair or replacement? Yes ☐ No ☒. If "Yes," explain in detail: _____

15. **NEIGHBORHOOD**
    Are you aware of any condition or proposed change in your neighborhood that could adversely affect the value or desirability of the property, such as noise or other nuisance, threat of condemnation or street changes? Yes ☐ No ☒.
    If "Yes," explain in detail: _____

16. **TOXIC SUBSTANCES**
    (a) Are you aware of any underground tanks or toxic substances present on the property (structure or soil) such as asbestos, PCBs, accumulated radon, lead paint, or others? Yes ☐ No ☒. If "Yes," explain in detail: _____
    (b) Has the property been tested for radon or any other toxic substances? Yes ☐ No ☒. If "Yes," explain in detail:

17. **CONDOMINIUMS AND OTHER HOMEOWNERS ASSOCIATIONS**
    (a) Is the property part of a condominium or other common ownership or is it subject to covenants, conditions, and restrictions (CC & R's) of a homeowner's association? Yes ☐ No ☐. (If your answer is "no", you may ignore the remainder of this section).
    (b) Is there any defect, damage, or problem with any common elements or common areas which could affect their value or desirability? Yes ☐ No ☐ Unknown ☐
    (c) Is there any condition or claim which may result in an increase in assessments or fees? Yes ☐ No ☐
        Unknown ☐. If your answer to (b) or (c) is "Yes," explain in detail: _____

18. **OTHER MATTERS**
    (a) Is there any existing or threatened legal action affecting the property? Yes ☐ No ☒
    (b) Do you know of any violations of local, state, or federal laws or regulations relating to this property?
        Yes ☐ No ☒
    (c) Is there anything else that you feel you should disclose to a prospective buyer because it may materially and adversely affect the value or desirability of the property, e.g., zoning violation, non-conforming units, setback violations, zoning changes, road changes, etc.? Yes ☐ No ☒
    If any of your answers in this section are "Yes," explain in detail: _____

The undersigned Seller represents that the information set forth in the foregoing disclosure statement is accurate and complete. Seller does not intend this disclosure statement to be a warranty or guaranty of any kind. Seller hereby authorizes the listing broker to provide this information to prospective buyers of the property and to real estate brokers and sales people. Seller understands and agrees that Seller will notify the listing broker in writing immediately if any information set forth in this disclosure statement becomes inaccurate or incorrect in any way through the passage of time.

Seller: _____ Date:_____ Seller:_____ Date:_____

N.J. BARGAIN AND SALE DEED WITH COVENANT AS TO GRANTOR'S ACTS

ALL-STATE LEGAL SUPPLY CO.

DEED

This Deed is made on   , 19

BETWEEN

whose address is

                                                          referred to as the Grantor,

AND

whose post office address is

                                                          referred to as the Grantee.
The words ''Grantor'' and ''Grantee'' shall mean all Grantors and all Grantees listed above.

Transfer of Ownership. The Grantor grants and conveys (transfers ownership of) the property described below to the Grantee. This transfer is made for the sum of

                                              The Grantor acknowledges receipt of this money.

Tax Map Reference. (N.J.S.A. 46:15-1.1) Municipality of
Block No.   Lot No.   Account No.
☐   No property tax identification number is available on the date of this Deed. (Check box if applicable).

Property. The property consists of the land and all the buildings and structures on the land in the   of
County of   and State of New Jersey. The legal description is:

Promises by Grantor. The Grantor promises that the Grantor has done no act to encumber the property. This promise is called a "covenant as to grantor's acts" (N.J.S.A. 46:4-6). This promise means that the Grantor has not allowed anyone else to obtain any legal rights which affect the property (such as by making a mortgage or allowing a judgment to be entered against the Grantor).

Signatures. The Grantor signs this Deed as of the date at the top of the first page.

Witnessed by:

--- (Seal)

---   --- (Seal)

STATE OF NEW JERSEY, COUNTY OF   SS.:
I CERTIFY that on   , 19   .

personally came before me and stated to my satisfaction that this person (or if more than one, each person):

(a) was the maker of the attached deed;
(b) executed this deed as his or her own act; and,

(c) made this Deed for $ as the full and actual consideration paid or to be paid for the transfer of title.
(Such consideration is defined in N.J.S.A. 46:15-5.)

_____

(Print name and title below signature)

N.J. MORTGAGE NOTE

ALL-STATE LEGAL SUPPLY CO.

Copyright© 1982 by ALL-STATE LEGAL SUPPLY CO.
One Commerce Drive, Cranford, N.J. 07016

MORTGAGE NOTE

This Mortgage Note is made on   , 19

    BETWEEN the Borrower(s)

whose address is

                                              referred to as ''I'',

    AND the Lender

whose address is

                                          referred to as the ''Lender''.

If more than one Borrower signs this Note, the word ''I'' shall mean each Borrower named above. The word ''Lender'' means the original Lender and anyone else who takes this Note by transfer.

    Borrower's Promise to Pay Principal and Interest. In return for a loan that I received, I promise to pay $ (called the ''principal''), plus interest to the Lender. Interest, at a yearly rate of   % will be charged on that part of the principal which has not been paid from the date of this Note until all principal has been paid.

    Payments. I will pay principal and interest based on a   year payment schedule with monthly payments of $ on the   day of each month beginning on   , 19   . I will pay all amounts owed under this Note no later than   , 19   . All payments will be made to the Lender at the address shown above or at a different place if required by the Lender.

    Early Payments. I have the right to make payments at any time before they are due. These early payments will mean that this Note will be paid in less time. However, unless I pay this Note in full, my monthly payments will remain the same.

    Late Charge for Overdue Payments. If the Lender has not received any monthly payment within   days after the due date, I will pay the Lender a late charge of   % of the monthly payment. This payment will be made along with the late monthly payment.

    Mortgage to Secure Payment. The Lender has been given a Mortgage dated   , 19   , to protect the Lender if the promises made in this Note are not kept. I agree to keep all promises made in the Mortgage covering property I own located at
in the   of
in the County of   and State of New Jersey. All of the terms of the Mortgage are made a part of this Note.

    Default. If I fail to make any payment required by this Note within   days after the due date, the Lender may declare that I am in default on the Mortgage and this Note. Upon default, I must immediately pay the full amount of all unpaid principal, interest, other amounts due on the Mortgage and this Note, the Lender's costs of collection and reasonable attorney fees. The Lender does not give up its right to declare a default due to any previous delay or failure to declare a default.

    Waivers. I give up my right to require that the Lender do the following: (a) to demand payment (called ''presentment''); (b) to notify me of nonpayment (called ''notice of dishonor''); and,(c) to obtain an official certified statement showing nonpayment (called a ''protest'').

    Each Person Liable. The Lender may enforce any of the provisions of this Note against any one or more of the Borrowers who sign this Note.

    No Oral Changes. This Note can only be changed by an agreement in writing signed by both the Borrower(s) and the Lender.

    Signatures. I agree to the terms of this Note. If the Borrower is a corporation, its proper corporate officers sign and its corporate seal is affixed.

Witnessed or Attested by:

--   -- (Seal)

                            -- (Seal)

N.J. MORGAGE

ALL-STATE LEGAL SUPPLY CO.

204 – NOTE MORTGAGE
Ind. or Corp. – Plain Language

C RVS —1

MORTGAGE

Prepared by: (Print signer's name below signature)
....

This Mortgage is made on , 19 .

BETWEEN the Borrower(s)

whose address is

referred to as ''I''.

AND the Lender

whose address is

referred to as the ''Lender''.
If more than one Borrower signs this Mortgage, the word ''I'' shall mean each Borrower named above. The word ''Lender'' means the original Lender and anyone else who takes this Mortgage by transfer.

Mortgage Note. In return for a loan that I received, I promise to pay $ (called ''principal''), plus interest in accordance with the terms of a Mortgage Note dated , 19 (referred to as the ''Note''). The Note provides for monthly payments of $ and a yearly interest rate of %. All sums owed under the Note are due no later than . All terms of the Note are made part of this Mortgage.

Property Mortgaged. The property mortgaged to the Lender (called the ''Property'') is located in the of County of and State of New Jersey. The Property includes: (a) the land; (b) all buildings that are now, or will be, located on the land; (c) all fixtures that are now, or will be, attached to the land or building(s) (for example, furnaces, bathroom fixtures and kitchen cabinets); (d) all condemnation awards and insurance proceeds relating to the land and building(s); and (e) all other rights that I have, or will have, as owner of the Property. The legal description of the property is:

5. Insurance. I must maintain extended coverage insurance on the Property. The Lender may also require that I maintain flood insurance or other types of insurance. The insurance companies, policies, amounts and types of coverage must be acceptable to the Lender. I will notify the Lender in the event of any substantial loss or damage. The Lender may then settle the claim on my behalf if I fail to do so. All payments from the insurance company must be payable to the Lender under a "standard mortgage clause" in the insurance policy. The Lender may use any proceeds to repair and restore the Property or to reduce the amount due under the Note and this Mortgage. This will not delay the due date for any payment under the Note and this Mortgage.

6. Repairs. I will keep the Property in good repair, neither damaging nor abandoning it. I will allow the Lender to inspect the Property upon reasonable notice to me.

7. Statement of Amount Due. Upon request of the Lender, I will certify to the Lender in writing: (a) the amount due on the Note and this Mortgage, and (b) whether or not I have any defense to my obligations under the Note and this Mortgage.

8. Rent. I will not accept rent from any tenant for more than one month in advance.

9. Lawful Use. I will use the Property in compliance with all laws, ordinances and other requirements of any governmental authority.

Eminent Domain. All or part of the Property may be taken by a government entity for public use. If this occurs, I agree that any compensation be given to the Lender. The Lender may use this to repair and restore the Property or to reduce the amount owed on the Note and this Mortgage. This will not delay the due date for any further payment under the Note and this Mortgage. Any remaining balance will be paid to me.

Tax and Insurance Escrow. If the Lender requests, I will make regular monthly payments to the Lender of: (a) $1/12$ of the yearly real estate taxes and assessments on the Property; and (b) $1/12$ of the yearly cost of insurance on the Property. These payments will be held by the Lender without interest to pay the taxes, assessments and insurance premiums as they become due.

Payments Made for Borrower(s). If I do not make all of the repairs or payments as agreed in this Mortgage, the Lender may do so for me. The cost of these repairs and payments will be added to the principal, will bear interest at the same rate provided in the Note and will be repaid to the Lender upon demand.

Default. The Lender may declare that I am in default on the Note and this Mortgage if:
    (a) I fail to make any payment required by the Note and this Mortgage within   days after its due date;
    (b) I fail to keep any other promise I make in this Mortgage;
    (c) the ownership of the Property is changed for any reason;
    (d) the holder of any lien on the Property starts foreclosure proceedings; or
    (e) bankruptcy, insolvency or receivership proceedings are started by or against any of the Borrowers.

Payments Due Upon Default. If the Lender declares that I am in default, I must immediately pay the full amount of all unpaid principal, interest, other amounts due on the Note and this Mortgage and the Lender's costs of collection and reasonable attorney fees.

Lender's Rights Upon Default. If the Lender declares that the Note and this Mortgage are in default, the Lender will have all rights given by law or set forth in this Mortgage. This includes the right to do any one or more of the following:
    (a) take possession of and manage the Property, including the collection of rents and profits;
    (b) have a court appoint a receiver to accept rent for the Property (I consent to this);
    (c) start a court action, known as foreclosure, which will result in a sale of the Property to reduce my obligations under the Note and this Mortgage; and
    (d) sue me for any money that I owe the Lender.

Notices. All notices must be in writing and personally delivered or sent by certified mail, return receipt requested, to the addresses given in this Mortgage. Address changes may be made upon notice to the other party.

No Waiver by Lender. Lender may exercise any right under this Mortgage or under any law, even if Lender has delayed in exercising that right or has agreed in an earlier instance not to exercise that right. Lender does not waive its right to declare that I am in default by making payments or incurring expenses on my behalf.

Each Person Liable. This Mortgage is legally binding upon each Borrower and all who succeed to their responsibilities (such as heirs and executors). The Lender may enforce any of the provisions of the Note and this Mortgage against any one or more of the Borrowers who sign this Mortgage.

No Oral Changes. This Mortgage can only be changed by an agreement in writing signed by both the Borrower(s) and the Lender.

Copy Received. I ACKNOWLEDGE RECEIPT OF A TRUE COPY OF THIS MORTGAGE WITHOUT CHARGE.

Signatures. I agree to the terms of this Mortgage. If the Borrower is a corporation, its proper corporate officers sign and its corporate seal is affixed.

Witnessed or Attested by:

-- (Seal)

--   -- (Seal)

STATE OF NEW JERSEY, COUNTY OF   SS.:
   I CERTIFY that on   , 19   ,

personally came before me
and acknowledged under oath, to my satisfaction, that this person (or if more than one, each person):
    (a) is named in and personally signed this document; and
    (b) signed, sealed and delivered this document as his or her act and deed.

....
            (Print name and title below signature)

STATE OF NEW JERSEY, COUNTY OF   SS.:
   I CERTIFY that on   , 19   ,

personally came before me, and this person acknowledged under oath, to my satisfaction, that:
    (a) this person is the   secretary of
                                   the corporation named in this document;
    (b) this person is the attesting witness to the signing of this document by the proper corporate officer who is
                 the   President of the corporation;
    (c) this document was signed and delivered by the corporation as its voluntary act duly authorized by a
        proper resolution of its Board of Directors;
    (d) this person knows the proper seal of the corporation which was affixed to this document; and
    (e) this person signed this proof to attest to the truth of these facts.

Signed and sworn to before me on
             , 19   ....
                          (Print name of attesting witness below signature)

....

NOTE MORTGAGE

Dated: *, 19*

                         Borrower(s),

        TO

                         Lender(s).

To the County Recording Officer of   County:

This Mortgage is fully paid. I authorize you to cancel it of record.

Dated   , 19   .... (Seal)
                                                               Lender

I certify that the signature of the Lender is genuine.

....

HUD-1 UNIFORM SETTLEMENT STATEMENT

ALL-STATE LEGAL SUPPLY CO.

HUD-1 UNIFORM SETTLEMENT STATEMENT
(Rev. August 1987)

OMB. No. 2502-0265
ALL-STATE LEGAL SUPPLY CO.
One Commerce Drive, Cranford, N.J. 07016

A.

U.S. DEPARTMENT OF HOUSING AND URBAN DEVELOPMENT

SETTLEMENT STATEMENT

B. TYPE OF LOAN

1. ☐ FHA   2. ☐ FmHA

3. ☐ CONV. UNINS.   4. ☐ VA   5. ☐ CONV. INS.

6. File Number:	7. Loan Number:
8. Mortgage Insurance Case Number:	

C. NOTE: This form is furnished to give you a statement of actual settlement costs. Amounts paid to and by the settlement agent are shown. Items marked "(p.o.c.)" were paid outside the closing; they are shown here for informational purposes and are not included in the totals.
NOTE: TIN = Taxpayer's Indentification Number.

D. NAME AND ADDRESS OF BORROWER:	E. NAME, ADDRESS AND TIN OF SELLER:	F. NAME AND ADDRESS OF LENDER:
G. PROPERTY LOCATION:	H. SETTLEMENT AGENT: NAME, ADDRESS AND TIN	
	PLACE OF SETTLEMENT:	I. SETTLEMENT DATE:

J. SUMMARY OF BORROWER'S TRANSACTION		K. SUMMARY OF SELLER'S TRANSACTION	
100. GROSS AMOUNT DUE FROM BORROWER:		**400. GROSS AMOUNT DUE TO SELLER:**	
101. Contract sales price		401. Contract sales price	
102. Personal property		402. Personal property	
103. Settlement charges to borrower *(line 1400)*		403.	
104.		404.	
105.		405.	
Adjustments for items paid by seller in advance		*Adjustments for items paid by seller in advance*	
106. City/town taxes to		406. City/town taxes to	
107. County taxes to		407. County taxes to	
108. Assessments to		408. Assessments to	
109.		409.	
110.		410.	
111.		411.	
112.		412.	
120. GROSS AMOUNT DUE FROM BORROWER		**420. GROSS AMOUNT DUE TO SELLER**	
200. AMOUNTS PAID BY OR IN BEHALF OF BORROWER:		**500. REDUCTIONS IN AMOUNT DUE TO SELLER:**	
201. Deposit or earnest money		501. Excess deposit *(see instructions)*	
202. Principal amount of new loan(s)		502. Settlement charges to seller *(line 1400)*	
203. Existing loan(s) taken subject to		503. Existing loan(s) taken subject to	
204.		504. Payoff of first mortgage loan	
205.		505. Payoff of second mortgage loan	
206.		506.	
207.		507.	
208.		508.	
209.		509.	
Adjustments for items unpaid by seller		*Adjustments for items unpaid by seller*	
210. City/town taxes to		510. City/town taxes to	
211. County taxes to		511. County taxes to	
212. Assessments to		512. Assessments to	
213.		513.	
214.		514.	
215.		515.	
216.		516.	
217.		517.	
218.		518.	
219.		519.	
220. TOTAL PAID BY/FOR BORROWER		**520. TOTAL REDUCTION AMOUNT DUE SELLER**	
300. CASH AT SETTLEMENT FROM/TO BORROWER		**600. CASH AT SETTLEMENT TO/FROM SELLER**	
301. Gross amount due from borrower *(line 120)*		601. Gross amount due to seller *(line 420)*	
302. Less amounts paid by/for borrower *(line 220)*		602. Less reductions in amount due seller *(line 520)*	
303. CASH (☐ FROM) (☐ TO) BORROWER		**603. CASH (☐ TO) (☐ FROM) SELLER**	

SUBSTITUTE FORM 1099 SELLER STATEMENT

_____

(Seller's Signature)

L. SETTLEMENT CHARGES

		PAID FROM BORROWER'S FUNDS AT SETTLEMENT	PAID FROM SELLER'S FUNDS AT SETTLEMENT
700. TOTAL SALES/BROKER'S COMMISSION based on price $ @ % =			
Division of Commission (line 700) as follows:			
701. $ to			
702. $ to			
703. Commission paid at Settlement			
704.			
800. ITEMS PAYABLE IN CONNECTION WITH LOAN			
801. Loan Origination Fee %			
802. Loan Discount %			
803. Appraisal Fee to			
804. Credit Report to			
805. Lender's Inspection Fee			
806. Mortgage Insurance Application Fee to			
807. Assumption Fee			
808.			
809.			
810.			
811.			
900. ITEMS REQUIRED BY LENDER TO BE PAID IN ADVANCE			
901. Interest from to @ $ / day			
902. Mortgage Insurance Premium for months to			
903. Hazard Insurance Premium for years to			
904. years to			
905.			
1000. RESERVES DEPOSITED WITH LENDER			
1001. Hazard insurance months @ $ per month			
1002. Mortgage insurance months @ $ per month			
1003. City property taxes months @ $ per month			
1004. County property taxes months @ $ per month			
1005. Annual assessments months @ $ per month			
1006. months @ $ per month			
1007. months @ $ per month			
1008. months @ $ per month			
1100. TITLE CHARGES			
1101. Settlement or closing fee to			
1102. Abstract or title search to			
1103. Title examination to			
1104. Title insurance binder to			
1105. Document preparation to			
1106. Notary fees to			
1107. Attorney's fees to			
(includes above items numbers; *)*			
1108. Title insurance to			
(includes above items numbers; *)*			
1109. Lender's coverage $			
1110. Owner's coverage $			
1111.			
1112.			
1113.			
1200. GOVERNMENT RECORDING AND TRANSFER CHARGES			
1201. Recording fees: Deed $; Mortgage $; Releases $			
1202. City/county tax/stamps: Deed $; Mortgage $			
1203. State tax/stamps: Deed $; Mortgage $			
1204.			
1205.			
1300. ADDITIONAL SETTLEMENT CHARGES			
1301. Survey to			
1302. Pest inspection to			
1303.			
1304.			
1305.			
1400. TOTAL SETTLEMENT CHARGES (enter on lines 103, Section J and 502, Section K)			

CERTIFICATION

I have carefully reviewed the HUD-1 Settlement Statement and to the best of my knowledge and belief, it is a true and accurate statement of all receipts and disbursements made on my account or by me in this transaction. I further certify that I have received a copy of the HUD-1 Settlement Statement.

_____ Seller   _____ Borrower

_____ Seller   _____ Borrower

To the best of my knowledge the HUD-1 Settlement Statement which I have prepared is a true and accurate account of the funds which were received and have been or will be disbursed by the undersigned as part of the settlement of this transaction.

_____ Settlement Agent   _____ Date

WARNING: It is a crime to knowingly make false statements to the United States on this or any other similar form. Penalties upon conviction can include a fine and imprisonment. For details see: Title 18 U.S. Code Section 1001 and Section 1010.

HOME INSPECTION REPORT

HouseMaster of America

September 15, 1997

Mr. & Mrs.

                                        Re:

Dear Mr. & Mrs.

Enclosed is the original and copy of our inspection report on subject property. This inspection was performed according to inspection industry standards and is for your exclusive use.

Also enclosed is our complimentary 90 day inspection guarantee. Please read through it to become familiar with its coverage and limitations.

We're pleased to be of assistance to you with your home purchase. Should you have any questions concerning your inspection or guarantee, please do not hesitate to contact our local office.

Good luck with your new home.

                              Sincerely yours,

                              Mary Ann Roberts
                              Office Manager

/mar
Enclosure

"The Home Inspection Professionals"®

HOME INSPECTION
LIMITED
GUARANTEE

TERMS AND CONDITIONS PRINTED ON REVERSE SIDE.

CENTRAL HEATING

CENTRAL COOLING

INTERIOR PLUMBING

INTERIOR ELECTRIC

MAIN ROOFING

FOUNDATION WALLS

KITCHEN APPLIANCES

ALL OFFICES INDEPENDENTLY OWNED AND OPERATED.

1. INTRODUCTION

The purpose of this complimentary Guarantee is to provide a HouseMaster home-buyer client with coverage for specified repair expense for a period of ninety (90) days from the inspection date This Guarantee is not designed to cover normal maintenance nor to replace available insurance. It applies only to owner occupied one and two family resale houses and condominiums (not common elements).

Your local HouseMaster licensee performed a visual inspection of the resale house described in the Inspection Report on the date noted. This Guarantee applies to the following house elements found to be in satisfactory condition and repairs to those house elements not noted or forecast in the Inspection Report:

A. **Central Heating.** Includes the main house heating system if reported by the HouseMaster Inspector to be less than ten (10) years old. If more than one system, the unit heating the master bedroom area would be the one covered.

B. **Central Cooling.** Includes the main house cooling system if reported by the HouseMaster Inspector to be less than seven (7) years old. If more than one system, the unit cooling the master bedroom would be the one covered.

C. **Interior Plumbing.** Includes the water, drain and vent piping throughout the house and the hot water heater.

D. **Interior Electric.** Includes the main electric panel box and wiring throughout the house.

E. **Main Roofing.** Includes sloped (greater than 2 on 12 slope) roofing materials, roof framing and roof backing over main house, if reported by the HouseMaster Inspector to be less than ten (10) years old.

F. **Foundation Walls.** Includes poured concrete and block foundation walls to the extent that their load-bearing ability is affected. Water penetration is not covered.

G. **Kitchen Appliances.** Includes built-in kitchen appliances reported by the HouseMaster Inspector to be less than six (6) years old.

2. COVERAGE

HouseMaster will pay up to an aggregate maximum of $10,000.00 per Guarantee for the cost of repair expense to covered elements subject to the following conditions:

A. Any element or component of an element inspected by the HouseMaster Inspector and judged to be in satisfactory condition and so recorded in the Inspection Report will be eligible for coverage under this Guarantee up to a maximum of $1,500.00 per element. Conversely, an element or component not inspected or not judged to be in satisfactory condition or any condition forecast or suggested correction or recommendation noted in the Inspection Report will not be covered.

B. There will be a $95.00 service fee or the actual fee, whichever is lower, per incident/per element. The HouseMaster client will be responsible for payment of these fees. HouseMaster will reimburse the client for the balance of the repair expense.

C. In no event will HouseMaster assume responsibility for repair claims (1) known prior to closing or occurring after the expiration date of the Guarantee, (2) on Inspection Reports not fully paid for, (3) where the work was completed prior to formal notification and reinspection by HouseMaster, (4) uncovered or should have been uncovered during the client's pre-closing inspection.

D. The Guarantee is provided for the exclusive benefit of the home-buying client. It may not be transferred or assigned to any other party without the written consent of HouseMaster.

E. If, in the sole judgement of HouseMaster, a repair of a covered element or component is not possible, HouseMaster will pay up to a maximum of $500.00, less the service fee, for the replacement of a similar style and quality element or component.

F. Client is responsible for arranging access to the property and the opening up of any surfaces needed to complete a repair. HouseMaster assumes responsibility to restore surfaces to a rough finish but not for resurfacing and decorating after the repair work is completed.

3. LIMITATIONS

Other than as provided by this Guarantee, HouseMaster assumes no liability to any party for damages which may result from the Inspection, the contents of the Inspection Report or this Guarantee. Nor does HouseMaster assume any liability for bodily injury caused by any of the inspected components or property damage to others. HOUSEMASTER IS NOT RESPONSIBLE FOR CONSEQUENTIAL OR SECONDARY DAMAGES or other conditions resulting from the failure or malfunction of the components of the house. HouseMaster specifically disclaims any liability for the adequacy of the capacity or the design of any component or its failure to comply with any local, state or national code. In addition, HouseMaster will not be liable for costs necessitated by normal maintenance or for damages which result from neglect or misuse, termites or other insects, shifting or settling of land, frost heaves, subsidence, dry rot, condensation, floods, surface water, waves or tidal waves, nuclear or air contamination, war or any act of aggression and other acts of God, or for losses recoverable under homeowner insurance, manufacturer and/or contractor warranties or service contracts, etc.

4. CLAIM PROCEDURE

Prior to any repair work, the HouseMaster client must notify the local HouseMaster office that performed the Inspection in writing during the term of this Guarantee. HouseMaster will forward a special Client Reporting Form to the client for their submission of a claim. The local HouseMaster office will advise the client on the repair completion procedure. In cases where the condition makes the house uninhabitable, HouseMaster may authorize, by telephone, reasonable emergency repairs. Any repairs made prior to notification and authorization by HouseMaster will void this Guarantee with respect to the element or component so repaired. HouseMaster assumes no liability for a recurrence of a settled claim condition. IN THE EVENT THAT A DISPUTE ARISES BETWEEN THE CLIENT AND HOUSEMASTER AS TO HOUSEMASTER'S LIABILITY UNDER THIS GUARANTEE, SUCH DISPUTE WILL BE PRESENTED TO A RECOGNIZED ARBITRATION ASSOCIATION, AT CLIENT'S EXPENSE, FOR RESOLUTION.

EXPRESS® REPORT

PROPERTY INFORMATION

Address: _____

_____

Owner(s): _____

Description: ○ Single Family   ○ Condominium

○ Two Family   ○ Other: _____

Reported/Estimated Age: _____ Years

INSPECTION COMPANY

Office: _____

_____

_____

_____

Telephone: _____

Inspector: _____

INSPECTION DETAILS

Client: _____   Report No: _____

Type Inspection: ○ Standard Home Inspection ○ _____

Date: _____   Time: _____   Status: ○ Occupied ○ Vacant ○ _____

Weather: _____   Approx. Temperature: _____

People Present For Inspection: _____

PURPOSE AND SCOPE OF INSPECTION

The purpose of this report is to render an opinion as to the condition of the major inspected elements of the referenced property on the date of inspection. Report findings are based on a limited time/scope inspection performed according to Terms and Conditions of the Inspection Order Agreement and in a manner consistent with home inspection industry standards. Information contained herein was prepared for the exclusive use of the client named above.

Evaluations are basically limited to a visual assessment, are not technically exhaustive and only include installed and specified structural, mechanical and electric systems components, unless otherwise stated.

Furthermore, no engineering, geological, design, environmental, or code compliance evaluations of the property were performed. Details related to these and similar limitations and exclusions, such as those listed under GENERAL INSPECTION GUIDELINES, can be found on the reverse side of this page and in applicable industry standards.

Due to the normal and stated limitations of a home inspection, no representations or guarantees are made with respect to latent deficiencies or any future conditions. The report, including all SUPPLEMENTAL INFORMATION and any addenda, should be reviewed in its entirety.

TERMINOLOGY

The following terms are used to describe inspected element conditions in the EXPRESS REPORT:

SATISFACTORY - Functional at the time of inspection. Element condition is sufficient for its minimum required function. Element is in working or operating order with no readily visible evidence of a substantial defect.

FAIR - Functional at the time of inspection but with limitations and/or exceptions. Element exhibits an existing defect or has a high potential for a defect to develop, is near or beyond its normal design life, has a limited service life, and/or does not meet normal condition expectations.

POOR - Not functional at the time of inspection or exhibiting conditions conducive to imminent failure. Element shows considerable wear or has a substantial defect, is missing when it should be present, and/or is not in working or operating order.

NOT CHECKED (NOT EVALUATED) - Element was disconnected or de-energized, was not accessible, was not visible, exhibited improper or unsafe conditions for inspection, was outside scope of the inspection, and/or was not inspected due to other factors, stated or otherwise.

NOT APPLICABLE - Elements or components were not present, were not observed, are not within the scope of the inspection, and/or were not inspected due to other factors, stated or otherwise.

SEE COMMENT - Review inspector comments, addenda, or SUPPLEMENTAL INFORMATION related to the specified element(s).

LIMITATIONS: Items listed under LIMITATIONS indicate conditions that may have impeded completion of a standard limited time/scope inspection pursuant to industry standards. If removal or elimination of the limitation occurs, inspection prior to closing is advised.

IMPORTANT NOTE: An element rated POOR requires immediate repair, replacement or other remedial work, or has a high probability of requiring such work in the very near future. An element listed in FAIR condition, has at least a moderate probability that repair, replacement or other remedial work will be required now or in the near future. If any decision about the property or its purchase would be affected by the cost of any remedial work, firm contractor quotations should be obtained prior to making any such decisions.

A SUBSTANTIAL DEFECT is a condition which may require an expenditure over $500 to repair, replace or otherwise correct, an expenditure which represents a significant portion of the estimated replacement cost of the listed element, and/or a defect that must be corrected now or in the near future for proper element function.

GENERAL INSPECTION GUIDELINES

Review important information on pertinent topics on the reverse of this and each report page.

- Construction Regulations
- Home Maintenance
- Aesthetic Considerations
- Environmental Exclusions
- Design and Adequacy

- Estimated Ages
- Design Life Range
- Element Descriptions
- National Standards
- Owner Questionnaire

- Remedial Work
- Wood Destroying Insects
- Elements Not Inspected
- Work in Progress
- ○ Owner Inspection

- ○ Relocation Inspection
- ○ Specific Element Inspection
- ○ Element Sampling
- ○ Condominium/Townhouse

- ○ New Construction
- ○ Cottage (Light) Construction
- ○ Vacant Building
- ○ Seasonal/Weather Factors

EXPRESS. REPORT

ROOFING

○ **NOT APPLICABLE**

Column headers (diagonal): SATISFACTORY, FAIR, POOR, SEE COMMENTS, NOT APPLICABLE, NOT CHECKED

PREDOMINANT ROOFING (#1): Description: ○ Moderate/Steep Slope ○ Flat/Low Slope ○ Shingle/Shake ○ Sheet/Rolled ○ Composition ○ Asphalt ○ Wood ○ Slate ○ Asbestos/Cement ○ Tile ○ Metal ○ Built-Up/Gravel ○ Not Determined ○ _____

Est. Age: _____ yrs.   Design Life Range: _____ - _____ yrs.

ROOFING (#2): ○ Same as #1   Description: _____
Location:_____ Est. Age: _____ yrs. Design Life Range: _____ - _____ yrs.

ROOFING (#3): ○ Same as #1   Description: _____
Location:_____ Est. Age: _____ yrs. Design Life Range: _____ - _____ yrs.

INSPECTION METHOD: ○ Ground w/Binoculars   ○ Ladder at Eaves   ○ Walked On   ○ _____

1 ○ ○ ○ ○ ○ ○ **ROOFING #1** _____
2 ○ ○ ○ ○ ○ ○ **ROOFING #2** _____
3 ○ ○ ○ ○ ○ ○ **ROOFING #3** _____
4 ○ ○ ○ ○ ○ ○ **FLASHING *** _____
5 ○ ○ ○ ○ ○ ○ _____
6 ○ ○ ○ ○ ○ ○ _____
7 _____
8 _____
9 _____
10 _____
11 _____
12 _____

13 **LIMITATIONS:** ○ Common Element ○ Height/Design ○ Snow Cover ○ Weather ○ Not Inspected _____ % ○ _____

> **NOTE:** Roofing type/material comments are intended to provide general descriptions only; actual materials were not verified. Rigid/Cementitious products may possibly contain asbestos. * Most roof leaks occur at flashings, however, assessment of flashing is limited to visible sections.

14 **SUPPLEMENTAL INFORMATION** - Review details related to the following items on reverse side of this page:
- ● Roofing Components
- ○ Flashings/Seal
- ○ Roof Underlayment
- ○ Multiple Layers
- ○ Low Slope Shingle
- ○ Eave Protection
- ○ Roof Drainage
- ○ Roofer Opinion
- ○ Roofing Materials
- ○ Roof Structure
- ○ Appearance

~~SAMPLE~~

ROOF ELEMENTS

○ **NOT APPLICABLE**

Column headers (diagonal): SATISFACTORY, FAIR, POOR, SEE COMMENTS, NOT APPLICABLE, NOT CHECKED

CHIMNEY (#1): Description: ○ Brick ○ Masonry ○ Stuccoed ○ Composition ○ Metal ○ w/ Enclosure
○ _____ Location:_____

CHIMNEY (#2): Description: ○ Brick ○ Masonry ○ Composition ○ Metal Vent ○ w/ Enclosure
○ _____ Location:_____

OTHER CHIMNEY(S): Description: _____ Location:_____

1 ○ ○ ○ ○ ○ ○ **EXTERIOR OF CHIMNEY #1†** _____
2 ○ ○ ○ ○ ○ ○ **EXTERIOR OF CHIMNEY #2†** _____
3 ○ ○ ○ ○ ○ ○ **SKYLIGHT(S)** _____
4 ○ ○ ○ ○ ○ ○ **VENTILATION COVER(S)** _____
5 ○ ○ ○ ○ ○ ○ **PLUMBING STACKS** _____
6 ○ ○ ○ ○ ○ ○ **GUTTERS** _____
7 ○ ○ ○ ○ ○ ○ **DOWNSPOUTS** _____
8 ○ ○ ○ ○ ○ ○ **FASCIA/SOFFITS††** _____
9 ○ ○ ○ ○ ○ ○ _____
10 ○ ○ ○ ○ ○ ○ _____
11 _____
12 _____
13 _____
14 _____

15 **LIMITATIONS:** ○ Common Elements ○ Height/Design ○ Snow Cover ○ Weather ○ Limited Access ○ _____

> **NOTE:** † Inspection of chimneys / vents are limited to readily visible external conditions. Flues, liners and footings are not generally visible for inspection. Review HEATING and FIREPLACE Sections for additional comments on chimneys/vents. †† Fascia/Soffit areas are generally inaccessible; they are prone to hidden decay/insect damage.

16 **SUPPLEMENTAL INFORMATION** - Review details related to pertinent topics on the reverse of this page:
- ● Chimney/Rooftop Elements
- ○ Chimney Height/ Clearance
- ○ Chimney Foundation
- ○ Flue/Liner Conditions
- ○ Flashing/Seal
- ○ Flue/Rain Guard
- ○ Spark Arrester
- ○ Mortarwork/Cap
- ○ Plumbing Stacks
- ○ Built-in Gutters/Drains
- ○ Roof Discharge
- ○ Downspout Into Ground
- ○ Splash Blocks/Extensions

EXPRESS. REPORT

EXTERIOR ELEMENTS

○ NOT APPLICABLE

PREDOMINANT SIDING (#1): Description: ○ Shingles/Shakes ○ Panels/Sheets ○ Lapped Board ○ Textured Coating ○ Masonry ○ Wood ○ Hardboard/Fiberboard ○ Aluminum/Metal ○ Vinyl/Coated ○ Brick/Veneer ○ Stucco ○ Asbestos/Cement ○ Not Determined ○ _____

SIDING (#2): Description: _____ Location: _____

SIDING (#3): Description: _____ Location: _____

PORCH/DECK (#1): Description: ○ Masonry/Concrete ○ Wood Frame ○ Enclosed ○ Screened ○ Covered ○ Porch ○ Balcony ○ Deck Location: _____

PORCH/DECK (#2): Description: _____ Location: _____

Column headers: SATISFACTORY / FAIR / POOR / SEE COMMENTS / NOT APPLICABLE / NOT CHECKED

#	SATISFACTORY	FAIR	POOR	SEE COMMENTS	NOT APPLICABLE	NOT CHECKED	
1	○	○	○	○	○	○	SIDING #1
2	○	○	○	○	○	○	SIDING #2
3	○	○	○	○	○	○	SIDING #3
4	○	○	○	○	○	○	WINDOWS
5	○	○	○	○	○	○	ENTRY DOOR(S)
6	○	○	○	○	○	○	STAIRS/STOOPS
7	○	○	○	○	○	○	PORCH/DECK #1
8	○	○	○	○	○	○	PORCH/DECK #2
9	○	○	○	○	○	○	RAILINGS
10	○	○	○	○	○	○	FOUNDATION COATING
11	○	○	○	○	○	○	
12	○	○	○	○	○	○	
13							
14							
15							
16							

17 **LIMITATIONS:** ○ Common Element ○ Weather ○ Vegetation ○ Under-Structure Inaccessible ○ Snow Cover ○ _____

NOTE: Exterior wood elements such as sidings, trimwork, decks, porches, and stairs are particularly prone to damage due to insects/decay. Concealed/latent conditions are not determinable. See INTERIOR Section for any additional comments.

18 **SUPPLEMENTAL INFORMATION -** Review details related to pertinent topics on the reverse of this page.

● Exterior Components   ○ Storm/Screens   ○ Exterior Faucets   ○ Wood Decay/Insects   ○ Deck At House
○ Window/Door Seals   ○ Drip Caps/Flashing   ○ Exterior Electric   ○ Railings   ○ Synthetic Stucco
○ Glazing/Putty   ○ Glass Surfaces   ○ Siding/Wood-Soil Clearance   ○ Supports/Foundation

SITE ELEMENTS

○ NOT APPLICABLE

PATIO: Description: ○ Concrete ○ Brick/Pavers ○ Flagstone ○ Roof Cover ○ Screened ○ Trellis ○ _____ Location: _____

WALKWAYS: Description: ○ Concrete ○ Brick/Pavers ○ Flagstone/Slate ○ Gravel ○ Unimproved

DRIVEWAY: Description: ○ Concrete ○ Asphalt ○ Pavers ○ Gravel ○ Unpaved ○ _____

RETAINING WALL(S): † Description: ○ Multiple Units ○ Concrete ○ Wood Timber ○ Brick/Masonry ○ Block ○ Rock/Stone Location(s): _____

#	SATISFACTORY	FAIR	POOR	SEE COMMENTS	NOT APPLICABLE	NOT CHECKED	
1	○	○	○	○	○	○	PATIO
2	○	○	○	○	○	○	WALKWAYS
3	○	○	○	○	○	○	DRIVEWAY
4	○	○	○	○	○	○	RETAINING WALL(S)†
5	○	○	○	○	○	○	WINDOW WELLS
6	○	○	○	○	○	○	SUB-GRADE ENTRYWAY
7	○	○	○	○	○	○	GROUND SLOPE AT FOUNDATION
8	○	○	○	○	○	○	SITE GRADING
9	○	○	○	○	○	○	
10	○	○	○	○	○	○	
11							
12							
13							

14 **LIMITATIONS:** ○ Common Elements ○ Weather ○ Vegetation ○ Snow Cover ○ _____

NOTE: Evaluation of any site element is limited to its effect on the house, unless otherwise indicated. Assessment of geological/soil conditions are outside the scope of this inspection. † Retaining wall evaluations are limited to walls at foundation/house areas, unless otherwise noted.

15 **SUPPLEMENTAL INFORMATION -** Review details related to pertinent topics on the reverse of this page.

● Site/Soil Factors   ○ Grading Provisions   ○ Window Wells/Areaways   ○ Vegetation/Landscaping   ○ Pool/Spa
○ Drainage from Surfaces   ○ Soil Conditions   ○ Sump Pump Discharge   ○ Lawn Irrigation   ○ Spa Support
○ Finished Surfaces   ○ Piles   ○ Splash Blocks/Extensions   ○ Seawalls/Docks   ○ Fencing/Sheds

SAMPLE

GARAGE

○ **NOT APPLICABLE**

Columns: SATISFACTORY / FAIR / POOR / SEE COMMENTS / NOT APPLICABLE / NOT CHECKED

DESCRIPTION: ○ Multiple Car (_____) ○ Attached ○ Under House ○ Detached ○ Carport ○ Wood Frame ○ Masonry ○ _____

ROOF: ○ Refer to ROOFING Section ○ Description: _____
Est. Age: _____ yrs. Design Life: _____ - _____ yrs. Inspection Method: _____

HOUSE/GARAGE SEPARATION: ✷ Description: ○ Not Applicable ○ Exposed Framing ○ Incomplete Cover ○ Covered Framing or Masonry ○ Solid Door ○ Self-Closing Door ○ _____

Insulation: ○ Not Determined ○ Incomplete Description: _____ Average (inches): _____

Vapor Retarder: ○ Not Determined ○ Not Found/Detected ○ Incomplete ○ Observed; Extent Indeterminate

ATTIC INSPECTION METHOD: ○ Entered ○ From Entry ○ Limited Entry ○ Inaccessible ○ _____

#	SAT	FAIR	POOR	SEE COMMENTS	N/A	NOT CHECKED	Item
1	○	○	○	○	○	○	**ROOFING**
2	○	○	○	○	○	○	**EXPOSED FRAMING**
3	○	○	○	○	○	○	**FLOOR SLAB**
4	○	○	○	○	○	○	**FOUNDATION**
5	○	○	○	○	○	○	**ATTIC VENTILATION**
6	○	○	○	○	○	○	**WALLS/CEILINGS**
7	○	○	○	○	○	○	**SIDING/TRIM**
8	○	○	○	○	○	○	**VEHICLE DOOR(S)**
9	○	○	○	○	○	○	**DOOR OPERATOR ✷✷**
10	○	○	○	○	○	○	**ELECTRIC**
11	○	○	○	○	○	○	
12	○	○	○	○	○	○	
13							
14							
15							

16 **LIMITATIONS:** ○ Vehicle(s) ○ Storage/Belongings ○ Common Element ○ Door(s) Locked ○ Not Inspected: _____% ○ _____

> **NOTE:** Additional garage comments may be noted in other sections of this report. ✷ Pertinent to Attached/ Under House garages only. Insulation and vapor retarder comments are based on a random spot check. ✷✷ A field test of door operators is limited to a visual assessment of auto retraction with application of reasonable resistance. Advise re-checking at occupancy and regularly to ensure proper operation.

17 **SUPPLEMENTAL INFORMATION** - Review details related to pertinent topics on the reverse of this page.
- ● Garage Components
- ○ Automatic Operator/Retraction
- ○ Door Hardware/Mechanisms
- ○ Wall/Ceiling Construction
- ○ Door to House
- ○ Insulation/Vapor Retarder
- ○ Electric/Strip
- ○ Mechanical Equipment
- ○ Detached Garage
- ○ Garage Conversion
- ○ Siding/Wood-Soil Clearance
- ○ Sub-Slab Excavation
- ○ Drainage
- ○ Leakage/Stain

SAMPLE

ATTIC

○ **NOT APPLICABLE**

Columns: SATISFACTORY / FAIR / POOR / SEE COMMENTS / NOT APPLICABLE / NOT CHECKED

DESCRIPTION: ○ Multiple Areas ○ Open Framing ○ Walk-Up/In ○ Finished Area(s) ○ No Void - Design Factor ○ Not Determined ○ _____

INSPECTION METHOD: ○ Entered ○ From Entry ○ Limited Entry ○ Inaccessible ○ _____

CONSTRUCTION: † Framing: ○ Rafters ○ Trusses ○ _____
Sheathing: ○ Structural Panels ○ Spaced Boards ○ _____

INSULATION: ○ Not Determined ○ Blanket/Batt ○ Loose Fill ○ _____ Average (inches) _____

VAPOR RETARDER: ○ Not Determined ○ Incomplete ○ Observed; Extent Indeterminate ○ Not Found/Detected

#	SAT	FAIR	POOR	SEE COMMENTS	N/A	NOT CHECKED	Item
1	○	○	○	○	○	○	**ROOF FRAMING**
2	○	○	○	○	○	○	**ROOF DECK/SHEATHING**
3	○	○	○	○	○	○	**VENTILATION PROVISIONS ††**
4	○	○	○	○	○	○	**ATTIC VENTILATOR(S)**
5	○	○	○	○	○	○	**WHOLE HOUSE FAN**
6	○	○	○	○	○	○	
7	○	○	○	○	○	○	
8							
9							
10							

11 **LIMITATIONS:** ○ Common Area ○ Design ○ Storage ○ Height/No Walkway ○ Not Inspected: _____% ○ _____

> **NOTE:** Stains/Leaks may be due to numerous factors; verification of status or cause, hidden damage is usually not possible. Any representations of insulation/vapor retarder materials or amounts is based on a limited visual check only. Wall insulation factors are not determinable. † Generally wood/wood products, unless otherwise noted. †† Natural Ventilation conditions are subject to changes due to weather, insulation work, etc.

12 **SUPPLEMENTAL INFORMATION** - Review details related to pertinent topics on the reverse of this page.
- ● Attic Components
- ○ Cathedral/Vaulted Ceilings
- ○ Truss Construction
- ○ Sheathing Conditions
- ○ Spaced Boards
- ○ Fire Retardant Plywood
- ○ Chimney/Vent Clearance
- ○ Ventilation Provisions
- ○ Attic Ventilators
- ○ Exhaust Vent Termination
- ○ Rafter Insulation
- ○ Insulation at Fixtures
- ○ Vapor Retarder
- ○ Insulation Levels
- ○ Electric/Wiring
- ○ Leakage/Stain

INTERIOR ELEMENTS

○ NOT APPLICABLE

Column headers (diagonal): SATISFACTORY, FAIR, POOR, SEE COMMENTS, NOT APPLICABLE, NOT CHECKED

PREDOMINANT TYPE STRUCTURE:
CEILINGS: ○ Wood Frame ○ _____ ○ Not Determined
WALLS: ○ Wood Frame ○ Masonry ○_____ ○ Not Determined
FLOORS: ○ Wood Frame ○ Slab (See Section Below) ○ _____ ○ Not Determined
WINDOW TYPE(S): ○ Not Determined ○ Awning ○ Double Hung ○ Casement ○ Sliders ○ Single Glaze
○ w/ Combo Storms/Screens ○ w/ Screens ○ w/ Double Glazing ○ w/ Storms ○_____
SMOKE DETECTORS: * ○ Not Determined ○ Battery ○ Hard Wired ○ Not Present
Locations Observed: _____

	SATISFACTORY	FAIR	POOR	SEE COMMENTS	NOT APPLICABLE	NOT CHECKED	
1	○	○	○	○	○	○	CEILINGS
2	○	○	○	○	○	○	WALLS
3	○	○	○	○	○	○	FLOORS
4	○	○	○	○	○	○	STAIRS
5	○	○	○	○	○	○	RAILINGS
6	○	○	○	○	○	○	WINDOWS **
7	○	○	○	○	○	○	ROOM DOORS **
8	○	○	○	○	○	○	SLIDERS **
9	○	○	○	○	○	○	
10	○	○	○	○	○	○	
11							
12							
13							
14							
15							
16							

17 **LIMITATIONS:** ○ Excess Furnishing/Storage ○ Suspended/Drop Ceilings ○ _____

NOTE: Construction descriptions including windows represent the predominant types/materials visible; finish materials are not considered. Carpeted floors and other floor, wall and ceiling coverings limit the ability to assess conditions. ** Window/Door evaluations are based on a spot check of random/representative units. * Smoke and carbon monoxide detectors are generally recommended for all houses; no determination of smoke detector operation/ placement was made, unless otherwise noted. An assessment should be made of smoke detector operation & positioning adequacy prior to occupancy.

SAMPLE

18 **SUPPLEMENTAL INFORMATION** - Review details related to pertinent topics on the reverse of this page.
- ● Interior Components
- ○ Wall/Ceiling Conditions
- ○ Moisture/Condensation
- ○ Window/Door Seals
- ○ Foam Insulation
- ○ Plaster Surfaces
- ○ Floor Structure
- ○ Roof Truss Uplift
- ○ Glass Surfaces
- ○ Leakage/Stain
- ○ Common Walls

SLAB CONSTRUCTION

○ NOT APPLICABLE

Column headers (diagonal): SATISFACTORY, FAIR, POOR, SEE COMMENTS, NOT APPLICABLE, NOT CHECKED

CONCRETE SLAB CONSTRUCTION: ○ Not Determined ○ Full House (Ground Level) ○ Part(s) of House:
○ Location: ○ Addition ○ Laundry/Utility Area ○ _____
PREDOMINANT SLAB COVER: † ○ Carpeting ○ Sheet Goods ○ Tile ○ Mixed ○ Not Determined
○ _____

	SATISFACTORY	FAIR	POOR	SEE COMMENTS	NOT APPLICABLE	NOT CHECKED	
1	○	○	○	○	○	○	EXTERIOR/EXPOSED EDGE
2	○	○	○	○	○	○	MAIN INTERIOR AREA
3	○	○	○	○	○	○	LAUNDRY/UTILITY AREA(S)
4	○	○	○	○	○	○	ADDITION(S)
5	○	○	○	○	○	○	
6	○	○	○	○	○	○	
7							
8							
9							
10							

11 **LIMITATIONS:** ○ Excess Storage/Furnishings ○ Exterior Vegetation ○ High Grade/Soil Levels ○ _____

NOTE: Comments in this section pertain to concrete slab on grade construction at living/habitable areas only. If applicable, see SUBSTRUCTURE, GARAGE, and INTERIOR sections for additional slab/floor comments. † The presence of floor covering (carpet, tile, etc.) limits ability to fully assess slab condition. Slab foundations are prone to movement in clay soil areas.

12 **SUPPLEMENTAL INFORMATION -** Review details related to pertinent topics on the reverse of this page.
- ● Inspection Considerations
- ○ Post Tension
- ○ Floor/Slab Surface
- ○ Water Penetration
- ○ WD Insect Treatment
- ○ Pier/Grade Beam
- ○ Sub-Floor (Slab) Ducts
- ○ Slab Structure

HouseMaster. "The Home Inspection Professionals"®

EXPRESS® REPORT

SUBSTRUCTURE

○ NOT APPLICABLE

BASEMENT: ○ None Observed ○ Full House ○ Unfinished ○ Finished Area(s) ○ ______
CRAWL SPACE: * ○ None Observed ○ Full House ○ Under Portions Of House ○ ______
○ Location #1: ______ #2: ______
CRAWL SPACE INSPECTION METHOD: ○ Not Applicable ○ No Visible Access ○ Entered ○ From Entry ○ Limited Entry ○ Inaccessible ○ ______
FOUNDATION WALLS/PIERS: ○ Block ○ Concrete ○ Brick/Stone ○ Pier ○ w/Curtain (Veneer) Wall ○ Wood ○ Not Determined ○ ______
HOUSE FLOOR STRUCTURE: ○ Wood Frame ○ Joist ○ Truss ○ Laminated ○ ______
Column(s): ○ Wood Post ○ Metal ○ Metal Screw Jack ○ ______
INSULATION: ○ Not Determined Description: ______ Ave. (inches): ______ Location: ______
VAPOR RETARDER: ○ Not Determined ○ Incomplete ○ Observed; Extent Indeterminate ○ Not Found/Detected

	SATISFACTORY	FAIR	POOR	SEE COMMENTS	NOT APPLICABLE	NOT CHECKED	
1	○	○	○	○	○	○	**FOUNDATION WALLS**
2	○	○	○	○	○	○	**PIERS/COLUMNS**
3	○	○	○	○	○	○	**FLOOR FRAMING**
4	○	○	○	○	○	○	**MAIN BEAM(S)**
5	○	○	○	○	○	○	**BASEMENT SLAB**
6	○	○	○	○	○	○	**STAIR/RAILING**
7	○	○	○	○	○	○	**CRAWL SPACE VENTILATION**
8	○	○	○	○	○	○	**CURTAIN (VENEER) WALLS**
9	○	○	○	○	○	○	
10	○	○	○	○	○	○	

11 ______
12 ______
13 ______
14 ______
15 ______
16 ______

17 **LIMITATIONS:** ○ Common Areas ○ Storage/Belongings ○ Finish Materials ○ Suspended/Drop Ceilings ○ Insulation ○ Water/Debris ○ Limited Clearance ○ Area Not Inspected: ______% ○ ______

> ***NOTE:*** *Review other areas of report for any additional comments on the structure. This report does not represent an engineering evaluation of the structure.*
> ** Crawl spaces located at or below grade are particularly prone to moisture and insect concerns; due to typical access restictions, evaluations are generally limited.*

SAMPLE

18 **SUPPLEMENTAL INFORMATION** - *Review details related to pertinent topics on the reverse of this page.*

● Structural Evaluations ○ Stone/Brick Foundation ○ Foundation Conditions
○ Screw Jack/Adjustable Columns ○ Balloon Framing ○ WD Insect Treatment
○ Engineered Lumber ○ Framing Conditions ○ Moisture/Condensation
○ Vapor Retarder/Insulation ○ Below Grade/Soil Contact ○ Curtain (Veneer) Walls
○ Ventilation Provision ○ Leakage/Stain

WATER PENETRATION

○ NOT WITHIN SCOPE OF THIS INSPECTION

SUBGRADE AREAS: ○ Not Applicable ○ Crawl Space Area(s) ○ Basement ○ Garage ○ Areas of House Slab ○ ______
SUMP PUMP(S): ○ Not Determined ○ Inaccessible ○ ______
Location: #1 ______ #2 ______

1 **INDICATIONS OF WATER PENETRATION CONDITIONS:** ○ Water Marks/Stains ○ Wet ○ Dampness ○ Mildew/Condensation ○ Indeterminate ○ Owner/Tenant Comment ○ ______

2 **GENERAL LOCATION OF OBSERVED CONDITIONS:** ○ House Slab Areas ○ Basement ○ Crawl Space(s) ○ Lower Level ○ Garage ○ Multiple Areas ○ ______

3 **SUMP PUMP(S):** ○ Satisfactory ○ Fair ○ Poor ○ Not Applicable ○ Not Checked ○ ______

4 **INDICATIONS OF POSSIBLE PRIOR REMEDIAL WORK:** ○ Owner Statement ○ Construction/ Coatings ○ Drainage/Grading ○ Excavation Work ○ Indeterminate ○ ______

5 **LIMITATIONS:** ○ Common Area ○ Inaccessible Areas ○ Recent Work/Refinishing ● Limitations as listed in SUBSTRUCTURE or SLAB CONSTRUCTION Sections ○ ______

6 **DETAILS:** ______

> ***NOTE:*** *Review all sections of the report for any comments on roof, plumbing or other leakage/infiltration concerns. This section is limited to an assessment of At-Grade/Subgrade moisture/water penetration conditions readily visible at time/date of inspection. Moisture/water penetration conditions are subject to unpredictable changes; future conditions can not be determined. Confirm past history/status of any concerns with owner and local authorities.*

7 **SUPPLEMENTAL INFORMATION** - *Review details related to pertinent topics on the reverse of this page.*

● Water Penetration ○ Sump Pump Discharge ○ Fixture Drain to Sump
○ Check Valve ○ Back Water Valve
○ Drainage Systems ○ Floor Drains
○ Window Wells ○ Exterior Entryway
○ Grading/Roof Drains ○ Moisture Barriers

KITCHEN

○ NOT APPLICABLE

BUILT-IN APPLIANCES [est. ages (in years) in brackets.]:
○ Countertop Range [_____]   ○ Wall Oven [_____]   ○ Freestanding Range/Oven [_____]
○ Garbage Disposal [_____]   ○ Dishwasher [_____]   ○ Compactor [_____]   ○ Refrigerator [_____]
○ _____ [_____]   ○ _____ [_____]
○ Ventilators: ○ Recirculating Fan   ○ Exhaust Fan   ○ Down-flow ○ _____
LOCATION (If multiple kitchens): #1 _____   #2 _____

	SATISFACTORY	FAIR	POOR	SEE COMMENTS	NOT APPLICABLE	NOT CHECKED	
1	○	○	○	○	○	○	**PLUMBING/SINK(S)**
2	○	○	○	○	○	○	**FLOOR(ING)**
3	○	○	○	○	○	○	**ELECTRIC**
4	○	○	○	○	○	○	**COOKING UNIT(S)**
5	○	○	○	○	○	○	**DISHWASHER**
6	○	○	○	○	○	○	**DISPOSAL**
7	○	○	○	○	○	○	**VENTILATOR(S)**
8	○	○	○	○	○	○	**CABINETRY/COUNTERTOP**
9	○	○	○	○	○	○	

10 **LIMITATIONS:**   ○ No Power/Gas   ○ Countertop / Cabinet Storage / Obstructions   ○ _____

SUPPLEMENTAL INFORMATION -
Review pertinent topics on the reverse of this page.
● Kitchen Components
○ Drain Trap
○ Drainage
○ Sink/Faucets
○ Water Flow
○ Spray Attachment
○ Dishwasher Air Gap
○ Wet Bar/Island Sink
○ Cross Connection
○ GFCI Test
○ Ventilators Discharge
○ Flex Gas Piping
○ Laundry Vent

NOTE: *Appliances are evaluated/inspected at inspector option; evaluations, when performed, do not include the full range of any appliance cycle/mode. Appliance service lives will vary with unit quality and maintenance.*

BATHROOMS

○ NOT APPLICABLE

DESCRIPTION/LOCATION:
BATH #1.: _____   BATH #2.: _____
BATH #3.: _____   BATH #4.: _____
OTHER FIXTURES: _____
Ground-Fault Circuit-Interrupter(s) (GFCI): ○ Yes ○ No ○ Indeterminate ○ _____
Whirlpool Bath: * ○ Not Applicable ○ Location: _____

SAMPLE

		SATISFACTORY	FAIR	POOR	SEE COMMENTS	NOT APPLICABLE	NOT CHECKED	
BATH #1	1	○	○	○	○	○	○	**SINK(S)**
	2	○	○	○	○	○	○	**TOILET**
	3	○	○	○	○	○	○	○ **BATHTUB/** ○ **STALL SHOWER** *
	4	○	○	○	○	○	○	**TILEWORK OR ENCLOSURE** **
	5	○	○	○	○	○	○	**VENTILATION**
	6	○	○	○	○	○	○	**FLOOR/WALLS/CEILING**
	7	○	○	○	○	○	○	**ELECTRIC**
BATH #2	8	○	○	○	○	○	○	**SINK(S)**
	9	○	○	○	○	○	○	**TOILET**
	10	○	○	○	○	○	○	○ **BATHTUB/** ○ **STALL SHOWER** **
	11	○	○	○	○	○	○	**TILEWORK OR ENCLOSURE** ***
	12	○	○	○	○	○	○	**VENTILATION**
	13	○	○	○	○	○	○	**FLOOR/WALLS/CEILING**
	14	○	○	○	○	○	○	**ELECTRIC**
BATH #3	15	○	○	○	○	○	○	**SINK(S)**
	16	○	○	○	○	○	○	**TOILET**
	17	○	○	○	○	○	○	○ **BATHTUB/** ○ **STALL SHOWER** **
	18	○	○	○	○	○	○	**TILEWORK OR ENCLOSURE** ***
	19	○	○	○	○	○	○	**VENTILATION**
	20	○	○	○	○	○	○	**FLOOR/WALLS/CEILING**
	21	○	○	○	○	○	○	**ELECTRIC**
BATH #4	22	○	○	○	○	○	○	**SINK(S)**
	23	○	○	○	○	○	○	**TOILET**
	24	○	○	○	○	○	○	○ **BATHTUB/** ○ **STALL SHOWER** **
	25	○	○	○	○	○	○	**TILEWORK OR ENCLOSURE** ***
	26	○	○	○	○	○	○	**VENTILATION**
	27	○	○	○	○	○	○	**FLOOR/WALLS/CEILING**
	28	○	○	○	○	○	○	**ELECTRIC**
	29	○	○	○	○	○	○	**OTHER FIXTURE(S):**

SUPPLEMENTAL INFORMATION -
Review pertinent topics on the reverse of this page.
● Bathroom Components
○ Drain Traps
○ Old Fixtures/Faucets
○ Toilet Seal/Tank
○ Shower Base/Pan
○ Basement Shower
○ Shower Diverter
○ Door/Glass Enclosure
○ Door/Enclosure
○ Water Flow
○ Drainage
○ Drain Mechanisms
○ Caulking/Grouting
○ Tilework/Backing
○ Ventilator Discharge
○ Moisture/Mildew
○ Cross Connections
○ GFCI Test
○ Heaters

○ Review Bathroom related comments in the Plumbing Section.

30 **LIMITATIONS:**   ○ Water Off   ○ Winterized   ○ _____

NOTE: * Whirlpool Bath unit evaluations are limited to fixture flow and drainage; mechanical/electric equipment is not evaluated.
** Stall Shower pans are not visible for evaluation. *** Tile work or enclosure item addresses wall covering at bathtub/stall shower only.

ELECTRIC

○ NOT APPLICABLE

Column headers: SATISFACTORY / FAIR / POOR / SEE COMMENTS / NOT APPLICABLE / NOT CHECKED

SERVICE LINE: ○ Underground ○ Overhead ○ Aluminum ○ Copper ○ Not Determined
Est. Line Capacity: _____ Amps   Est. Voltage: ○ 120/240 Volt ○ 120 Volt
MAIN DISTRIBUTION PANEL: Est. Capacity: _____ Amps ○ Indeterminate ○ w/Sub Panels
○ Circuit Breaker ○ Fuse   Location: _____
SERVICE DISCONNECT(S): ○ None ○ Multiple ○ Single Main: Est. _____ Amps
○ Indeterminate   Location: ○ In Distribution Panel ○ Exterior ○ _____
MAJOR APPLIANCE (240 VOLT) CIRCUIT(S): ○ Aluminum ○ Copper ○ Not Determined
HOUSEHOLD (120 VOLT) CIRCUITS: ○ Aluminum ○ Copper ○ Not Determined
GFCI: ○ In Panel ○ At Receptacle(s) ○ Multiple Units ○ None Observed ○ _____

1 ○○○○○○ **SERVICE DISCONNECT PANEL** _____
2 ○○○○○○ **DISTRIBUTION PANEL** _____
3 ○○○○○○ **SUBPANEL(S)** _____
4 ○○○○○○ **GFCI TEST*** _____
5 ○○○○○○ **WIRING/CONDUCTORS** _____
6 ○○○○○○ **DEVICES **** _____
7 ○○○○○○ _____
8 ○○○○○○ _____
9 _____
10 _____
11 _____
12 _____
13 **LIMITATIONS:** ○ Power Off ○ Panel(s) Not Accessible ○ Secured Cover ○ _____

NOTE: Review electric comments in other report sections. Representations of wire sizes/types are based on a limited visual check at panel and random interior locations. * Ground-Fault Circuit-Interrupter (GFCI) evaluation is based on check utilizing built-in tester only unless otherwise noted. ** Represents an assessment of receptacles on exterior walls, in garage, kitchen and bathrooms and randomly representative installed fixtures/devices throughout house.

14 **SUPPLEMENTAL INFORMATION -** Review details related to pertinent topics on the reverse of this page.

● Electrical Components ○ System Ground ○ Breaker/Fuse/Wire Size ○ Low Voltage Lighting ○ Non-Grounding Receptacles
○ Service Line ○ Panel Conditions ○ Service Disconnect ○ Light Fixtures/Switches ○ Receptacle Polarity
○ Service Limitations ○ GFCI Test ○ Sub-Panel Ground ○ Electric Distribution ○ Aluminum (120V) Wiring
○ Panel Capacity ○ Circuit Taps ○ Knob & Tube Wire ○ Wire Splices

COOLING

○ NOT APPLICABLE

Column headers: SATISFACTORY / FAIR / POOR / SEE COMMENTS / NOT APPLICABLE / NOT CHECKED

SYSTEM #1: Description: ○ Electric Central Air Conditioning ○ Evaporative Cooler ○ Gas Absorption
○ Room Units ○ Unitary/Packaged Unit(s) ○ _____ Location: _____
○ Electric Heat Pump: † ○ Air Source ○ Water/Ground Source ○ _____
○ Supplemental Heat (HP): † ○ Electric Coils ○ Indeterminate ○ None Observed ○ _____
Make: _____ Est. Age: _____ yrs. Design Life Range: _____ - _____ yrs.
SYSTEM #2: Description: ○ Same as System #1 ○ _____ Location: _____
Make: _____ Est. Age: _____ yrs. Design Life Range: _____ - _____ yrs.
GENERAL DISTRIBUTION: †† ○ Ducted/Registers ○ Unitary/Fan Coil Units ○ Central Supply
○ Individual Room Supply ○ Exceptions: _____

1 ○○○○○○ **SYSTEM #1** _____
2 ○○○○○○ **SYSTEM #2** _____
3 ○○○○○○ **OUTDOOR UNIT(S)** _____
4 ○○○○○○ **INDOOR BLOWER/FANS †††** _____
5 ○○○○○○ **CONDENSATE REMOVAL** _____
6 ○○○○○○ **EXPOSED DUCTWORK †††** _____
7 ○○○○○○ **THERMOSTAT(S) †††** _____
8 ○○○○○○ _____
9 ○○○○○○ _____
10 _____
11 _____
12 _____
13 **LIMITATIONS:** ○ Cool/Cold Weather ○ HP Cool Mode Only ○ HP Heat Mode Only ○ Programmable Thermostat ○ _____

NOTE: Cooling System operation cannot be assessed in cool/cold weather. Internal components, including indoor unit coils, are generally unobservable. † Refer to HEATING Section for supplemental heat comments & additional details. †† Represents predominant distribution to habitable areas. ††† Additional information may be included in the HEATING Section on shared components.

14 **SUPPLEMENTAL INFORMATION -** Review details related to pertinent topics on the reverse of this page.

● Cooling/Heat Pumps ○ Outdoor Unit ○ Condensate Removal ○ Ductwork Insulation ○ Window/Wall Unit(s)
○ Pre-Test Power ○ Refrigerant Tubing ○ Blower/Filter(s) ○ Ceiling Fan(s) ○ Ventilation Provisions
○ Service Disconnect ○ Supplemental Heat (HP) ○ Distribution System

HEATING

○ **NOT APPLICABLE**

Column headers (diagonal):
- SATISFACTORY
- FAIR
- POOR
- SEE COMMENTS
- NOT APPLICABLE
- NOT CHECKED

HEATING UNIT (#1): Description: ○ Hot Air ＊ ○ Hot Water ○ Steam ○ Heat Pump (HP-see Cooling)
○ Heat Coils ○ _____ Location: _____
Fuel: ○ Nat. Gas ○ LP-Propane ○ Oil ○ Electric ○ Solar ○ Coal/Wood ○ _____
Distribution: ○ Ducted/Registers ○ Piped/Radiators ○ Radiant ○ Unitary/Baseboard ○ _____
Make:_____ Est. Age: _____ yrs. Design Life Range: _____ – _____ yrs.

HEATING UNIT (#2): Description: ○ Same as System #1 ○ _____
Fuel: _____ Distribution: _____ Location: _____
Make:_____ Est. Age: _____ yrs. Design Life Range: _____ – _____ yrs.

ROOM HEATING: ＊＊ ○ Central Source ○ Individual Room Source ○ Exceptions: _____

	Sat	Fair	Poor	SeeC	N/A	NC	
1	○	○	○	○	○	○	**HEATING UNIT #1**
2	○	○	○	○	○	○	**HEATING UNIT #2**
3	○	○	○	○	○	○	**BURNER(S)**
4	○	○	○	○	○	○	**GAS/FUEL LINES @ UNIT**
5	○	○	○	○	○	○	**VENT CONNECTOR(S)**
6	○	○	○	○	○	○	**BLOWER(S) ＊＊＊**
7	○	○	○	○	○	○	**CIRCULATOR PUMP(S)**
8	○	○	○	○	○	○	**DISTRIBUTION SYSTEM(S) ＊＊＊**
9	○	○	○	○	○	○	**HEAT COIL(S)**
10	○	○	○	○	○	○	**EXPOSED FUEL TANK**
11	○	○	○	○	○	○	**THERMOSTAT(S) ＊＊＊**
12	○	○	○	○	○	○	
13	○	○	○	○	○	○	

14 _____
15 _____
16 _____
17 _____

SAMPLE

18 **LIMITATIONS:** ○ Power Off/No Fuel ○ Common Element ○ Winterized ○ Programmable Thermostat ○ HP Heat Mode Only ○ _____

NOTE: ＊ *Due to normal design constraints, the heat exchanger in a hot air furnace cannot be fully assessed within the scope of a standard inspection. Complete heat exchanger evaluation requires use of special equipment. Independent evaluation by a specialist is advised, particularly if unit is older and/or exhibits wear.*
＊＊ *Predominant method of heat supply to habitable rooms.* ＊＊＊ *COOLING Section may contain additional comments.*

19 **SUPPLEMENTAL INFORMATION** - *Review details related to pertinent topics on the reverse of this page.*

- ● Heating Systems
- ○ Blower/Filters
- ○ Flue/Venting
- ○ Unit/Vent Clearance
- ○ Combustion Air
- ○ Heat Exchanger
- ○ Sub-Floor Ducts
- ○ Heat Distribution
- ○ Radiant Heating
- ○ LP Gas/Tanks
- ○ Boiler Relief Valve
- ○ Flue/Vent Damper
- ○ High Efficiency Unit
- ○ Gas Lines/Valves
- ○ Buried Fuel Tank
- ○ Flex Gas Piping
- ○ Garage Location
- ○ ACM Insulation
- ○ Electronic Air Cleaner
- ○ Humidifier
- ○ Programmable Thermostat
- ○ Air Exchanger
- ○ Mixed Fuel Units

FIREPLACE

○ **NOT APPLICABLE**

Column headers (diagonal):
- SATISFACTORY
- FAIR
- POOR
- SEE COMMENTS
- NOT APPLICABLE
- NOT CHECKED

FIREPLACE (#1): Description: ○ Brick ○ Stone ○ Freestanding ○ Metal ○ w/Metal Liner ○ w/Gas Igniter
○ w/ Gas Burner ○ w/ Exterior Air Supply ○ _____ Location: _____
FIREPLACE (#2): Description: _____ Location: _____
OTHER: † ○ Not Applicable Description: ○ Freestanding Stove(s) ○ Fireplace Insert(s) ○ Primary Heat Source
○ _____ Location(s): _____

	Sat	Fair	Poor	SeeC	N/A	NC	
1	○	○	○	○	○	○	**FIREPLACE #1**
2	○	○	○	○	○	○	**FIREPLACE #2**
3	○	○	○	○	○	○	**GAS BURNER(S)**
4	○	○	○	○	○	○	**STOVE(S)†**
5	○	○	○	○	○	○	**INSERT(S)†**
6	○	○	○	○	○	○	
7	○	○	○	○	○	○	

8 _____
9 _____

10 **LIMITATIONS:** ○ Decorative Unit Only ○ Stove/Insert † ○ _____

NOTE: *Evaluations are limited to a visual assessment of readily accessible components; flues, interiors and operational conditions were not evaluated. Review chimney comments also.* † *Stove/Insert inspections, if performed, do not include code/fire safety compliance assessments; it is recommended that a qualified specialist and/or local authorities perform a thorough evaluation of the unit and its installation. Any comments/ratings herein are based on a limited external check.*

11 **SUPPLEMENTAL INFORMATION** - *Review details related to pertinent topics on the reverse of this page.*

- ● Fireplaces/Stoves
- ○ Drafting
- ○ Firebox
- ○ Hearth Extension
- ○ Damper Operation
- ○ Creosote/Cleaning
- ○ Ash Pit/Clean-out
- ○ Unit/Vent Clearances
- ○ Combustion Air

PLUMBING

WATER SUPPLY & WASTE DISPOSAL: No verification of the type or method of water supply or waste disposal was made as part of this inspection. Verify type systems prior to purchase.

WATER PIPING: ∗ Description: ○ Not Determined ○ Copper ○ Galvanized ○ Plastic ○ Lead ○ Brass
○ _____

SHUT OFF LOCATION: WATER: ○ At Meter ○ Not Determined ○ _____
GAS: ○ At Meter ○ Not Determined ○ Not Applicable ○ _____

WASTE/DRAIN/VENT LINES: ∗ Description: ○ Not Determined ○ Copper ○ Galvanized ○ Cast Iron
○ Plastic ○ w/Waste Pump (Sanitary Waste) ○ _____

WATER TREATMENT SYSTEM: ∗∗ ○ Not Determined ○ Not Observed ○ Water Softener ○ Filter
○ _____

○ **NOT APPLICABLE**

Columns: SATISFACTORY · FAIR · POOR · SEE COMMENTS · NOT APPLICABLE · NOT CHECKED

#	Item
1	WATER PIPING
2	WATER FLOW AT FIXTURES
3	DRAIN/WASTE/VENT PIPING
4	FIXTURE DRAINAGE
5	INTERIOR WASTE PUMP
6	EXTERIOR FAUCET(S)
7	LAUNDRY SINK
8	GAS PIPING ∗∗∗
9	
10	
11	
12	
13	
14	

15 **LIMITATIONS:** ○ Water Off ○ Winterized ○ Fixtures Not Functional ○ _____

NOTE: Due to typical construction constraints, evaluation of plumbing components is limited to readily accessible areas. See other report sections for additional plumbing system comments. ∗ Any listing of piping types represents predominant materials observed. ∗∗ Water Treatment Systems must be independently evaluated. ∗∗∗ Gas/Fuel piping comments/ratings are based on visual conditions only.

SAMPLE

16 **SUPPLEMENTAL INFORMATION** - Review details related to pertinent topics on the reverse of this page.

- ● Plumbing System
- ○ Water Supply Flow
- ○ Pressure Regulator
- ○ Old/Mixed Water Piping
- ○ Plastic Water Piping
- ○ Ejector/Waste Pumps
- ○ Cross Connections
- ○ Backflow Preventer
- ○ Pipe Insulation
- ○ Laundry Discharge
- ○ Methods/Materials
- ○ Pipe Supports
- ○ Water Hammer
- ○ Vent Piping
- ○ Clean-outs
- ○ Floor Drains
- ○ Leakage/Stain
- ○ Private Water Supply
- ○ Private Waste Disposal

WATER HEATER

WATER HEATER (#1): Description: ○ Standard Tank ○ Tankless ○ Heat Exchanger ○ Off Boiler
○ w/Separate Storage Tank ○ _____ Location: _____
Fuel: ○ Natural Gas ○ LP-Propane ○ Electric ○ Oil ○ Solar   Est. Capacity (Gal): _____
Make: _____ Est. Age: _____ yrs. Design Life Range: _____ - _____ yrs.

WATER HEATER (#2): Description: ○ Same as #1 ○ _____
Fuel: _____ Est. Capacity (Gal.): _____ Location: _____
Make: _____ Est. Age: _____ yrs. Design Life Range: _____ - _____ yrs.

○ **NOT APPLICABLE**

Columns: SATISFACTORY · FAIR · POOR · SEE COMMENTS · NOT APPLICABLE · NOT CHECKED

#	Item
1	WATER HEATER #1
2	WATER HEATER #2
3	VENT CONNECTOR(S) †
4	GAS/FUEL LINES @ UNIT
5	RELIEF VALVE(S) ††
6	
7	
8	
9	
10	

11 **LIMITATIONS:** ○ Water Off ○ No Power/Fuel ○ _____

NOTE: No determination of hot water volume/temperature adequacy was made, unless otherwise noted. † Related comments may be recorded in HEATING Section. †† Evaluation of the Temperature Pressure Relief Valve (TPRV) is restricted to a visual assessment of its installation; no operational check was performed.

12 **SUPPLEMENTAL INFORMATION** - Review details related to pertinent topics on the reverse of this page.

- ● Hot Water Supply
- ○ TPRV Discharge
- ○ Thermal Blanket
- ○ Electric Metering
- ○ Seismic Restraint
- ○ Clearances/Elevation
- ○ Overflow Pan
- ○ Buried Fuel Tanks
- ○ Flex Gas Piping
- ○ Flue/Venting Conditions

TITLE
INSURANCE
POLICY

LAWYERS TITLE INSURANCE
CORP.

Service available throughout the United States, Canada, Puerto Rico, the Bahamas, and the U. S. Virgin Islands.

National Division, Branch and Agency offices and Approved Attorneys are located throughout the operating territory.

Lawyers Title
Insurance Corporation
NATIONAL HEADQUARTERS
RICHMOND, VIRGINIA

RESIDENTIAL TITLE INSURANCE POLICY

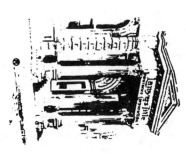

POLICY ISSUED THROUGH

Lawyers Title
Insurance Corporation
NATIONAL HEADQUARTERS
RICHMOND, VIRGINIA

(PLS 19459)

Lawyers Title Insurance Corporation

RESIDENTIAL TITLE INSURANCE POLICY
One-To-Four Family Residences

POLICY NUMBER 101-00- 417916

OWNER'S INFORMATION SHEET

Your Title Insurance Policy is a legal contract between you and the Company.

It applies only to a one-to-four family residential lot or a condominium unit. If your land is not either of these, contact us immediately.

The Policy insures you against certain risks to your land title. These risks are listed on page one of the Policy.

The Policy is limited by:

- EXCLUSIONS on page 1
- EXCEPTIONS in Schedule B
- CONDITIONS on page 2

You should keep the Policy even if you transfer the title to your land.

If you want to make a claim, see Item 3 under Conditions on page 2.

You do not owe any more premiums for the Policy.

This sheet is not your insurance Policy. It is only a brief outline of some of the important Policy features. The Policy explains in detail your rights and obligations and our rights and obligations. Since the Policy — and not this sheet — is the legal document:

YOU SHOULD READ THE POLICY VERY CAREFULLY

If you have any questions about your policy, contact the issuing office shown on Schedule A or

Consumer Affairs Dept.
Lawyers Title Insurance Corporation
P. O. Box 27567
Richmond, Virginia 23261

TABLE OF CONTENTS

Lawyers Title
Insurance Corporation

NATIONAL HEADQUARTERS
RICHMOND, VIRGINIA

SCHEDULE A — RESIDENTIAL TITLE INSURANCE POLICY

CASE NUMBER	DATE OF POLICY	AMOUNT OF INSURANCE	ENDORSEMENT(S)	POLICY NUMBER

The Policy Amount will automatically increase by 10% of the amount shown above on each of the first five anniversaries of the Policy Date.

This number must be the same as the Policy number on the Owner's Information Sheet.

1. Name of Insured:

2. Your interest in the land covered by this Policy is:

   Fee simple

3. The land referred to in this Policy is described as follows:

   In compliance with Chapter 157, Laws of 1977, premises herein are Lot
   in   on the Tax Map of the Township of West Windsor.

   The property conveyed to the Insured by Deed from Canal Pointe Associates,
   Inc., dated July 23, 1987 and recorded   in Book   of Deeds
   for Mercer County at page

POLICY ISSUED THROUGH

Kenneth H Morsk
Countersignature Authorized Officer or Agent

(11/1/S-7/193.04)

Issued at (Location)

This Schedule is valid only when attached to the Residential Title Insurance Policy and Schedule B.

Policy 101—Litho in U.S.A.
035-0-101-2900/1

ALTA Residential Title Insurance Policy — 1979

ORIGINAL

Lawyers Title Insurance Corporation
RESIDENTIAL TITLE INSURANCE POLICY

SCHEDULE B

CASE NUMBER

POLICY NUMBER

EXCEPTIONS

In addition to the Exclusions, you are not insured against loss, costs, attorneys' fees, and expenses resulting from:

1. Any facts about the land which a correct survey would disclose and which are not shown by the public records.

2. Real estate taxes for 1987 paid through the third quarter.

3. Possible additional taxes and assessments for the year 1987 assessed or levied under R.S. 54:4-63.1 et seq.

4. Terms of Farmland Assessment Act of 1964.

5. Cross Easement and Shared Maintenance Agreement recorded in Deed Book 2300 page 19, which refers to a Closing Agreement and amended by Deed Book 2337 page 504.

6. Declaration of Covenants running with the land recorded in Deed Book 2300 page 39 and revised Declaration of Covenants running with the land dated May 8, 1986 and recorded in the Mercer County Clerk's Office on May 8, 1986 in Deed Book 2337 page 439.

7. Deed of Easement (Greenbelt) from Canal Pointe Associates, Inc. to Township of West Windsor recorded December 10, 1985 in Deed Book 2318 page 357 and Utility Easements in Deed Book 2356 page 497 and Deed Book 2356 page 503 recorded September 18, 1986, Deed Book 2372 page 139 recorded January 5, 1987, Deed Book 2378 page 77, recorded February 13, 1987, and Right-Of-Way Agreement in Deed Book 2343 page 9, recorded June 26, 1986.

8. Deed of Easement (Sanitary Sewer and Access) from Canal Pointe Associates, Inc. to Township of West Windsor recorded December 10, 1985 in Deed Book 2318 page 376.

9. Terms, conditions, restrictions, and provisions as contained in the Master Deed recorded September 23, 1986 in Deed Book 2357 page 585 and First Amendment recorded September 23, 1986 in Deed Book 2357 page 799 and Deed Book 2377 page 783.

10. Drainage Basin Agreement recorded September 22, 1986 in Deed Book 2357 page 87.

11. Conservation and Maintenance Agreement recorded September 22, 1986 in Deed Book 2357 page 103.

12. Consent to Detention Basin Easement Agreement recorded May 8, 1986 in Deed Book 2337 page 515.

13. Agreement with Windsor Cablevision, Inc. recorded in Deed Book 2343 page 9.

14. Right of Way Agreement recorded May 8, 1986 in Deed Book 2339 page 638.

15. The policy insures that Canal Pointe Condominium is a valid condominium in accordance with N.J.S.A. 46:8B-1 et seq.

16. Mortgage by   to COLUMBIA SAVINGS AND LOAN ASSOCIATION, dated July 23, 1987 and recorded August 27, 1987 in Book   of Mortgages for Mercer County at page   showing an original principal amount of $150,000.00.

OWNER'S COVERAGE STATEMENT

This Policy insures your title to the land described in Schedule A - if that land is a one-to-four family residential lot or a condominium unit. Your insurance, as described in this Coverage Statement, is effective on the Policy Date Shown in Schedule A. Your insurance is limited by the following:

EXCLUSIONS on page 1   EXCEPTIONS in Schedule B   CONDITIONS on page 2

We insure you against actual loss resulting from:

any title risks covered by this Policy - up to the Policy Amount; and

any costs, attorneys' fees, and expenses we have to pay under this policy

1. Someone else owns an interest in your title.
2. A document is not properly signed, sealed and acknowledged, or delivered.
3. Forgery, fraud, duress, incompetency, incapacity, or impersonation.
4. Defective recording of any document.
5. You do not have any legal right of access to and from the land.
6. There are restrictive covenants limiting your use of the land.
7. There is a lien on your title because of:
   - a mortgage or deed of trust
   - a judgment, tax, or special assessment
   - a charge by a homeowner's or condominium association
8. There are liens on your title, arising now or later, for labor and material furnished before the Policy Date - unless you agreed to pay for the labor and material.
9. Others have rights arising out of leases, contracts, or options.
10. Someone else has an easement on your land.
11. Your title is unmarketable which allows another person to refuse to perform a contract to purchase, lease, or make a mortgage loan.
12. You are forced to remove your existing structure - other than a boundary wall or fence - because:
    - it extends onto adjoining land or onto any easement
    - it violates a restriction shown in Schedule B
    - it violates an existing zoning law
13. You cannot use the land for a single-family residence, because such a use violates a restriction shown in Schedule B or an existing zoning law.
14. Other defects, liens, or encumbrances.

Company's Duty to Defend Against Court Cases

We will defend your title in any court case that is based on a matter insured against by this Policy. We will pay the costs, attorneys' fees, and expenses we incur in that defense. We can end this duty to defend your title by exercising any of our options listed in Item 4 of the Conditions.

This Policy is not complete without Schedules A and B.

Lawyers Title Insurance Corporation

(SEAL — LAWYERS TITLE INSURANCE CORPORATION · S E A L · 1925 · RICHMOND)

By: _Robert C. Dawson_
President

Attest: _[signature] III_
Secretary

EXCLUSIONS

In addition to the Exceptions in Schedule B, you are not insured against loss, costs, attorneys' fees, and expenses resulting from:

1. Governmental police power, and the existence or violation of any law or government regulation. This includes building and zoning ordinances and also laws and regulations concerning:
   - land use
   - improvements on the land
   - land division
   - environmental protection

   This exclusion does not limit the zoning coverage described in Items 12 and 13 of Covered Title Risks.

2. The right to take the land by condemning it, unless a notice of taking appears in the public records on the Policy Date.

3. Title Risks:
   - that are created, allowed, or agreed to by you
   - that are known to you, but not to us, on the Policy Date — unless they appeared in the public records
   - that result in no loss to you
   - that first affect your title after the Policy Date — this does not limit the labor and material lien coverage in Item 8 of Covered Title Risks

4. Failure to pay value for your title.

5. Lack of a right:
   - to any land outside the area specifically described and referred to in Item 3 of Schedule A; or
   - in streets, alleys, or waterways that touch your land

   This exclusion does not limit the access coverage in Item 5 of Covered Title Risks.

CONDITIONS

1. DEFINITIONS

a. Easement - the right of someone else to use your land for a special purpose.

b. Land - the land or condominium unit described in Schedule A and any improvements on the land which are real property.

c. Mortgage - a mortgage, deed of trust, trust deed, or other security instrument.

d. Public Records — title records that give constructive notice of matters affecting your title - according to the state law where the land is located.

e. Title - the ownership of your interest in the land, as shown in Schedule A.

2. CONTINUATION OF COVERAGE

This policy protects you as long as you:

• own your title; or

• own a mortgage from anyone who buys your land; or

• are liable for any title warranties you make

This Policy protects anyone who receives your title because of your death.

3. HOW TO MAKE A CLAIM

If anyone claims a right against your insured title, you must notify us promptly in writing.

Send the notice to Lawyers Title Insurance Corporation, P. O. Box 27567, Richmond, Virginia 23261. Please include the Policy number shown in Schedule A, and the county and state where the land is located.

Our obligation to you could be reduced if:

• you fail to give prompt notice; and

• your failure affects our ability to dispose of or to defend you against the claim

4. OUR CHOICES WHEN YOU NOTIFY US OF A CLAIM

After we receive your claim notice or in any other way learn of a matter for which we are liable, we can do one or more of the following:

a. Pay the claim against your title.

b. Negotiate a settlement.

c. Prosecute or defend a court case related to the claim.

d. Pay you the amount required by this Policy.

e. Take other action which will protect you.

f. Cancel this Policy by paying the Policy Amount, then in force, and only those costs, attorneys' fees, and expenses incurred up to that time which we are obligated to pay.

5. HANDLING A CLAIM OR COURT CASE

You must cooperate with us in handling any claim or court case and give us all relevant information.

Unless you can show that payment was reasonable and necessary, we will not reimburse you for money you pay, or agree to pay:

• to settle disputes; or

• to cover expenses and attorneys' fees

We will repay you for all expenses that we approve in advance.

When we prosecute or defend a court case, we have a right to choose the attorney. We can appeal any decision to the highest court. We do not have to pay your claim until your case is finally decided.

6. LIMITATION OF THE COMPANY'S LIABILITY

a. We will pay up to your actual loss or the Policy Amount in force when the claim is made — whichever is less.

b. If we remove the claim against your title within a reasonable time after receiving notice of it, we will have no further liability for it.

If you cannot use any of your land because of a claim against your title, and you rent reasonable substitute land or facilities, we will repay you for your actual rent until:

• the cause of the claim is removed; or

• we settle your claim

c. The Policy Amount will be reduced by all payments made under this Policy — except for costs, attorneys' fees, and expenses.

d. The Policy Amount will be reduced by any amount we pay to our insured holder of any mortgage shown in this Policy or a later mortgage given by you.

e. If you do anything to affect any right of recovery you may have, we can subtract from our liability the amount by which you reduced the value of that right.

7. TRANSFER OF YOUR RIGHTS

When we settle a claim, we have all the rights you had against any person or property related to the claim. You must transfer these rights to us when we ask, and you must not do anything to affect these rights. You must let us use your name in enforcing these rights.

We will not be liable to you if we do not pursue these rights or if we do not recover any amount that might be recoverable.

With the money we recover from enforcing these rights, we will pay whatever part of your loss we have not paid We have a right to keep what is left.

8. OUR LIABILITY IS LIMITED TO THIS POLICY

This Policy, plus any endorsements, is the entire contract between you and the Company. Any title claim you make against us must be made under this Policy and is subject to its terms.

LEGAL (METES AND BOUNDS) DESCRIPTION

Dated: 9/24/93
File No.:

METES AND BOUNDS DESCRIPTION
LOTS   &   IN BLOCK
TOWNSHIP OF MONROE
MIDDLESEX COUNTY, NEW JERSEY

BEGINNING at a point in the Northerly line of Tyndale Avenue, said point being located a distance of 175.00' Westerly from the intersection of the Southwesterly line of Monmouth Road with the Northerly line of Tyndale Avenue and from said point running; THENCE

1. Along the Northerly line of Tyndale Avenue, North 77 degrees 30 minutes West, 100.00' to a point; THENCE

2. North 11 degrees 31 minutes East, 100.00' to a point; THENCE

3. South 77 degrees 30 minutes East, 100.00' to a point; THENCE

4. South 11 degrees 31 minutes West, 100.00' to a point in the Northerly line of Tyndale Avenue, said point being the Point or Place of BEGINNING.

Being known and designated as Lots   in Block   as shown on the Tax Maps of the Township of Monroe, Sheet No.   Being also known and designated as Lots   as shown on a certain unfiled map entitled "Appleby Estate, Spotswood, Monroe Township, Middlesex County, N.J.". Said map is on record at the Middlesex County Clerk's Office.

Being commonly known as
New Jersey.

This description is made in accordance with a survey Prepared by Fletcher Engineering, Inc., dated September 4, 1993 in File No. 48193.

SURVEY

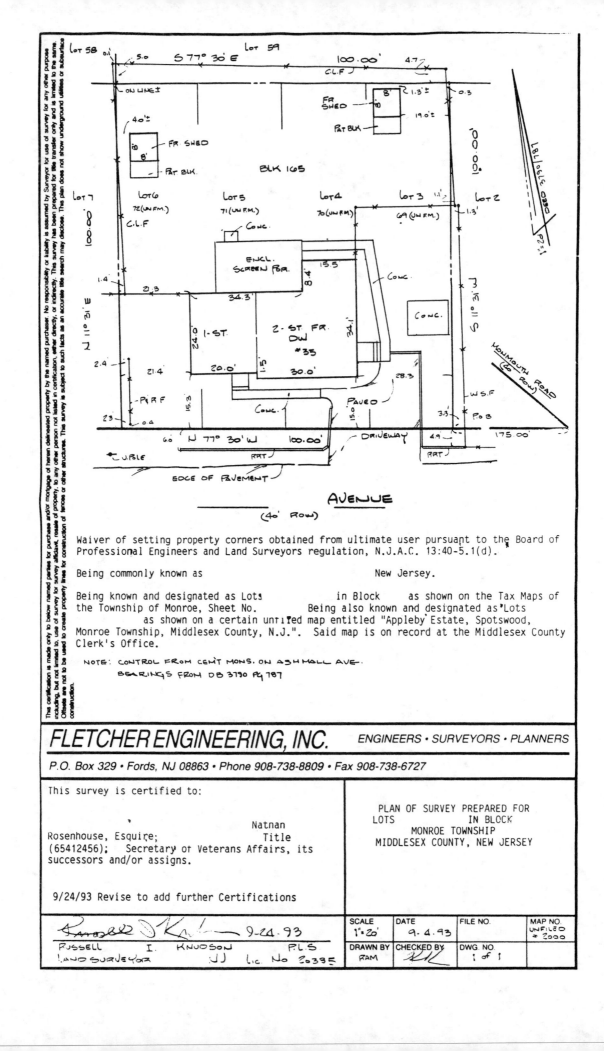

Waiver of setting property corners obtained from ultimate user pursuant to the Board of Professional Engineers and Land Surveyors regulation, N.J.A.C. 13:40-5.1(d).

Being commonly known as   New Jersey.

Being known and designated as Lots   in Block   as shown on the Tax Maps of the Township of Monroe, Sheet No.   Being also known and designated as Lots   as shown on a certain untitled map entitled "Appleby Estate, Spotswood, Monroe Township, Middlesex County, N.J.". Said map is on record at the Middlesex County Clerk's Office.

NOTE: CONTROL FROM CENT MONS. ON ASH MALL AVE.
      BEARINGS FROM DB 3790 Pg 787

FLETCHER ENGINEERING, INC.   ENGINEERS · SURVEYORS · PLANNERS

P.O. Box 329 • Fords, NJ 08863 • Phone 908-738-8809 • Fax 908-738-6727

| This survey is certified to:

Rosenhouse, Esquire;   Natnan Title
(65412456); Secretary of Veterans Affairs, its successors and/or assigns.

9/24/93 Revise to add further Certifications | PLAN OF SURVEY PREPARED FOR
LOTS   IN BLOCK
MONROE TOWNSHIP
MIDDLESEX COUNTY, NEW JERSEY |

Russell J. Knudson 9-24-93	SCALE 1"=20'	DATE 9.4.93	FILE NO.	MAP NO. UNFILED # 2000
RUSSELL I. KNUDSON P.L.S LAND SURVEYOR NJ Lic No 20385	DRAWN BY RAM	CHECKED BY	DWG. NO. 1 of 1	

GLOSSARY

ABSTRACT OF TITLE: History of title and ownership of a parcel of land culled from a search of public records, summarizing transfers of title and liens against the property.

ACCELERATION PROVISION: Clause in a mortgage creating a condition that if terms are breached, the holder has the option to declare the entire debt immediately due and payable. Option to call in the mortgage where there is a "due on sale" provision and the mortgagor transfers title.

ACKNOWLEDGMENT: A formal declaration before a public official that a person has signed an instrument or document and a verification of this fact by the official, usually a notary public, who signs and affixes his stamp and seal.

ADJUSTABLE RATE MORTGAGE (ARM): A loan whose interest rate fluctuates to keep up with a financial index, such as the one-year treasury bill rate, cost of funds for savings and loan interest, or national average mortgage contract interest rate. The lender usually adds a "margin" or number of percentage points to the index to calculate the ARM interest rate at each adjustment. Limits on periodic adjustments in interest rates are known as **Caps**. There is usually a yearly cap and a lifetime cap.

ADVERSE POSSESSION: The hostile, exclusive, and continuous possession of another's land under a claim of title. Possession for a statutory period may be a means of acquiring title. For instance, if you held yourself out as an owner of a particular plot of land, used it and paid the taxes on that property, after holding it continuously for the requisite statutory period of time you can be declared the owner by a court. This is also called "squatter's rights." The law, particularly as to the requisite period, varies from state to state.

AFFIDAVIT OF TITLE: A sworn statement by seller certifying the history of his ownership and his marital status and verifying that there are currently no defects or encumbrances to title except for liens to be paid at closing.

AGENT: One who acts or has the power to act for another. Under the law of agency a fiduciary relationship is created when a property owner, as the principal, executes a listing agreement or management contract authorizing a licensed real estate broker to be his or her agent. An agent owes undivided loyalty to his principal to represent him without conflicting interest.

AMORTIZED LOAN: Gradual payment of principal as well as interest through regular installments. The payments remain level but the amount allocated to principal and interest changes as each payment is credited. As the principal is reduced the amount of interest decreases as the interest rate is applied against a lower principal balance.

ANTITRUST LAWS: Acts prohibiting conspiracies in restraint of trade, such as price-fixing by brokers to fix commission rates or allocations of customers or markets to minimize competition.

APPRAISAL: Report setting forth the opinion of an expert as to the value of property. Sometimes there is a confusion with the term "assessment," which is the opinion of the value of the property for taxation purposes, which is usually lower than market value.

APPRECIATION: Increase in the value of property due to economic or related causes, such as inflation or demand for location.

ASSIGNMENT: The written transfer of a right or interest in property.

ATTACHMENT: The seizure of property by court order at the commencement of a legal action to make it available for application to a person's debts by a judgment creditor.

BALANCE: The amount due at any given time for the payoff of a loan.

BALLOON PAYMENT: Final payment on a loan in a lump sum, where the loan was not fully amortized by the installments paid. For instance, where there is a 10-year loan with payments based on a 20-year schedule, there will be a balance of principal due at the end of 10 years, when the loan is due.

BARGAIN AND SALE DEED: A deed without covenants or warranties by the grantor, other than the implied representation that he has the right to convey title.

BENEFICIARY: Recipient of the proceeds of a life insurance policy or one who receives a monetary gift or property under a will.

BREACH OF CONTRACT: Default or non-performance in meeting the terms of an agreement, such as failure to pay when due.

BROKER: Licensee acting as agent for buyer or seller for an agreed commission or fee, whose function it is to bring willing and able parties together in a transaction, usually involving real estate.

BUILDING CODE: Governmental regulations specifying minimum standards for the construction or alteration of structures to protect the public.

BUILDING PERMIT: Written permission by authorized governmental official to construct, alter or demolish an improvement.

BUY-DOWN: Funds paid to lender by parties to a real estate transaction to reduce monthly payments on mortgage for the early years of the loan.

CAPITAL GAIN: Taxable profit on the sale of an asset (difference between the sales price and the adjusted cost basis of the property).

CAVEAT EMPTOR: Let the buyer beware (a Latin phrase).

CHAIN OF TITLE: The succession of ownership of a particular property tracing its derivation back to a given starting point from its present owner.

CLOSING STATEMENT: A written accounting of debits and credits prepared for a closing or transfer of title summarizing all of the funds paid or received. A federal act (the Real Estate Settlement Procedures Act or RESPA) requires a uniform statement for all covered transactions. This statement shows each of the parties all costs and disbursements of the transaction.

CLOUD ON TITLE: An undischarged lien or encumbrance impairing the title to real estate, which can be removed by release, quitclaim or lawsuit to quiet title. Any lien or encumbrance detracting from the marketability of the title and preventing a title company from issuing unconditional insurance to an owner and/or lender.

COMMISSION: Fee paid to broker or agent for procuring a buyer for property (almost invariably paid by seller as a percentage of the purchase price.)

COMMON ELEMENTS: The undivided areas of a condominium property used by the owners for their safety, convenience or recreation, such as walkways, roads, tennis courts, or swimming pools. Each condominium owner has an undivided proportional interest in these areas.

COMMUNITY PROPERTY: The law in certain states (Arizona, California, Idaho, Louisiana, Nevada, New Mexico, Texas and

Washington) dictating that each spouse has an equal interest in all of the assets acquired by either of them during the marriage.

CONDEMNATION: Exercise by a governmental body or entity authorized by statute of the power to take private property for a definite public use for just compensation to the private owner.

CONDOMINIUM: Form of real estate ownership of a dwelling unit in a multi-unit complex where each owner owns his own unit plus an undivided percentage of common areas, such as walkways, recreation and other shared areas.

CONSIDERATION: Anything of value given as an inducement for one to enter into an agreement. Every contract must be supported by something given in exchange, even a promise.

CONTINGENCY: Condition in an agreement that must be satisfied before the agreement becomes binding.

CONTRACT: A legally enforceable promise based on consideration embodying a meeting of the minds of the parties as to a common objective, the breach of which gives rise to a legal remedy.

CONVENTIONAL LOAN: A loan not insured or guaranteed for a fixed term at a fixed rate of interest usually given by a lender for the purchase or refinance of a residence. The vast majority of mortgage loans are of this familiar type.

COOPERATIVE: A form of ownership where the entire complex is owned by the cooperative corporation and each individual member owns a share of stock and a proprietary lease giving him the right to occupy a residential unit. There is usually much greater power and control in the board of directors than in a condominium, particularly as to consent for sale of stock.

CORPORATION: A fictional entity with perpetual existence used to conduct business in its own name. The use of this form of ownership gives the stockholders limited liability, limiting their risk to the amount of their investment, and immunizes their individual assets.

COUNTEROFFER: The rejection of an offer by a qualified acceptance made by the offeree conditioned on the acceptance of new or modified terms.

COVENANT: A promise or commitment made under oath, usually contained in real estate documents such as deeds, mortgages and leases. One consequence is that the time to sue is longer than on other contractual obligations.

CREDIT: Charge in your favor; as distinguished from debit, a charge against you.

DECEDENT: One who dies leaving an estate and heirs, whether with a valid will (testate) or without (intestate).

DEED: Instrument whereby title or an interest in real estate is passed from one person or entity to another, recorded in the central recording office of the appropriate governmental subdivision.

DEED RESTRICTIONS: Limitations on the future use of a particular property usually created by a developer of a tract to preserve the residential nature and value, which runs with the land and can be enforced by any landowner in the subdivision. For instance, a restriction that no business shall be conducted on any lot in the tract.

DEFAULT: Breach of performance of the terms of an agreement, such as one contained in a mortgage note or bond, giving rise to certain remedies (such as foreclosure.) For instance, non-payment of installment on mortgage or non-payment of taxes or assessments within the prescribed time gives rise to a breach.

DEPRECIATION: Reduction in value of land or property based upon location and/or economic forces. For example, if a developer overbuilds and cannot sell all of the new homes, he will lower his price and all of the homes in the development will go down in market value.

DEVELOPER: Builder who has assembled a tract of land and subdivided the tract into individual lots and built dwellings based on an integrated plan, including off-site improvements such as streets, sidewalks, curbs and utilities.

DUAL AGENCY: Where an agent represents two principals, usually with adverse (opposing) interests (like both seller and buyer). This is an attempt to overcome the built-in conflict of interest that seller's brokers must deal with.

DURESS: Pressure imposed by one side over the other in a contractual relationship dominating the will of the party on whom it is practiced, who enters the agreement involuntarily. Forcing a party to enter into a contract by threat of force or economic harm.

EARNEST MONEY: Deposit given at the inception of an agreement to show good faith intention to complete the transaction.

EASEMENT: Right granted by a landowner giving another permission to use the land in a limited way, such as a utility easement. The party granting the easement usually cannot build over the land on which it is granted and the grantee agrees to maintain the area and not cause any damage to the property.

EMINENT DOMAIN: The right of condemnation given to a governmental or private entity such as a utility to acquire ownership of private property for public use conditioned upon just compensation to the owner.

ENCROACHMENT: An improvement extending and intruding upon the adjacent property of another owner that can affect the marketability of the property.

ENCUMBRANCE: An easement, right, claim, lien or restriction on the use of land that may diminish its value or prevent its sale until removed.

EQUITY: Value of property above any indebtedness pertaining to it.

ESCROW: An instrument or funds held in trust pending the occurrence of a specific event or compliance with a condition. Usually held by one of the attorneys or a named trustee based upon specific instructions for release.

ESTATE TAXES: Federal taxes payable by an estate on a decedent's property.

EVICTION: Legal process to dispossess a tenant or occupant who is in possession of real estate.

EXCLUSIVE-AGENCY LISTING: Where one agent has the listing to sell an owner's real estate for a commission upon stated terms for a specific period of time, reserving to the owner the right to sell without a commission to any buyer not found by the broker.

EXCLUSIVE-RIGHT-TO-SELL LISTING: A listing giving the broker the exclusive right to a commission no matter who introduces the buyer, even the owner, if sold during the listing period.

EXECUTED CONTRACT: A contract in which all the parties have performed and all conditions have been complied with.

EXECUTION: The act of signing a contract or other legal instrument. Also a process to enforce a judgment where the debtor's property is seized by a judicial officer and sold.

FEE SIMPLE ABSOLUTE: The highest form of real estate ownership. Distinguished from a life estate, which is ownership only during the life of the life tenant.

FHA LOAN: Loan insured by the Federal Housing Agency made by an approved lender in accordance with strict regulations.

FIDUCIARY RELATIONSHIP: A relationship of trust and confidentiality, such as between attorney and client, principal and agent and trustee and beneficiary.

FIXTURE: Item of personal property affixed to the realty, which cannot be removed without substantial damage, e.g. gas range.

FORECLOSURE: Legal procedure where lien on property given as security for a debt or loan is sold to satisfy the obligation, cutting off all ownership rights.

FRAUD: Misrepresentation and deception inducing one to relinquish lawful right, property or funds. False statement of fact or opinion relied upon to the detriment of one to whom it is made.

GENERAL WARRANTY DEED: The highest form of deed, in which the grantor warrants clear title to not only the immediate grantee but to a remote grantee. Other forms of deed are: bargain and sale with covenant against grantor, bargain and sale and quitclaim.

GRADUATED-PAYMENT MORTGAGE (GPM): One where the monthly interest and principal payments increase by a certain percentage each year for a certain number of years in order to make up for the early years' reduced payments. The disadvantage is negative amortization: Instead of the principal balance reducing, it increases to make up for the lower payments during the earlier years.

GRANTEE: The recipient of title from the grantor.

GRANTOR: The transferor of title to the grantee.

HEIR: Successor and inheritor under the laws of descent when the owner of land dies intestate (without a valid will). One who inherits land under a will is called a devisee. The term is regularly confused with beneficiary.

HOME EQUITY LOAN: Usually a second mortgage on real property for a loan or line of credit. The interest is usually tax deductible if you itemize.

HOMEOWNER'S INSURANCE POLICY: Packaged multi-peril policy covering residence owner for common risks and naming mortgagee as lienholder. Covers risks such as fire, burglary, and liability and can be for fair market value or replacement value.

HOMESTEAD: In certain states land declared by the owner to be the family home, which is exempt from judgment for debt.

IMPROVEMENT: Structure or amenities, such as utilities, sidewalks, streets or curbs, which enhances the value of the property.

INDEPENDENT CONTRACTOR: One who performs a contracted work, where the owner specifies the result but not the manner or details of how the job is to be done.

INFLATION: Gradual reduction of the purchasing power of money resulting from economic forces.

INHERITANCE TAXES: State tax on the privilege of a beneficiary to receive inheritance from an estate, which tax is technically payable by the beneficiary. The federal tax is on the privilege of the decedent to leave property to his beneficiaries and is called an estate tax.

INSTALLMENT CONTRACT: A real estate contract in which the purchaser pays the purchase price to the seller in periodic payments until a certain time, not necessarily the time of final payment, when title is transferred to the purchaser (sometimes called "contract for deed"). The purchaser pays the balance due or gets a mortgage from a lender or the seller takes back a purchase money mortgage.

INTEREST: Charge made by a lender for the loan of funds. In effect, a rental fee payable until the funds are repaid.

INTESTATE: One who dies without a valid will resulting in his property passing to his legal heirs in accordance with the laws of descent. These laws dictate who receives property in order of classification by closeness of blood lines.

JOINT TENANCY: A form of undivided ownership of real property by two or more persons characterized by the incident of survivorship where upon the death of a joint owner his interest passes to the surviving joint tenant. Where the joint tenancy is between husband and wife it is called a tenancy by the entirety.

JUDGMENT: The result of an adjudication in a lawsuit which, if for money, can become a lien on real estate owned by the judgment debtor. Where a verdict is rendered by a judge or jury it results in a judgment, which gives rise to enforcement remedies such as execution sale.

LACHES: An equitable principle applied to bar a legal claim because of an unreasonable delay or failure to assert a legal right in a timely manner.

LAND: The surface of the earth extending upward into space and downward to the center of the earth. Some landowners sell mineral rights to oil drilling, mining or chemical companies. In places like New York City, air rights have also been sold.

LEASE: Contract allowing the possession, use and occupancy by tenant of real property owned by landlord upon specified terms.

LEASE PURCHASE: Tax or financing technique in which the purchase of real property is preceded by a lease where at least a portion of the rent is credited to the purchase price on exercise by tenant of the option to purchase.

LEGAL DESCRIPTION: Description of real estate by metes and bounds (courses and distances) or by reference to a filed map or tax map.

LEGALLY COMPETENT PARTIES: Those of legal age and sound mind who have the capacity to enter into a binding contract.

LICENSE: Privilege or right granted by the federal government, state, county or municipal governing body to conduct a business or profession sometimes conditioned on an examination testing competency.

LIEN: A charge or claim on property giving the holder the right to enforce a court-ordered sale to satisfy the debt.

LIQUIDATED DAMAGES: Predetermined compensation to a party for breach (non-compliance or non-performance) of an obligation by the other party.

LISTING AGREEMENT: Agreement between an owner and broker for the sale of the owner's realty for a limited period at a designated commission.

MARKETABLE TITLE: A clear title insurable by a reputable title insurance company at regular rates.

MARKET VALUE: The probable price at which real estate will be sold based upon supply and demand.

MECHANIC'S LIEN: Charge or claim on property filed pursuant to law by subcontractor or materialman to the extent that the value of the property has been enhanced. The law creates a lien on the property to protect people in this protected class who have a contractual relationship with the contractor but not the owner of the real estate.

METES-AND-BOUNDS DESCRIPTION: A legal description of property expressing its boundaries by courses (directions) and distances measured from stakes or other fixed objects known as monuments.

MORTGAGE: Lien given on real estate as security for a debt or obligation wherein the holder has the remedy of foreclosure upon default. The sheriff or other official conducts a public sale where the property is sold to satisfy the amount due.

MORTGAGEE: The lender in a mortgage loan transaction.

MORTGAGOR: The borrower in a mortgage loan transaction.

MULTIPERIL POLICIES: Insurance policies covering fire, casualty, hazard, burglary and public liability. Homeowner's policies are package policies covering a multitude of risks. Most commercial policies cover these risks by separate policies.

OFFER AND ACCEPTANCE: Essential components of a valid contract. The combination of these two factors constitute a "meeting of the minds," which is the essence of an agreement.

OPTION: Agreement to keep offer open for a designated period of time usually granted for a consideration paid, the exercise of which must conform to specific notice requirements and other conditions, such as the payment of a deposit.

PARTNERSHIP: Association of two or more individuals to carry on a business for profit as co-owners.

PARTY WALL: Wall located on the boundary line of property used in common by the owners of the two properties.

PERSONAL PROPERTY: Movables or chattels which are not real estate.

PHYSICAL DETERIORATION: Decline in value of property resulting from decay and neglect.

POWER OF ATTORNEY: Written instrument giving one the power to act as agent (attorney in fact) in the name of another (principal). A "durable" power of attorney remains in effect even if the principal becomes incompetent. All powers of attorney expire on the death of the principal.

PREPAYMENT PENALTY: A charge imposed by a lender for paying off a loan before its due date. Illegal in many states.

PRINCIPAL: Person for whom an agent or attorney in fact acts.

PRIORITY: Preference or seniority of claim or lien. For instance, a first mortgage has priority over a subordinate mortgage, judgment or mechanic's lien placed on record against the property subsequent to the recording of the first mortgage.

PRIVATE MORTGAGE INSURANCE (PMI): Coverage given to a lender to insure a given percentage of its lien for which the mortgagor pays a premium. The lender relies on the insurer to guarantee that portion of the loan that it would not have granted without the insurance.

PROBATE: Legal process of lodging a will for proof with a probate court or surrogate to determine who will inherit the property of a decedent. The surrogate is the public official charged with the duty of keeping the records and qualifying the named executors, who carry out the wishes expressed in the will.

PROMISSORY NOTE: Legal instrument evidencing an obligation, which makes formal proof of the underlying debt unnecessary.

PRORATIONS: Division of expenses at closing between buyer and seller based upon those that are prepaid or in arrears. Adjustments are based upon the date of closing.

PUFFING: Exaggerated claims as to features or value of real estate.

PURCHASE-MONEY MORTGAGE (PMM): Mortgage taken back by a seller in a real estate transaction for a portion of the price.

QUITCLAIM DEED: Deed in which grantor transfers only his right, title and interest in the real property without covenants or warranties. This, however, does not relieve the grantor of his obligations under any mortgage and note affecting the property.

READY, WILLING AND ABLE BUYER: Prospective purchaser prepared to buy property on terms acceptable to seller having the unconditional present ability to complete the transaction. Usually the standard by which it is judged whether a broker has earned a commission.

REAL ESTATE: See "Land."

REAL PROPERTY: See "Land."

REALTOR: Registered trademark of local Realtor boards affiliated with National Association of Realtors.

RECORDING: The act of filing of an instrument affecting the title to real estate in the central recording office of the governmental subdivision having jurisdiction, such as county clerk's office.

REDEMPTION: The act of curing a default and reinstatement of rights of a defaulting property owner.

REGULATION Z: Requires lenders to disclose to borrowers the true interest rate on a mortgage loan. Required by federal law (RESPA).

RENT: See "Lease."

REPLACEMENT COST: The actual cost of restoration of original property that was damaged or destroyed in a casualty, such as fire, flood, or hurricane.

REVERSE-ANNUITY MORTGAGE (RAM): A loan arrangement in which a homeowner receives periodic payments based upon his equity in the property, which loan is repaid upon sale of the property or death of the owner.

RIPARIAN RIGHTS: Right of owner of property bordering on a river, lake or ocean, including access to and use of the water.

SALE AND LEASEBACK: Sale by owner of real estate and, as part of the same transaction, signing a long-term lease to remain in possession.

SALESPERSON: Person selling real estate under the supervision of a licensed broker.

SATISFACTION OF MORTGAGE: Discharge acknowledging the payment of a mortgage debt.

SECONDARY MORTGAGE MARKET: A market for the purchase of existing mortgages; as distinguished from primary mortgage market where mortgages are originated.

SETBACK: A building and zoning regulation requiring vacant space between the property line and the building line.

SHARED-APPRECIATION MORTGAGE (SAM): A mortgage in which the borrower gets a favorable interest rate in exchange for agreeing to share a portion of the profit upon sale of the property with the lender.

SPECIAL WARRANTY DEED: A deed in which the warranties are limited: The grantor guarantees only against defects in title arising during the period of his ownership and not against defects in title existing before that time.

SPECIFIC PERFORMANCE: An extraordinary legal remedy in which a court orders a party to carry out the terms of a contract, particularly suitable to real estate because every parcel is regarded as unique. A condition for the granting of this remedy by a court is a showing that monetary damages will not be adequate to grant relief and that irreparable injury will ensue if the party sued is not ordered to perform. For example, no two parcels of real property have the same view and exposure to light and air and if the seller defaults the court probably will order the seller to convey title to the buyer of that parcel.

STATUTE OF FRAUDS: The law that requires certain instruments to be in writing in order to be legally enforceable.

STATUTE OF LIMITATIONS: The period of time within which a law suit must be commenced or thereafter barred.

STATUTORY LIEN: A lien imposed on real property by law, such as a tax lien.

SUBDIVIDER: Developer of land, who gets governmental permission, on conditions to divide tract into separate, usable lots.

SUBDIVISION: The division of a tract into lots and blocks shown on a filed map, subject to local ordinances and regulations.

SUBORDINATION: The relegation of a security to an inferior position, such as subordination of a first mortgage to a new construction mortgage.

SUBROGATION: Acquisition of the rights of another to make a claim or sue, usually upon payment to the assignor by an insurance carrier.

SUIT TO QUIET TITLE: Action to settle or establish a clear title where there is a dispute or "cloud" on the title. "Quieting" the title refers to the removal of the encumbrance or other alleged defect to make title marketable and insurable.

SUPPLY AND DEMAND: The economic forces that dictate the market value of property.

SURETY BOND: Undertaking by an insurance company guaranteeing the debt, default or miscarriage of a required performance.

SURVEY: Plot plan showing the measured boundaries and area of a lot and location of structures, encroachments and easements.

TAX LIEN: A charge against property having priority over other liens created by operation of law and giving the right to the holder to sell the property in satisfaction of the balance due.

TAX SALE: Court-ordered sale of real property to cover delinquent taxes.

TENANCY BY THE ENTIRETY: Joint ownership of real property by husband and wife where survivor becomes absolute owner upon death of spouse. Recognized by less than one-half of the states in this country. Not recognized in those states having community property.

TENANCY IN COMMON: A co-ownership in which each owner holds an undivided interest in the entire property where the interest of each owner can be inherited and is not subject to survivorship.

TENANT: See "Lease."

TESTATE: One who dies leaving a valid will. One who dies without a valid will is said to have died intestate.

TESTATOR/TESTATRIX: Male/Female who makes a valid will.

TIME IS OF THE ESSENCE: Words used in a contract or written notice requiring strict and punctual performance at a given time and place.

TITLE: Evidence of ownership of real estate transferred by deed.

TITLE INSURANCE: Policy covering the owner and/or mortgagee of real estate against loss resulting from defect in title. For a one-time premium the policy insures marketability of the title.

TRUST: A confidential relationship in which property is held and administered for the benefit of another called the beneficiary.

TRUST DEED: An instrument creating a mortgage lien.

TRUSTEE'S DEED: Deed signed by a trustee transferring title to property held in trust.

UNIFORM COMMERCIAL CODE: Uniform law codifying regulations pertaining to commercial transactions, such as sales, banking, warehouse receipts, or liens on personal property.

UNMARKETABLE TITLE: Defective title that is usually uninsurable for title insurance unless defects and encumbrances are satisfied or removed.

USURY: Interest exceeding the maximum rate legally permitted.

VARIANCE: An exception to the requirements of a zoning ordinance allowing the use or construction of a structure otherwise prohibited. When the zoning code official of the municipality rejects a building and zoning permit, an appeal must be made to the zoning board of adjustment or similar body to prove hardship or special need and no detriment to neighboring properties or to the master zoning plan.

WRAPAROUND MORTGAGE: Form of mortgage financing in which the new mortgage is placed in a subordinate position and the existing mortgage remains in place with the owner paying the new mortgagee on both mortgages. Permission from the first mortgagee must be obtained if the mortgage has a "due on sale" provision.

YIELD: Return on investment.

ZONING ORDINANCE: Regulation by a municipality under its police power of the use and character of real estate. Zones are designated where certain uses are permitted and others are prohibited. The principal purposes of zoning are to prevent congestion, noxious odors, noise and other factors that will reduce the value of real property.

INDEX

A

C

F

P